David M. Stanley, S.J.

JESUS IN GETHSEMANE

PAULIST PRESS   *New York/Ramsey*

IMPRIMI POTEST
William F. Ryan, S.J.
Provincial, Province of Upper Canada

NIHIL OBSTAT
J. Brian Peckham, S.J.
Censor Deputatus

IMPRIMATUR
† Aloysius M. Ambrozic
Auxiliary Bishop of Toronto

October 22, 1979

Library of Congress
Catalog Card Number: 80-80576

ISBN: 0-8091-2285-5

Published by Paulist Press
Editorial Office: 1865 Broadway, New York, N.Y. 10023
Business Office: 545 Island Road, Ramsey, N.J. 07446

Printed and bound in the
United States of America

CONTENTS

For
Pamela and David

hoc amicitiae pignus perennis

FOREWORD

This book represents the fruits of a project which, in one way or another, has occupied me intermittently during the past several years. I began by teaching courses to university and clerical students on its principal themes in Rome, San Francisco, and Toronto. I have attempted to grapple with a number of problems presented by the pertinent New Testament texts, and I confess that I have not yet discovered completely satisfactory solutions to all of the difficulties they contain. Thus, this present stage, the publication of my own views on the varying interpretations by the sacred writers of the significance of Jesus' prayer and struggle in Gethsemane, should be regarded as the newest phase in what may well be a continuing dialogue with these authors, as well as with many contemporary scholars whose insights into the meaning of the texts have provided me both enlightenment and encouragement.

During recent years I have also given a number of Ignatian retreats to various small groups of exercitants, for three, six, or eight days, during which some or all of the Gospel texts devoted to this moving and mysterious episode in the earthly life of Jesus were proposed for the contemplation of those making the Spiritual Exercises. Since a number of those participating in these directed retreats have professed to find assistance for the living of the Gospel, by concentrating their attention in prayer upon this important mystery, I have been encouraged to put my reflections on this fascinating and fruitful topic at the disposition of a larger audience.

Another field of inquiry which has engaged my attention

during the past decade is that to which I have devoted the first chapter of this book, the contemplation of episodes in the life of Jesus as interpreted in such diverse, if not contradictory ways by the evangelists. The first of several articles on this intriguing subject was published in *Theological Studies* in 1968.[1] In March 1972 I attempted to clarify the method I had advocated in the earlier article by applying it to the ancient monastic practice, *lectio divina*, the meditative reading of the Bible, referred to in the Rule of St. Benedict. This took the form of a talk at the annual meeting of the American Benedictine Abbots and Priors held in New Subiaco Abbey, Arkansas.[2] In July 1973 an international symposium on Ignatian spirituality took place at the University of San Francisco, for which I wrote a brief study on "Revitalizing Our Prayer Through the Gospels."[3] A few months before the symposium I received the most helpful reactions to my suggestions from two distinguished panelists, George W. MacRae, S.J., Stillman professor at the Harvard Divinity School, and Joseph F. Conwell, S.J., of Gonzaga University in Spokane, a specialist in Ignatian spirituality. I then composed a "revised version" of my communication which I actually read at the symposium.[4] Meantime in the *Supplement* to *The Way* during the summer of 1972 John Ashton, S.J., an English scripturist, published some criticisms of my original article in a thoughtful and provocative study of "The Imitation of Christ."[5] In writing the present Chapter 1, I have taken all of these responses into account.

Basic Orientation of This Study

My primary purpose in composing this study of Jesus' prayer and struggle in Gethsemane is an essentially "practical" one. I simply wish it to be of some service to the increasing number of contemporary Christians who manifest an ever-growing interest in that discourse with God through the risen Lord in the Spirit, which we call Christian prayer. The term, of course, stands for an almost endless variety of forms and attitudes adopted by the believer in the approach to God. George MacRae, in his reflections on my first contribution to the San

Francisco symposium alluded to above, asked a very fundamental question, as to "whether prayer is a given, an absolute. . . . Is prayer immune to change? It is not, of course, but plotting the course of its change remains a task for our spirituality."[6] As I shall suggest later on, one important element to be taken into consideration in tracing the evolution of Christian prayer is the changing conception of Christ that varies with each culture and with different periods of history.

For the moment I should like to alert the reader to an aspect of this study which deserves to be stated with a certain emphasis. While this exploration of the profound mystery of Jesus' prayer during "the days of his flesh" (Heb 5:7) is not intended as a scholarly work, given the goal of assisting others to pray from the Gospel texts, given also the deliberate omission of the paraphernalia of biblical scholarship, yet I believe that it is not irrelevant to point out that this book has been written out of what I have judged to be the best results of modern biblical criticism.

I do not hesitate to underline this point, because I am convinced that the findings of New Testament scholarship can be a powerful ally for the man of faith in his perennial search for God in Christ. Now it is surely no secret that, since the middle of the nineteenth century, a critical approach to the Gospels has been viewed with uneasiness, suspicion, even hostility, by not a few earnest, devout Christians. In our own day it has become necessary to insist on a positive attitude toward biblical science, since in certain constituencies of the Christian churches, now enjoying a resurgence of pentecostalism or charismatic renewal, there has been a simultaneous renaissance of biblical fundamentalism.

This mentality, unfortunately so frequently allied with piety, is essentially a form of anti-intellectualism applied to the interpretation of the biblical text. It is a mind-set which ingenuously decides *a priori* the sense of a scriptural passage without knowing or caring to inquire into the kind of literature (poetry, myth, legend, saga, parable, chronicle) to which a given text belongs. Thus, when the Bible asserts that the waters of the flood covered "the highest mountains everywhere" (Gen 7:19), the fundamentalist looks for evidence of a universal deluge. In his view, to adopt any other viewpoint is simply a denial of faith! Now it ought to carry considerable weight with Catholics at least to be reminded that Pius XII over thirty years ago, through his innovative letter on the promotion of biblical studies in the Catholic Church, *Divino afflante Spiritu*, did in fact "unequivocally repudiate fundamentalism in Catholic exegesis"—to borrow the trenchant phrase of John L. McKenzie.[7]

The Scholar and the Community of Faith

We may be permitted here to ask: Just what is the function of the scholar in the religious community? To some, at a first glance, it might seem the scholar has no place at all. The scholar greatly resembles the little boy in the nursery rhyme "who is always asking *Why?*" I have always treasured the remark of the late, regretted Gustave Weigel, S.J., himself a scholar of some eminence: "The postulate of all scholarly investigation is the nagging existence of mystery." The religious community, on the other hand, is the collectivity of "the people with the Book," that is, with the answers. If the scholar is filled with an insatiable desire to see, the community of faith is filled with "the conviction of things not seen" (Heb 11:1). Yet, I venture to suggest, the scholar has a vital role in the life of the Church. He has, in fact, a twofold function: (1) to draw the attention of the unbeliever to the supreme importance of the question of God and his claims upon man; and (2) to educate the believer to cherish the values inherent in a rational, reverent approach to the mystery of the kingdom of God. These points require further amplification.

In the first place, it is the scholar's responsible role to keep the discussion of religion and its problems before the general public. These supremely important issues must, by reason of their worth, be set above questions of politics, sociology, psychology, even material well-being. They demand a position of prominence and security beyond the interests of Madison Avenue, 42nd Street, or Wall Street. And I submit that it is only the person with expertise in the theological disciplines who is equipped to perform this task worthily. The theologically unschooled believer can *live* his faith effectively, beautifully. He is, however, in no position to debate its issues publicly. The simple, earnest believer—should he attempt such a hazardous project—exposes himself to the danger of degrading the faith. He may well be led, through frustration and anger at his inability to cope with his adversary, to defy reason. Or he may also, in his uncritical enthusiasm, run the risk of making the very idea of God ridiculous in the eyes of the unbeliever. When, after the discovery of the Dead Sea scrolls some thirty years ago, it was suggested in the popular press that these documents found at Qumran had definitively disproved the originality of Christianity, not a few Christians were gravely disturbed, rejected such insinuations angrily, or capitulated to a rationalism compromising to their faith. They had apparently forgotten, or were unaware, that the evangelist Matthew, for instance, with his insistence upon Jesus' fulfillment of Old Testament prophecy was asserting that not everything in Jesus' message and mission was without precedent in Israel's history.

Secondly, it is the scholar's role within "the household of the faith" (Gal 6:10) to assist his fellow-believer in liberating himself from superstition on the one hand, and from agnosticism on the other. Specifically, the biblical scholar is a person equipped to hold out against concordism and the "double truth," because he is convinced that it is the same God who graciously gave us the precious revelation of himself through the Bible and also imparted to us the spirit of inquiry, the insatiable capacity for ever asking "Why?" The assumption of the concordist that the Bible and science are merely saying the same thing in different words is naive. Without apparently seeing the implications of irreverence behind his attitude, he gleefully shouts, "The Bible was right after all!"

To confine our attention to the four Gospels, since we shall be occupied chiefly with certain passages from these books in our investigation of Jesus' prayer in Gethsemane, I suggest that the age-old practice of attempting to "harmonize" the contradictions between one evangelist and another is not only unhelpful to the safeguarding of one's Christian faith, but a positive detriment to any attempt to pray from the Gospels. This frame of mind is the result, in part, of a kind of scrupulosity, an over-anxiety to assert at any cost the "historicity" of our Gospels. To refute the confident assertion by certain nineteenth-century "liberal" historians that our Gospels were not "historical" documents, but tracts of a "tendentious character" (written as they obviously are by believers for believers), the Christian apologists attempted to demonstrate that the Gospels were indeed "historical" (in the sense defined by their opponents!), whereas they should have admitted the "confessional" nature of these sacred books, after denying the validity of certain assumptions by their learned opponents. It is to the great credit of a distinguished theologian like Avery Dulles, S.J. that he has shown in a superb and brief monograph, *Apologetics and the Biblical Christ*,[8] that in fact such apologetic tactics were ineffectual because of faulty methodology which rendered invalid many a misguided, if bravely loyal attempt to "defend" the faith. To liberate many Catholics trained by such apologetics from a deep-seated rationalism (which believes it can "prove" Jesus' resurrection or his "divinity") is still very much a piece of unfinished business for the religious scholar.

Some Presuppositions

It may be helpful, for the sake of clarity, to mention certain assumptions which it is necessary to make in undertaking a study like this. First, the basic historical character of the incident in Jesus' life is accepted as much more plausible than the hypothesis adopted, for instance, by Martin Dibelius that the entire episode was created in the very early Church with the help of psalms and other Old Testament citations to inspire courage in believers under threat of persecution, or to concretize the sufferings of the Messiah for the community of faith.[9] Admittedly the incident is unique in the life of Jesus, revealing as it appears to do, especially in Mark (and Matthew), an attitude toward his own death at variance with the calm acceptance of the divine will that is implied in his other predictions of it. Admittedly also there is a certain problem about the assertion of the three Synoptic evangelists that the disciples fell asleep: how then did anyone witness Jesus' humiliating struggle and his almost desperate prayer to the Father? There is, on the other hand, no reason to deny the evident influence of certain Old Testament allusions or citations upon some details of the Gospel narratives. Indeed, it is well known that, to interpret the meaning of many happenings in Jesus' life, particularly of his Passion, the sacred writers had recourse to "the Scriptures" of Israel as an indication of the declared will of God for Jesus. The astute observations of R. S. Barbour are pertinent and help to point out the right path. "We do not indeed know just how it was, for the accounts are not mutually consistent either in detail or in the interpretation they offer; but therein lies their value. They attempt a description which they cannot compass; had they done more, or had they been simply the deposit of the early Christians' faith in the light of their reading of the Scriptures, in either case we should have a Christ held captive by his Church."[10]

One may still ask: Why did the Gospel writers judge it fitting to preserve this puzzling incident? To such a question several answers suggest themselves. It is in effect a dramatic summary of the entire Passion story, in fact, of Jesus' entire earthly history, particularly as Paul viewed it as a "beggaring of himself" by him who was rich (2 Cor 8:9), a disclosure of God's "Son in the likeness of sinful flesh" (Rom 8:3) or, as a primitive pre-Pauline Christian hymn describes it, "an emptying of himself," a self-humiliation (Phil 2:7–8). In addition, as will be seen, the episode came to be regarded in the early Church as a kind of school of Christian prayer. And the values of the story held for a realistic belief in the humanity of Jesus, in the face of early docetist tendencies, are surely obvious.

A second pre-supposition needs to be mentioned: we accept as the best working-hypothesis what is known as the Two-Source theory. This widely accepted reconstruction seeks to explain the inter-relationships between the first three Gospels by the theory that Matthew and Luke are largely dependent on two previous written documents, Mark's Gospel and a (hypothetical) sayings-source known as "Q" (from the German word for "source," *Quelle*). Accordingly, in our examination of the Gospel narratives of Gethsemane, we shall begin with Mark.

A third assumption is drawn from the consensus of modern New Testament scholarship, namely, that the primitive pre-Gospel Passion narrative(s) began only with the account of Jesus' arrest.[11] In fact, this seems to be suggested from the manner in which the fourth evangelist begins his Passion narrative proper (see Jn 18:1ff). Accordingly it appears probable that it was Mark, who wished to include in his Passion story an account of the institution of the Eucharist at the Last Supper, who found it useful to draw on earlier accounts (already in writing) of Jesus' struggle and prayer as a link between the Supper and the arrest. This does not necessarily mean that Mark transposed an incident, which in fact occurred at some other point in Jesus' public life, to this juncture in the Passion. Indeed, the fact that John—who, as will be seen, locates a scene reminiscent of the Synoptic Gethsemane episode at the very close of the public ministry (Jn 12:20–36)—is careful to place the great prayer of Jesus (ch. 17) just before his narrative of Jesus' arrest in the garden (18:1ff.) provides an indication of an historical tradition that was too important to be completely ignored.

The Approach to Our Theme

Because of the "practical" aim of this investigation into the prayer of Jesus in Gethsemane, I propose to begin by discussing the significance for Christian living of the contemplation of Jesus' earthly history (Chapter 1). In Chapter 2 we shall examine the various statements concerning Christian faith contained in the four Gospels, in order to appreciate as deeply as possible the quite individual conceptions of faith entertained by these sacred writers. This will prove of assistance in the examination of the passages which they devote to Gethsemane, as well as in the discovery of the relationship which each inspired author perceived between faith and Christian prayer.

In reviewing the pertinent scriptural passages concerned with our topic we shall follow the historical sequence of their composition, so far as it is possible, in order to evaluate the development in the understanding of this difficult episode. Thus, Chapter 3 will deal with three attempts by anonymous Christians of the very early Church to interpret Jesus' attitudes toward his own sufferings and death. The pre-Gospel essays that have survived by being incorporated into the New Testament assume the form of a (liturgical?) hymn, celebrating as priestly actions the sufferings of Jesus during his mortal life (Heb 5:7–10), or that of a brief narrative of Jesus' reactions and his prayer before his arrest in the garden. There are, we shall find, two such accounts, commonly denominated as Source "A" and Source "B," since they are sufficiently recoverable by an analysis of the Marcan narrative of Gethsemane (Mk 14:32–42). Modern critics are generally agreed that Mark has, in creating his own somewhat original interpretation of the incident, employed two written sources already in existence when he came to write his Gospel.

We shall next assess the creativeness of Mark as the first writer to put together a written Gospel, by reviewing the general character of the Marcan Passion narrative as well as investigating the meaning he has seen in the Gethsemane scene (Chapter 4). In Chapter 5 we shall study the Matthean narrative, with particular attention to the imaginative and didactic manner in which Matthew has revamped the written account by Mark. In order to grasp the very different interpretation which Luke has put upon Jesus' prayer "in a garden" we shall begin by recalling Luke's highly novel concept of what a Gospel ought to be and the points in his theological outlook, peculiar to himself, which have presided over his two-volume work on the origins of Christianity. Thus we shall be in a better position to grasp the meaning he has intuited in the incident with which we are chiefly concerned (Chapter 6). Finally, we shall turn to the radical revision made in the tradition by the fourth evangelist with regard to Jesus' struggle (Jn 12:27–36) and his final prayer before his arrest (Jn 17:1–26). This will constitute the contents of Chapter 7. A final chapter will attempt to summarize the results of the entire investigation.

NOTES

1. "Contemplation of the Gospels, Ignatius Loyola, and the Contemporary Christian," *Theological Studies* 29 (1968) 417–443. This essay is also included in *Prayer: The Problem of Dialogue with God,* papers of the 1968 Bea Institute Symposium, edited by Christoper F. Mooney, S.J. (Paramus/New York, Toronto/London, 1969), pp. 49–77.

2. "A Suggested Approach to *Lectio Divina,*" *The American Benedictine Review* 33 (1972) 439–455.

3. *The Way, Supplement* 19: *Apostolic Spirituality and Reform I* (1973) 3–12.

4. See the brochure published by *Program To Adapt the Spiritual Exercises* (Jersey City, 1973), *Revitalizing Our Prayer Through the Gospels.*

5. *The Way, Supplement* 16: *Prayer and the Ignatian Exercises, New Directions* (1972) 28–45.

6. The reader is referred to the essay cited in n. 4, pp. 1–2.

7. "Problems of Hermeneutics in Roman Catholic Exegesis," *Journal of Biblical Literature* 77 (1958) 198.

8. *Woodstock Papers,* No. 6 (Westminster, Md., 1963).

9. Martin Dibelius, "Gethsemane," *The Crozer Quarterly* 12 (1938) 254–265.

10. R. S. Barbour, "Gethsemane in the Tradition of the Passion," *New Testament Studies* 16 (1969–70) 251.

11. See X. Léon-Dufour, S.J., art. "Passion" in *Dictionnaire de la Bible: Supplément,* vol. 6 (1960), cols. 1424–1425.

I

CONTEMPLATION OF JESUS' EARTHLY HISTORY AND CHRISTIAN LIVING

In our own day the Church through the *Constitution on Divine Revelation (Dei Verbum)* promulgated by Vatican II has reaffirmed the place of privilege rightly accorded to the Bible, together with "sacred tradition," "as the supreme rule of faith."[1] The Council asserted that "the Christian religion itself . . . must be fed as well as ruled by Sacred Scripture." Indeed, it went so far as to avow that "the Church has always venerated the divine Scriptures even as she does the very body of the Lord, since from the table both of God's word and of Christ's body she never ceases to receive the bread of life and hand it out to the believer, particularly at the sacred liturgy." To this remarkable affirmation of the superlative values for Christian living to be found in the Bible is appended a strong recommendation, in which "this sacred synod earnestly and with particular emphasis urges upon all Christian believers, especially members of religious families, that they acquire 'the supreme advantage of knowing Jesus Christ' (Phil 3:8) by the assiduous reading of the divine Scriptures. . . . Consequently, they should gladly put themselves to school to the sacred text. . . . They must moreover bear in mind that prayer should accompany the reading of Sacred Scripture, in order that there may ensue a dialogue between God and man." It should be noted that this practice of Bible reading is not regarded as something magical; the exhortation presupposes some preparation and instruction by homilies at the liturgy, by "courses" (*institutiones*) geared to the promotion of an intelligent reading of the Bible, or "other aids" (for instance, competent, popular books about Scripture).

It is however in the fifth chapter of *Dei Verbum*, devoted to the New Testament, that we find several observations apposite to the theme we wish to discuss here, the high place which the contemplation of Jesus' earthly history should occupy in the life of the Christian. It is significant that the document takes, as its point of departure, "the word of God," that is, God in his definitive *historical* self-disclosure to mankind, and specifically through what Paul calls "the Gospel" (Rom 1:16). This dynamic reality, be it noted, is not a written Gospel, nor even the apostolic kerygma: it "is God's dynamic power (*dynamis*) leading, for everyone with faith, to salvation." It is this existential, divine reality which "is set forth and displays its force in an outstanding manner in the writings of the New Testament." This statement is immediately followed by a summary of Jesus' earthly history. "It is to these realities that the New Testament writings give continuous, divine testimony."[2]

But among these precious books a distinction must be made, insofar as their value for Christian spirituality is concerned; and it is to the four Gospels that the place of honor is accorded by the Council. "The Gospels have a special preeminence, and rightly so, for they provide the principal witness to the life and teaching of the incarnate Word, our Savior." Here again the concern of the Council with history is not to be overlooked. The canonical Gospels were not the first contribution to Christian sacred literature: they were preceded historically by the writing of all the Pauline letters, at least. Yet the evangelists, not Paul, are the specially privileged witnesses to the way in which Christians of the first and second generation nourished their faith and love and hope upon what Jesus had said and done during his mortal life in this world. That such is the sense in which Vatican II intended to assert the "pre-eminence" of our Gospels may be gathered by the confirmatory function it ascribes to the other books of the New Testament. These, it says, "confirm what concerns Christ as Lord: his authentic teaching is more fully stated; the saving power of Christ's divine activity is announced; the origins of the Church and her marvelous growth are told, while her final consummation in glory is pointed out."

This brief but highly pregnant statement of values reaches its climax as the chapter ends, when attention is focused upon the activity of the Spirit. It is this new, active presence that has realized Jesus' promise to "be present to his apostles"; for it is "as Paraclete that the Spirit would lead them into the fullness of truth." The prominence given to the Holy Spirit in this conciliar document cannot (and should not) be overlooked. Both Paul (2 Cor 3:6) and John (Jn 6:63a) denominate the Spirit as "the life-giver." At the same time, both Paul and John present Jesus glorified as life-giver (1 Cor 15:45; Jn 6:63b), for both one and the other think of the risen Lord as the bearer of the Spirit. For John this giving of the Spirit by Jesus occurs, proleptically, with his dying breath: "And bowing his head he handed over the Spirit" (Jn 19:30). In Paul's eyes the Spirit is rightly recognized as "the Spirit of Christ" (Rom 8:9b), or, better, "the Spirit of his [God's] Son" (Gal 4:6). In the Pauline view of salvation, which remains eschatological, we learn that "in union with Christ all will be brought to life" (1 Cor 15:22), or "the One who raised Christ from death will revivify even your mortal bodies through his Spirit dwelling within you" (Rom 8:11). The goal of Christian existence for Paul is the "transformation into the image of his [God's] Son, so that he [the Son] may be the eldest of a large family of brothers" (Rom 8:29). This transformation-process has already begun in this life: "All of us with unveiled face, while we behold as in a mirror the glory of the Lord, are being transformed into the same image from glory to glory—and this by the Lord who is Spirit" (2 Cor 3:18). Yet it is the consummation of this transforming action which is called the object of Christian hope in "Lord Jesus Christ as Savior," since it is he "who will transform our wretched bodies in conformity with his glorious body by virtue of that dynamism that enables him to subject everything to himself" (Phil 3:20–21). For Paul, no less than John, the risen Jesus is the bearer of the Spirit.

It is however peculiar to John to show the relationship of the Spirit to the Christian comprehension of the earthly life of Jesus; and hence it is not accidental that the chapter in *Dei Verbum* on the New Testament concludes, as has been seen, with a citation from the Fourth Gospel. For this evangelist, the principal significance of Jesus' mission is to be bearer of "the truth" from the unseen God, that is, to disclose to men God's loving relationship to them. This mission, as will be seen in the next chapter, fails for various reasons during Jesus' public ministry.[3] It is specifically the role of the Spirit as "advocate" or "defense counsel" to bring to mind within the disciples the values inherent in Jesus' earthly life (Jn 14:26; 16:8–15). Thus the disclosure of the "God no man has ever seen" (Jn 1:18), through the completely human life of the Word become flesh as Jesus, is properly the function of the "Spirit of truth" who alone can "unveil" its message (Jn 16:14) to the man of faith.

This important activity of the Spirit as revealer of divine truth deserves to be recalled nowadays, when in the enthusiasm of the charismatic revival it may be in danger of being forgotten. Paul, in his own way, has also reminded us of this salient feature of the Spirit: "We have not received the spirit of the world, but the Spirit that comes from God, in order that *we may know* the acts of God's graciousness toward us" (1 Cor 2:12). A genuinely Christian experience of the Spirit brings to the man of faith a more profound understanding of God and his designs for us, particularly as these are revealed through Jesus' earthly history, to which as the Council states the Gospels "provide the principal witness," and so occupy a place of "special pre-eminence" in Christian spirituality.

Some Problems in Contemplating Jesus' History

It remains to mention certain difficulties which arise for not a few present-day Christians in their attempts to contemplate the Gospel texts. The stress on the *historical* character of

the divine revelation in *Dei Verbum*, while indeed most congenial to the modern mentality (as contrasted with the viewpoint
of "classical," Scholastic theology, where history found little
place) presents a problem, that of "bridging the distance." Not a
few Christians are uncomfortable with the experience that the
Bible in general, and even the Gospels in particular, speak in an
idiom and out of a culture that is alien, coming to us, as it does,
from the far-away past. It may well be that this strangeness of
the biblical texts has prompted those experiments in liturgy in
which testimonies by twentieth-century figures (Gandhi, Teil-
hard de Chardin, Simone Weil, Dietrich Bonhoeffer, Dag Ham-
marskjöld) are employed in place of readings from Scripture.
Whatever be the view taken of such substitutions, such practices
clearly indicate a felt difficulty with the understanding of the
sacred texts.

And indeed, as Heinrich Schlier, the distinguished German
Neutestamentler, has observed, one must acknowledge that any of
our Gospels is truly "historical testimony to a distant past."[4]
The Gospel of Matthew, let us say, like any letter of Paul, is a
piece of writing conditioned by the particular era and culture
and intended audience for which it was at one time composed. It
is only by grasping, at least to a degree, these various facets of
the historical relativism of any part of the Bible that such a document becomes less foreign to us, more readily comprehensible
and acceptable for its testimony to Jesus Christ. To put it simply, this very feature of our inspired Scriptures is an imperious
invitation to examine it critically, putting questions to it, seeking to grasp its author's intention and meaning. What should be
remembered is that only thus can one, *as a believer*, display the
proper respect and reverence for God's decision to enter our human history at various times in the past in order to disclose his
purpose for man and to reveal something of himself.

Not indeed that such an enterprise is not fraught with risk.
As Schlier candidly admits, the understanding of any scriptural
text I thus question "shares all the uncertainty of the scientific
historical approach."[5] Quite recently in the Bellarmine Lecture
for 1976, George W. MacRae, S.J. has commented upon the age-
old tendency of Christians to seek a kind of certainty in the area

of God's self-revelation "which is exempt from the laws and the limitations of human discourse. The Church had allowed itself, and many Christians still do, to yearn for that point at which God will speak directly, not through the muddled confusion of human utterance: there must be somewhere some words of God that are immune to the interpretive processes that we of necessity have to exercise when we try to understand one another."[6] Fr. MacRae sagely remarks that "in that yearning the Church sought a privilege that was not granted even to the Son of God. In the incarnation, God entrusted his Son to humanity in its fullest sense.... God can be portrayed as taking the risk of revealing himself in the human.... If God speaks to us in the language of humanity, then we must interpret God's speech as we interpret the language of humanity. The Church must not shy away from accepting that same risk which God may be said to have taken in the greatest mystery of our faith."[7] Accordingly, if my entire, single-hearted intent in prayer is simply to "meet" the God of history in his Son Jesus, the God who has thereby accepted the hazard of revealing himself through the historical process (whether of Israel's history or of Jesus' earthly life), and subsequently through a set of writings that are correctly assessed as "historical testimony to a distant past," then I must be prepared to "bridge the distance" and to accept the ambiguities and ambivalence of the historical. To refuse this risk, to demand a dogmatic assurance from ecclesiastical authority about the "correct" meaning of the Bible, is, in point of fact, to refuse to surrender in love to the God of history.

A second difficulty that is frequently felt by not a few who attempt to pray from the Gospels is concerned specifically with the contemplation of the narratives of Jesus' life. Many experience a sense of frustration when they try to pray about many of these stories. This is caused, no doubt, in part by the exotic nature of these ancient documents, as has already been mentioned. For some it may arise from a feeling that this type of meditative reading is more study than prayer. Again, it can be the result of the failure (often largely unconscious) to appreciate the special character of, for instance, the post-resurrection narratives, or the Infancy episodes in Matthew and Luke. Yet even the narratives of Jesus' public life can pose problems, particularly for the imagination. And here it must be acknowledged that "the form of the stories about Jesus reveals little about the place, indeed that the evangelist may never have known it. This is often the case with Luke, but one would be reluctant to regard Luke as a poor subject for contemplation."[8] If while at prayer over these narratives I try in imagination to recreate a scene, despite the discreet silence of the sacred writer, is this anything more than a kind of pious make-believe? And how can I put myself in touch with Jesus in reality by such pious (if well-intentioned) fraud? Surely sincerity at prayer would appear to demand that if, as is frequently the fact, in the course of preserving these stories for a particular purpose (for example, instruction, apologetics, ethics, liturgy) the tradition has permitted many concrete details to be lost, or has possibly omitted them deliberately, I should be much better advised to grasp *why* such concrete details are missing, rather than attempt to substitute for them some imaginings of my own. Surely a realistic approach to these stories, especially in prayer, where realism would seem to be crucial, demands that I reckon with what the modern New Testament critic calls their "setting in life" (*Sitz im Leben*)—a phrase which refers, *not* to Jesus' historical life, but to that of the primitive Christian communities. As George MacRae has correctly seen, "the emphasis of modern Gospel scholarship on the creative mediation of the early Christian communities and of their literary leaders should be a liberating example for modern contemplation of the Gospel passages."[9] We shall return shortly to this point in order to underscore the values for prayer which it can be made to exhibit.

A third problem that is often voiced in our day by religious may be put in the form of objection: "Why attempt to relate to our Lord through the pages of the Gospels, especially since they are not readily comprehensible without considerable biblical expertise, when I can more easily experience the presence of the risen Christ in my work, in other people, in the myriad ups and downs of day-to-day living?" Certainly it must be granted that this awareness of Christ's presence to my own history is of paramount importance for faith-development, and one which present-day theology has beneficially set into prominence. This kind of "contemplation in action," so thoroughly Ignatian, speaks with special allure to the modern Christian. Yet surely in this enterprise, which can be fraught with dangers for the unwary and the naive (falling in love with another human being can be confused with falling in love with Jesus), our Gospels, when prayerfully and reflectively read, can offer many valuable clues to the discovery of the Lord Jesus' presence in my own work and in other people. The assistance which the Gospel narratives offer will be the more readily perceived and appreciated once I realize that these stories about Jesus have in large measure attained their present form by the fact that two or three generations of Christians in the primitive Church had already fed their faith from them. To put it simply, the Gospels are indeed not more biographies of Jesus than they are autobiographies of the earliest Christians. Thus a faith-filled contemplation of the Gospels can teach me the essentially social or societal character of Christian prayer. If I put myself to school to Mark, let us say, I am put in contact not only with this single evangelist, but with his community, with all those anonymous Christians who, in one way or another, contributed to Mark's creation of the first Gospel ever written. Thus I am invited, in my reading of Mark, to meet not only Jesus or this evangelist; I am put into contact with the Church.

Here the analogy drawn by Vatican II in *Dei Verbum* between the Eucharistic body of the risen Christ and the scriptural word can be instructive. It is basic to Christian belief in this august sacrament to hold that the risen Lord Jesus is bodily present to me as an individual and to the celebrating community. But this Eucharistic presence of Christ is not to be regarded as an isolated or merely individual presence, if one takes seriously Paul's teaching in 1 Cor 12:12–27 on "the body of Christ." I heartily endorse the view of Pierre Benoit, O.P.: "This famous expression of St. Paul . . . is not simply a metaphor borrowed from the classical comparison of the 'social body'; on the contrary it must be taken in a most realistic sense. . . . Christians are the members of Christ because their union with him joins their bodies to his body in the same risen life. . . . Consequently the body of Christ, his personal body, crucified and raised up again, bears within itself the bodies of the brethren whom he forms to his image (Rom 8:29). The implications of this for the Eucharist are clear. Since this sacrament gives us the body of Christ, it unites us by that very fact to all our brethren whom it bears within itself."[10] Accordingly, the sacramental experience of Christ through the reception of the Eucharist is also a sacramental experience of the community, of the Church. And consequently this sacrament readies the believer for those encounters with Christ in others which are so appealing to modern Christians.

With regard to the contemplation of the Gospels, which as we have seen are avenues not only to the risen Christ but also to those communities of Christians who contributed to their formation, does not Vatican II by the comparison alluded to imply that this is a significant part of "the bread of life" from "the table of God's word" that the Church receives and hands out to the faithful, "particularly at the sacred liturgy"? George Mac-Rae's comment is noteworthy: "To the extent that prayer focuses on the Gospels it is necessarily linked both with the community that transmitted and shaped their content and the community that interprets them. Prayer, like faith, must always be personal, but it is never really 'private.' To the extent that Paul serves as a model or connecting link in the process of reflecting upon the traditions about Jesus, one should be aware of the tension within Pauline theology between the person of Christ as individual, who is experienced in prayer, and the person of Christ as collectivity, the body of Christ, who is experienced in and through the Christian community itself. In the early Church it was only Paul who articulated the doctrine of the collective body of Christ, but I believe this same tension between two modes of encountering Christ is inherent throughout the experience of early Christianity."[11]

There is a fourth problem related to the contemplation of Jesus' earthly history which must be mentioned here, even though the answer to it will appear only later in this chapter. I refer to a question, often anxiously posed by devout Christians, who perhaps only recently have begun in their prayer-life to reckon with the truth that the Christ who today exists is indeed the risen Christ. "Have I been wrong in trying to pray to the agonizing Jesus, to Jesus at the Last Supper, to the infant Jesus?" I venture to suggest that this is an important question, and one to which a positive answer can ultimately be given.

In the fifth place there is a problem of a more general nature, with regard to the contemplation of the Gospels, which the thinking Christian has often wrestled with: How can the past *as past* affect my contemporary existence? How can the "historical Jesus," the search for whom is still a never-ending quest for most New Testament critics, act upon me in the twentieth century? In one sense the answer of modern man must be "no": the past *as past* no longer exists, and so cannot have any influence upon the present. And yet, particularly in medieval piety, beginning with the spirituality of St. Bernard, the imitation of Christ has left a marked influence. Anyone acquainted with Ignatian spirituality is aware how important for the Spiritual Exercises this practice has always been.[12] Indeed, at least St. Paul, among the New Testament writers, appears to have laid great store by the imitation of Christ and of himself.[13] Yet two contemporary English Jesuits have quite persuasively pressed home a number of objections to this traditional Christian practice.[14]

One might indeed reply to such difficulties and questions by remarking that the past once mythicized can have a profound influence upon successive generations of, for instance, the citizens of any given country. Here one must be careful not to misunderstand the sense in which myth is being employed. To the popular mind, myth is a story that is a figment of the imagination. Most people think of mythology as the collection of tales about pagan gods or ancient heroes who never existed. To think of myth thus is to discredit it as lacking any truth or significance, except possibly usefulness as bedtime stories for children. There is another meaning attaching to the myth, as it appears in studies of the history of culture, or ethnology. "Myth is always an attempt to express, and thereby to make comprehensible, some truth about the world and man's existence in it, a truth inaccessible and unknown in itself, but capable of being expressed in and by symbols. . . . What is essential is that it should attempt to formulate transcendental reality, to reach something beyond the flux of phenomena that envelops human existence, to pin down an absolute in which the human mind can rest with some feeling of security."[15] If one accepts this descriptive definition of the myth elaborated by R. A. F. MacKenzie, S.J., then it becomes possible to admit that the past can have influence, enduring and vital influence, upon the present. In this sense the "for us men and for our salvation," prefixed to the factual statements in the Nicene Creed concerning Jesus' birth and death, expresses the mythical. It is this element, when assented to in the act of justifying faith, which gives its perennially efficacious sense to the historical death of Jesus *sub Pontio Pilato*.

Heinrich Schlier in the article cited earlier[16] has expressed this dynamic quality of Scripture in a somewhat different manner. While Schlier is concerned with isolating the various principles for scriptural interpretation laid down by the Bible itself, yet what he has to say can be useful in learning how to contemplate Jesus' earthly history from our Gospels. He asserts that the Bible is to be understood "as documenting a claim expressed in God's self-utterance in Jesus Christ."[17] This divine claim upon the obedience of the man of faith, consigned to a series of contingent historical writings, can be heard when the initial spadework of grasping the sense of, for example, John's Gospel has been done. "The aim of exegesis must be to hear God's claim, expressed by and in Scripture. For this and no other is the truth of Scripture . . . the peremptory claim of the promise and advent in history of God's fidelity historically fulfilled in the act of judgment and grace in Jesus Christ."[18] Now to hear this divine challenge and to submit to it with "the obedience of faith" (Rom 1:5) is clearly the purpose of contemplating the Gospels. Once again we must remind ourselves that without some serious attempt to grasp the thrust and purpose of the sacred text to the degree that this is possible for any Christian, this claim of the truth cannot be heard, or assimilated, or lived by the believer. Schlier remarks astutely, "Significant historical texts, themselves fixed by historic events, seek to beget history. They tend to be texts in the history of the very person reading them."[19] If Jesus' life as presented by one or other evangelist is to be permitted to make its appeal to me, however little I know of Jesus, it is necessary that I open my heart and accept the testimony of the sacred writer and his interpretation of the meaning for me of a particular episode in this sacred history.

The Evangelists' Experience of Receiving the Tradition

After our review of some of the problems that arise for the twentieth-century Christian in his attempts to learn to pray from the Gospels, it is time to seek for some answers. I suggest that there are *four points* upon which modern Gospel studies have shed considerable light, and these will be found to contain the answers to the questions we have been formulating. The *first point* is that there is a consensus among modern Gospel critics that not one of our evangelists was an "eyewitness" to the events of Jesus' public ministry and death, even though two of these books bear the names of two of the Twelve, Matthew and John. Actually the ascription of various New Testament books to a certain author stems from a later ecclesiastical (not necessarily reliable) source. There is no need to introduce a demonstration of this solidly grounded, almost universally accepted view of modern scholarship. Suffice it to say that, in regard to the Fourth Gospel, certain features of the book demand the intervention of two, possibly three, editors/authors.[20] Thus the writer who created the crucifixion scene speaks of the one who actually witnessed the events on Calvary as someone distinct from himself. "Now the man who saw this has given his testimony, and his testimony is reliable; and *he* [Christ?] knows that he speaks the truth, in order that you too may come to believe" (Jn 19:35).

Rather than delay to defend the opinion that none of the evangelists personally knew Jesus during his earthly life, it seems more useful to point out a significant and positive consequence of this fact. Each evangelist had of necessity to receive from the Jesus-tradition, already created by one or two generations in the primitive Church, the data about Jesus' words and actions which he chose to incorporate into his Gospel. For the greater part such traditions were still being passed on by word of mouth (preaching, instruction, defense of the faith), although Mark, the first Gospel-writer, made use (as will be seen) of certain essays about isolated episodes that had already been set down in writing. There were certainly, by the time the first Gospel came to be created, very early accounts of Jesus' Passion (including his death and post-resurrection appearances) written up for use in the liturgy of various communities.

Now it is of the utmost importance to appreciate the peculiar features of the content of this tradition. Some of these were pointed out in a significant document issued by the Pontifical Biblical Commission, April 21, 1964, "The Historical Truth of the Gospels."[21] Three stages in the evolution of the Gospel-tradition are traced: that of the public life of the "historical Jesus"; then the post-resurrection creation of the apostolic preaching; finally, the composition of the four Gospels. It is the second stage which is of present concern here. "The apostles proclaimed above all the death and resurrection of the Lord as they bore witness to Jesus. They faithfully explained his life and words, while taking into account in their method of preaching the circumstances in which their listeners found themselves. After Jesus rose from the dead and his divinity was clearly perceived, faith, far from destroying the memory of what had transpired, rather confirmed it, because their faith rested on the things Jesus did and taught. . . . On the other hand . . . the apostles transmitted to their hearers what was really said and done by the Lord with that fuller understanding which they enjoyed, having been instructed by the glorious events of the Christ and taught by the light of the Spirit of truth. So . . . they also interpreted his words and deeds according to the needs of their listeners. . . . They preached and employed various modes of speaking suited to their own purpose and the mentality of their listeners. . . . These modes of speaking . . . must be distinguished and assessed. . . ."[22] It will have been noted that this apostolic, evangelical tradition is admittedly already an *interpretation* of Jesus' actions and teaching in the light of the post-resurrection faith. It was moreover an *adaptation,* accommodated to the audience, that is, a rephrasing of what Jesus had actually said, a recasting of stories about him. Lastly, it was an *articulation* in new "modes of speaking," dictated at once by the orientation of the apostolic proclamation and by "the mentality of their listeners." Consequently, to think that in our Gospels we have the "very words of Jesus" is not only ingenuous (the original Greek texts contain very few Aramaic words, the language of Jesus), but deleterious to the correct conception of tradition as well as unhelpful to our attempts to pray from the Gospels. It is unhelpful because it neglects one very important element, the personal appropriation by numbers of primitive Christians of Jesus' earthly history.

It is useful for our purpose to reflect upon the experience of receiving the traditions about Jesus which each Gospel writer underwent. And here it is Paul, above all, who will prove of invaluable assistance. Paul, of course, was not acquainted with Jesus during his earthly life (2 Cor 5:16b). After he received the gift of Christian faith through the intervention of the risen Lord on the Damascus road, he had still to learn about what Jesus had said and done from the evangelical traditions, which he was undoubtedly taught by those who instructed him in Christianity. Paul moreover attests frequently by his letters to the high value he set upon these traditions regarding Jesus. He declares to the Corinthians, "I handed on to you as of supreme importance what I in my turn had received [in tradition]" (1 Cor 15:3). Scarcely a genuinely Pauline letter omits to speak of receiving or handing on this tradition (2 Corinthians is a notable exception: see 1 Thes 2:13; 4:1-2; 2 Thes 2:15; 3:6; Phil 4:7; 1 Cor 11:2; Gal 1:9; Rom 6:17; Col 2:6).

Two statements regarding tradition by Paul deserve to be noted and commented upon. "For I received [as tradition] *from the Lord* what I in my turn handed on to you, how the Lord Jesus, on the night he was handed over, took bread. . . . " (1 Cor 11:23). The italicized phrase strikes a curious note. For Paul the (liturgical) tradition regarding Jesus' promulgation of the Lord's supper was received by him from the risen Christ! How is this to be explained? Even more emphatic is his assertion to the Galatian churches about his own reception of his Gospel. "The Gospel preached by me is not of human origin; *nor did I receive it from any human being,* nor was I taught it except through a *revela-*

tion by Jesus Christ" (Gal 1:11–12). Can this strong statement be construed to mean, as certain commentators have suggested, that all the knowledge acquired about Jesus by Paul, who had no personal experience of Jesus' earthly life, was imparted to him through visions? That would indeed make Paul a crank and a visionary! More significantly, such an hypothesis contradicts Paul's own concern to learn precisely about the evangelical traditions from authoritative sources such as Peter. For in this same letter to Galatia, written actually to vindicate his own authority and independence as an apostle, Paul states: "Then after three years I went up to Jerusalem to consult Cephas, and I remained with him two weeks" (1:18); and "I went up as the result of a revelation, and I laid before them the Gospel I am proclaiming among the pagans . . . to make sure that the race I had run, and was running, should not be run uselessly" (2:2).

Yet, of course, we still are confronted with the question: Why, if Paul in fact learned the Jesus-tradition from his fellow Christians, does he declare so apodictically that he did not receive these data "from any human being, nor was I taught, except through a revelation of Jesus Christ"? I suggest the key to this anomaly is to be found in Paul's intense awareness that to receive this tradition was no merely natural process of data-gathering. It was in truth a personal experience of the action of the risen Lord Jesus, who was the agent transmitting the traditions concerning his earthly life to Paul.

What indication that this is Paul's conviction can be found in his letters? What attitude does he adopt toward the teaching and deeds of Jesus? Is it correct to conclude, as some students of the Pauline letters sometimes do, that Paul displayed little if any interest in Jesus' earthly history? I suggest there are indications that, if Paul does not often cite sayings of Jesus and only once (1 Cor 11:23–25) includes a narrative from his earthly life, yet he clearly treasures the teaching and the life of Jesus as of superlative value for Christian living. One piece of evidence is readily available. Whenever Paul alludes to some point of Jesus' teaching, he never refers to a "saying (*logion*) of Jesus," as does the modern critic; he speaks rather of a "word of *the Lord,*" that is, the risen Christ (1 Thes 4:15; 1 Cor 7:10; 9:14; Rom 14:14). It is as emanating from the exalted Lord Jesus (in Paul's eyes) that the teachings preserved in the Gospel traditions possess authority. When Paul himself communicates such injunctions he thinks of himself simply as an intermediary or instrument of the risen Christ. "And now, my brothers, we beg and exhort you by our union with Lord Jesus: you must continue living your lives by virtue of the tradition, received from me, regarding the way we ought to live to please God—indeed, you must even excel yourselves! For you know what injunctions we gave you *through the Lord* Jesus" (1 Thes 4:1–2). "If anyone considers himself a prophet or led by the Spirit, then let him recognize that what I write is *the Lord's command!*" (1 Cor 14:37). In his own case Paul has personally felt the dynamic action of the risen Christ as he received the tradition concerned with the earthly Jesus. "The Lord laid down the injunction that those who preach the Gospel should earn their living by the Gospel" (1 Cor 9:14). "I know, I have been convinced of this *by Lord Jesus*, nothing is impure in itself" (Rom 14:14). Moreover, it is clear that Paul regards the evangelical tradition as a reality that is beyond the merely human. "So, since Jesus was delivered to you [by tradition] as Messiah and Lord, live your lives in union with him. Be rooted in him; become built upon him; be consolidated in the faith you were taught; let your hearts overflow with thankfulness. Be on your guard! Do not allow your minds to be seduced by hollow and delusive speculations, based on tradition of man-made teaching and centered on the elemental spirits of the world, and not on Christ!" (Col 2:6–8). Thus, while there can be no question that Paul actually had been taught what we should call the "content" of the tradition from his predecessors in the faith, Paul does not make such a distinction. The imperative or authoritative character of this teaching, for him, does not stem from the accuracy of "eye-witnesses," their reliability, or the fidelity of the transmission of these traditions. Their "special pre-eminence" (Vatican II) as testimony to "the life and teaching of the incarnate Word, our Savior" springs from his own experience and faith that they are truly the "utterance of Christ" (Rom 10:17), capable of effecting that "hearing," or openness of man's innermost heart, that leads to faith. Thus there are two important elements to be noted in Paul's attitude toward these "sayings of the Lord": they have been communicated to him by the risen Christ, *and* his personal experience of this dynamic action upon himself attests their universal value for Christian living.

In similar fashion Paul speaks of the actions of the earthly Jesus as deeds of the Lord. In his narrative of the institution of the Eucharist, it is to "the Lord Jesus" that the words and actions are attributed (1 Cor 11:23). Paul asserts that the Jews "killed the Lord Jesus" (1 Thes 2:15), that the powers of evil "crucified the Lord of glory" (1 Cor 2:8). Thus for Paul Jesus' mortal life is of consequence for Christian living as *the pre-history of the exalted Christ,* who commands faith.

One finds an analogous mode of speaking in Luke's Gospel. Alone of the evangelists, Luke retrojects the resurrection-title "the Lord" back into his narrative of the public ministry, and he does this some sixteen times. This seems to imply that this evangelist desires the reader to think of Jesus' activity and teaching, *already in his mortal existence,* as of a piece with his activity in his risen life. Indeed, it is not entirely implausible that when he summarizes his Gospel in the opening sentence of Acts, Luke deliberately employs the expression "all that Jesus *began* to perform and to teach" and is not simply under Semitic influence. At any rate, our evangelist has with great frequency used "the Lord" to denominate Jesus, beginning with the narrative of the miracle at Naim (Lk 7:13), "And the Lord on seeing her was moved to pity." It is "the Lord" who "appointed a further seventy-two" (10:1). Mary sits "at the feet of the Lord" (10:39), and "the Lord" replies to Martha's complaint (10:41). The series comes to an end with the story of Peter's denials: "And the Lord turned around and looked upon Peter; and Peter remembered the saying of the Lord. . . ." (22:61). By this technique Luke appears to regard the words and actions of the historical Jesus as those of the risen Lord, *insofar as they are significant for Christian faith.* Such a conviction, I believe, springs from Luke's personal experience of receiving the Gospel traditions from those he has called "the original eye-witnesses who also became ministers of the word" (Lk 1:2).

The fourth evangelist alludes several times to the experience of Jesus' disciples after his resurrection, by which they come to grasp the meaning of his actions as "signs" and the true sense of his mysterious utterances during his public ministry. This privileged experience of Jesus' followers John denominates as "remembering," although he evidently intends the term to connote far more than mere historical recall, since it leads to genuine faith in Jesus. Note the evangelist's comment on the enigmatic saying, "Destroy this sanctuary, and in three days I will raise it up again" (2:19). "He however was speaking about the sanctuary of his body. Consequently, after his resurrection his disciples *remembered* what he had said, and they *believed* the Scriptures and *the word* Jesus had uttered" (2:20).

There is a similar gloss which John appends to his narrative of the messianic entry by Jesus into Jerusalem, where he cites combined texts from Zechariah and Zephaniah. "At the time, his disciples did not understand, but after Jesus had been glorified they *remembered* that this had been written about him and that this had happened to him" (12:16). Here the post-resurrection experience of the disciples provides an understanding of the Christological orientation of Old Testament prophecy. They were brought to see how Jesus had fulfilled Israel's Scriptures.

To what does John ascribe this new post-resurrection awareness by Jesus' disciples? We learn this from Jesus' words at the Last Supper. "I have told you all this while I am still here with you; but the Paraclete, the Holy Spirit, whom the Father will send in my name, will teach you everything and *will make you remember* all I have told you" (14:25–26). Thus "remembering" is a spiritual experience, not merely a mnemonic exercise. It is the effect of the new presence of the Holy Spirit, promised by Jesus and sent to his own after Jesus' glorification.

Does this evangelist say anything about the experience of those who receive the Gospel traditions in a later period? There is at least one clear statement which John has placed in the mouth of the risen Lord at his appearance to Thomas, words which formed (in the original ending of this Gospel) the final utterance of Jesus himself. "Happy those who, though they never saw me, yet have come to believe" (20:29b). The beatitude-form is employed in our Gospels to express an already existent state of happiness in relation to God and his Christ. While such a state obviously belongs to the eschatological "end-time," it is brought forward by the judgment pronounced in the beatitude and is in truth already to some degree a present possession.

This evangelist has the deepest respect for "the original eye-witnesses" and certainly considers them to be "happy," but the radical reason for his creation of a new beatitude is the new presence of Jesus (though visibly absent) through "another Paraclete" (14:16), the Spirit of truth. Hence what John has to say about the function of the Holy Spirit, particularly in his discourse after the Last Supper, may, I venture to suggest, be taken as his chief grounds for pronouncing the final beatitude on those who have never personally known Jesus "in the days of his flesh." And this awareness of the Spirit is, in John's view, initially experienced in the reception of the traditions concerned with Jesus' earthly history. Such would appear to be the import of Jesus' prayer before his Passion for "those who through their [i.e., the first disciples'] word [the apostolic preaching] come to believe in me, in order that they all may be one. Inasmuch as you, Father, are in me and I am in you, [I pray] that they in turn may be one in us, that the world may believe you have sent me." Thus far Jesus' prayer for these future disciples is much like that for the unity of those who personally knew and followed him (17:11b), to whom "I have given your word" (v. 14), and whom Jesus sends forth to challenge "the world" (v. 18). But now John appears to add something more to Jesus' prayer for these later disciples. "And I have given to them *the glory* you have given me" (v. 23). John uses the word "glory" in its technical sense of the divine self-revelation; thus Jesus' glory given him by the Father is his entire earthly life, climaxed and brought to its successful consummation by his death, whereby he reveals the unseen God. This self-disclosure of Jesus is his "glory," and this he bestows upon those "who, though they never saw me, yet have come to believe." Now it is precisely this revelation of Jesus' identity that, for John, is properly the function of the Spirit, since it is "he who *will glorify me*. For he will take what is mine, and unveil it for you" (16:14). By "what is mine" John means the reader to understand the whole of Jesus' earthly history, whose true significance can be "unveiled" only through the action of the Spirit. Thus the reception of the Jesus-tradition by those who never saw Jesus in his lifetime is, in John's view, truly a "spiritual" experience.

With regard to the Gospels of Mark and Matthew it is more difficult to point to specific evidence that the reception of the tradition by these writers was a supernatural experience. A remark by Matthew, in which he not inconceivably refers to himself, may be read in this sense. "For this reason every scribe become a disciple of the kingdom of heaven is like a householder who can produce from his storeroom the new as well as the old" (Mt 13:52). Moreover, this evangelist's introduction of a series of ten "formula citations"[23]—a unique feature of his Gospel—may also be taken as evidence of Matthew's attitude toward his own reception of the tradition. These quotations of Old Testament texts, apparently translated directly from the Hebrew, are a gloss by Matthew (nothing similar is found in either Mark or Luke) by way of commentary on Jesus' actions.

The Gospel Narrative, Record of Author's Reactions to Episode

My second point is, in a sense, implicit in the first, but I wish to draw attention to a consequence of it which will prove helpful in contemplating the scenes of Jesus' public life by the prayerful perusal of the text of a given evangelist. My *second* point is that one ought to be very much aware that any Gospel narrative is *primarily* the record of its author's personal reaction to the tradition he has received regarding a particular episode in the life of Jesus. This is simply the application to our prayer of an important discovery of contemporary Gospel criticism. In our day considerable light has been thrown on the significance which an individual evangelist has attached to an event in Jesus' life by analyzing the way, often highly creative and personal, in which he has re-edited the story as handed on to him in tradition. Almost always it is the writer's own conception of Jesus and his mission which presides over this refashioning of his narrative. It may be (as in the case of Matthew) the picture he has formed for himself of the Church in his own day which determines the manner in which he tells his version, for instance, of the storm on the lake.[24] Or, as with Luke, it may be the view taken of the profound puzzle of the lack of comprehension of "the original eye-witnesses" who followed Jesus. In Luke's eyes no blame attaches to the Twelve for this failure to pierce the mystery: "Its meaning was concealed from them" (Lk 18:34c); "They did not comprehend this saying; it appeared so obfuscated for them, lest they perceive its meaning; and they remained too frightened to ask him about this saying" (Lk 9:45).

Indeed, not infrequently the results of such editorial work on the part of our evangelists stand in rather obvious contradiction, one with another. Thus the observant reader of the various Gethsemane episodes might well ask himself whether the disciples ran away at Jesus' arrest (as in Mark and Matthew), or whether they remained at Jesus' side (as Luke implies), or whether they were dismissed by Jesus himself and allowed safe-conduct by Jesus' captors (as with John). Much more distressing, because seemingly of far greater importance, is what form the words of Jesus, in instituting the Eucharist, took at the Last Supper. Paul, our earliest written version (1 Cor 11:23–25), differs notably from Mark (14:22–24) or Matthew (26:26–28), or even Lk 22:19–20, and especially from Jn 6:51c.

Let us reassure ourselves of one thing before going any further. The various episodes concerning Jesus in the Gospels do tell us—and faithfully tell us—about Jesus! Their basic historical value cannot reasonably be called into question. That Jesus came with a message from God, proclaiming the imminent coming of God's sovereignty in human history, that he realized that his message was the final, definitive summons to men to accept through himself God's ultimate self-disclosure, that his ministry had such serious implications and met such resolute, virulent opposition as to make his own death a necessary part of that ministry—all this belongs undeniably to the historicity of our Gospels. Moreover, Jesus must be credited with performing those "acts of power" or "signs" which we call miracles, since these are attested by the sacred writers as inextricably meshed

with Jesus' teaching. One cannot deny the miracles without rejecting the doctrine of Jesus. Indeed, it is only reasonable to expect that God would intervene in what may appear to some to
be a spectacular fashion, once one accepts in faith the fact that in
Jesus God has willed to utter his ultimate summons to mankind,
thus terminating his historical attempts at self-revelation.

Yet it is as well to admit that our modern preoccupation to
find out "just how it actually happened" betrays a large measure
of merely human curiosity which can distract us from the
search for that kind of truth we ought to be seeking primarily
from the sacred books. Vatican II has reminded us in *Dei Verbum*
that we ought to be searching for "that truth which God has
willed to consign to the sacred writings *for the sake of our salvation.*"[25] It is then saving truth, not scientific, or historical, or literary truth that the man of faith is to derive from contemplating
the Gospels. If it is correct to define an event as happening *plus
meaning*, as I believe it is, then it is precisely in the significance
of any event in Jesus' life that the saving element is to be found.
Now it is just this element which the evangelist's interpretation
of what Jesus said and did seeks to bring before the eyes of the
believing reader. It is moreover the accuracy of the insight of
the sacred writer which is guaranteed for us by the charism of
scriptural inspiration.

It is helpful, of course, to bear in mind that we do not have
in the Gospels a coldly objective, scientifically detached portrait
of Jesus or of the disciples. Each evangelist is profoundly and
personally involved through his faith in this saving story he has
created from the traditions he received. Thus this Gospel-histo-
ry is a *mediated* history, that is, we are brought (and should allow
ourselves to be brought) to meet Jesus and accept him through
the author's presentation of him. We are to endeavor to "see Jesus" as Mark or Matthew or John or Luke "saw" him. And, as
will be seen in detail in the following chapter,[26] Mark's Jesus is
distinctively different from the Jesus of Luke or John.

The question "Why four?" is often asked with respect to the
Gospels. Harald Riesenfeld is worth citing here. "If we had only
one Gospel, it might perhaps have been possible to picture an
imaginative self-consciousness within the framework of the life

of Jesus. But with the existence of four separate pictures of the appeal and the claim of Jesus, the hypothesis that the nerve-center of the figure of Jesus should be an invention of the early Church is quite unbelievable; what is more important, it cannot be proved."[27] Somewhat further on, Professor Riesenfeld discusses Oscar Cullmann's view of this question and comments: "Perhaps Cullmann gives a somewhat too one-sided explanation of this fact when he denies the 'biographical' outlook of the Gospels and only recognizes them as 'witnesses to faith.' Is it not rather the case that 'witness to faith' and 'biography'—not in the sense of a chronological biographical account, but as a reproduction of the impression made by the words and work of some personality—present in indestructible unity the reactions called forth by impulses proceding from a *bios?* For that reason it was intuitively realized in the early Church that a single Gospel is as little capable of apprehending the dimensions and plasticity of the person and message of Jesus as is a single portrait when it comes to reproducing the complicated richness of any individual personality. On the other hand, the early Church clearly felt that the harmonizing of the Gospels would lead to a result just as destructive as a reduction in the numbers of the Gospels."[28]

One aspect of this quadriform character of the Gospel, to which Professor Riesenfeld does not advert, is of some consequence for anyone attempting to pray from the Gospels. When at prayer I approach a particular narrative in any one of them, I ought not to neglect the personality of the evangelist through whose presentations I seek to relate to Jesus. To have my own "spiritual" experience of my Lord with the help of an evangelist, I should scrutinize as carefully as I can the various facets of his own experience of Jesus. I am, of course, to try to speak to Jesus as he reveals himself to me now in a specific mystery of his earthly life, but I should also address myself to the person (be it Mark, or Matthew, or Luke, or John) through whose eyes and heart and faith I am confronted with the Lord Jesus. I should be involved in dialogue with this sacred author, whose specially privileged experience of Christ has produced his own inspired account of Jesus. I am wise if I lean upon his assistance in my attempts to hear the claim of Jesus upon myself.

Accordingly, I should come gradually, through familiarity with the four Gospels, to cherish the distinctiveness, the differences, the contradictions in the pictures of Jesus which these four writers present to me. To try by some ingenious tour de force to flatten out these varying portraits, to make Luke or John conform to Mark, is not only to lack reverence for the creative work of the Spirit in these inspired writers. It is actually to impoverish the picture of Jesus which the Church has for centuries held out to all believers, and thus to impoverish my own image of Jesus. Each evangelist has an inestimable treasure to give me if only I can give up the mania for standardization and conformity, and my curiosity as to "what really happened."

The third and fourth points I wish to discuss will provide answers to one of the questions especially which were raised in the earlier section of this chapter. How can the Gospel narratives, as records of the past, insofar as they contain the story of Jesus' earthly life, exercise any influence upon our present-day Christian existence? Now it is true, nonetheless, that the men of the past although dead can still exert a profound influence upon the present. Socrates, for example, is dead these past two thousand years. Yet his memory and the fascination of his personality and virtuous life still retain their power. There is a very real sense in which Socrates survives, and his past life survives in that survival. This is largely the effect of the genius of Socrates' pupil, Plato, whose *Dialogues* have immortalized his master by perpetuating his ideas and his celebrated method of arriving at the truth. We may well ask (in fact, should ask) whether the memory of Jesus has lived on among us because of the four Gospels. Are Jesus, the attraction of his personality, and the appeal of his teaching the creation of the evangelists? These questions must be fairly and squarely confronted.

The Absence of Any Sense of Nostalgia in Our Gospels

It has been one of the lasting achievements of the method of Gospel-study, called, in English, Form criticism, to have dispelled the mistaken notion that the Gospels are simply biographies of Jesus of Nazareth. In the first flush of enthusiasm for this new discovery in the 1920s, the original Form critics like Martin Dibelius and Rudolf Bultmann displayed great skepticism with regard to the historical elements present in the Gospels. Yet, the gains in our knowledge of the life and practices of the very early Christian communities, which the application of Form criticism has unearthed, have been solid and manifold. Indeed, Catholics may take some pride in the thought that, through the document issued by the Pontifical Biblical Commission in 1964, to which we have already referred, the Catholic Church has officially approved this methodology as a valid technique for tracing the development of the Jesus-tradition.[29]

What has led the practitioners of Form criticism to the conclusion that the Gospels are not a "life" of Jesus, or even sources out of which such a life might be written? "The nature of the only real sources for the life of Jesus—the Synoptic Gospels—makes a biography impossible. The community which was most influential in the formation of the tradition was not concerned with a biography as such and did not transmit a connected, chronological, geographical outline of developments in the life of Jesus. It transmitted individual sayings and narratives, with the single exception of the passion narrative. Moreover, according to Dibelius and Bultmann, the individual units do not go back to Jesus. The Church formulated them for its purposes! We do not delete 'additions' here and there and get back to a primitive form from Jesus' day; we get back to the form which originated in the Church."[30] Even if one might reasonably query the contention that the "biographical" was in no sense an interest of the very early Church, yet it remains true that it was the day-to-day life of the young Christian communities with its various needs which was responsible for the selection, preservation, and even the development of certain episodes, as well as many sayings from the public life of Jesus. Sometimes these interests were liturgical; hence the varying formulations of the words of institution, or the transcription of a baptismal formula (Mt 28:19), or the preservation in two distinct forms of the dominical prayer (Mt 6:9–13; Lk 11:2–4). Often it was an ascetical interest which retained Jesus' saying about fasting in Christianity (Mk

2:18–22). The need of the young Church to defend her belief that Jesus was in truth the Messiah, indeed the Son of God, led her to conserve whatever episodes or utterances of Jesus might be interpreted in this sense. In fact, since Jesus in his own lifetime appears not to have admitted that he was Messiah (much less, Son of God), the insight of Christian faith prompted the religious genius who authored the Fourth Gospel to embark upon the monumental and highly creative development for which his book is famous. Again, if Jesus during his public teaching invoked the mysterious figure "the Son of Man," it was, it seems, as someone distinct from himself and the ultimate vindicator of the truth of his teaching. "Now I tell you, everyone who will acknowledge me before men, the Son of Man will acknowledge you before the angels of God; but anyone who disowns me before men will be disowned before the angels of God" (Lk 12:8–9). As a result of Jesus' vindication by his resurrection and with the advent of Christian faith, the Church expressed her belief in Jesus' divinity by reformulating many "Son of Man" sayings so as to affirm the identity of Jesus as the Son of Man.

The above examples of certain interests in the very early Christian communities which presided over the preservation and formation of the Jesus-tradition must suffice here as a demonstration of one of the most significant features of our Gospels—their notable lack of any nostalgia for "the good old days" of Jesus' earthly life. None of the four evangelists ever implies the least desire to go back to that dearly loved, most precious period in history when the Twelve enjoyed such familiarity with Jesus; not one of them fancies it as a vanished golden age to which he longs to return. Luke, as he writes the conclusion of his Gospel, after describing Jesus' leave-taking of the little band of first disciples at his ascension into heaven, remarks in a somewhat offhand way, "And they returned to Jerusalem with great joy, and spent all their time in the temple area blessing God" (24:52–53). It appears well nigh unbelievable: Jesus has left them forever—and his abandoned followers are filled with joy! Mark, with what would seem to be an ironical twist, concludes his book by drawing attention to the terror and disobedience of three women confronted at the empty tomb by a youth in a white robe. "And they fled out of the tomb: they were beside themselves with terror; and they said nothing to anyone, since they were afraid" (16:8). How then, the reader may well ask, did the great good news of Jesus' resurrection ever get out?

This lack of nostalgia for the privileged familiarity which the Twelve enjoyed with the earthly Jesus is the more remarkable when it is recalled how each evangelist, in his own way, is careful to remind us that the old intimacy with Jesus was never part of the post-resurrection confrontations by their Lord with his disciples. On the contrary, the disciples are filled with fears, thinking at first that the risen One is a ghost (Lk 24:37); and even after his urging that they touch him, "they kept doubting for joy" (v. 41). Or they continue ill at ease in his presence near the lake of Tiberias, knowing who he is, yet filled with inhibitions which prevent their asking "Who are you?" (Jn 21:22). And at the appointed rendezvous on the mountain in Galilee, as Matthew reports, "upon seeing him they made an obeisance—yet some doubted" (28:17).

Finally, each of the Gospel writers makes it only too plain that the period of Jesus' presence to his disciples during the public life was actually a time of their ignorance of him, their lack of appreciation of his aims and goals, incomprehension of his mission, and frightened obtuseness at his repeated mention of his future sufferings. Mark's Gospel has indubitably made its name by its author's repeated insistence upon what Wilhelm Wrede happily dubbed "the messianic secret." In fact, it is a mystery that keeps the reader in suspense until after the death of Jesus himself, when a pagan Roman centurion declares, "Truly this man was God's Son!" (15:39). The author of the Fourth Gospel goes out of his way, as he writes a special conclusion to his story of Jesus' public life, to pronounce it a complete, or almost total failure. "In spite of the many signs Jesus worked in their presence they would not believe in him. . . . For all that, even among those in authority, many found faith in him; yet they would not profess their faith openly on account of the Pharisees, for fear of being excommunicated from the synagogue. They set a higher priority on their reputation with men than on the glory of God" (12:37–43). More poignant and tragic still is the failure of Jesus' closest disciples, as late as the last meal they shared with him before the Passion, to grasp even the simplest hints he gives them regarding his imminent departure from them. Peter thinks of it as a long, possibly a dangerous journey, offering to accompany Jesus, and he is puzzled to have Jesus refuse his companionship (13:36–38). Thomas, admitting their collective ignorance of Jesus' ultimate destination, finds it unreasonable of Jesus to assume that they know the road he travels (14:3–5). Philip, obviously hoping for a theophany like those depicted in the Old Testament, betrays his profound ignorance of Jesus' true identity (14:7–11). And Judas, not Iscariot, ingenuously voices his disillusionment with Jesus' failure to stage a well-publicized manifestation of himself (14:22–24). Moreover, it is this same fourth evangelist, as noted earlier, who originally concluded his book with the paradoxical beatitude pronounced by the risen Jesus, "Happy those who, though they never saw me, yet have come to believe!" (20:29b). Happy indeed as were the Eleven, privileged as was their experience of Jesus' public ministry and death, and essential for our faith as that collective experience actually was, yet it is *we*, John has Jesus tell us as we read this Gospel, who are the happy ones. The writer who penned that macarism was certainly not an advocate of nostalgia for the good old days!

The Crucial Significance of Jesus' Resurrection

This brings us to the *fourth* (and final) point. Despite the obvious fact that each Gospel writer devotes most of his book to recounting what Jesus said and did during "the days of his flesh," yet not one of the evangelists is in any way concerned to record Jesus' past as past. Rather one receives the distinct impression again and again that what is recounted is presented somehow as a contemporary reality which can and must exert its influence upon my Christian life in the twentieth century. For one thing, as we have seen, the traditions concerning Jesus recorded in the Gospels were preserved and selected out of many others precisely because of some need or interest or concern of the very early communities or of one of their members. The fourth evangelist in his explicit statement of purpose avows his concern with the deepening of faith in his Christian reader. "These things have been written down, in order that you may deepen your faith . . . and possess eternal life" (Jn 20:31). Luke declares that he writes out of a contemporary concern, to give a more thoroughgoing instruction to the lordly Theophilus (possibly a convert of Luke's) and so provide a more solid foundation for this neo-Christian's faith. "I, in my turn, noble Theophilus, after thorough and complete research into their origins, have resolved to write an ordered narrative for you, in order that you may possess a deeper knowledge of the solid basis for what you heard in the catechesis" (Lk 1:3–4). Not preoccupation with the past, but conviction about the contemporary relevance of what he writes has motivated Luke in the writing of his Gospel.

Yet what precisely has brought it about that our Gospels are not mere history, and certainly not biography? Why is it that their authors, insofar as they expressly state their purpose in composing these books, do not intend to record the past of Jesus *as past*, but as, in a very real sense, of on-going importance and significance for subsequent generations of Christians? The answer to these questions is a brief and simple one: the resurrection of Jesus has occurred between his earthly life and the writing of our Gospels.

Yet, if the answer is a simple one, it demands a nuanced understanding (insofar as it is possible to comprehend this greatest mystery of our Christian faith), an understanding we can acquire only by putting ourselves to school to the four evangelists and to Paul. In fact, for the sake of clarity, I should like to resume what these sacred writers have to say about Jesus' resurrection under *four* headings.

First, it is of paramount importance to realize that all these inspired writers unambiguously present the resurrection as an event unique and unparalleled in history. One of the clearest proofs of this awareness on the part of the authors of the New Testament is the fact that nowhere is any attempt ever made to describe the actual resurrection of Jesus as it happened. Accordingly, as Bultmann somewhere sagaciously remarked, it is not to be pictured as the resuscitation of a corpse. For that sort of happening is precisely what *is* described several times by the evangelists in the raising to life of Jairus' dead daughter (Mk 5:35–42), or of the widow's son at Naim (Lk 7:1–17), or of Lazarus of Bethany (Jn 11:8–44). It is important to perceive that in each of these instances the dead person was brought back to this present, mortal existence. Consequently, the beneficiaries of such a great favor did not escape the inevitable necessity of facing death a second time.

Jesus Christ, unlike these people, *has not come back to this life.* Such is *not* the meaning of his resurrection, and the discreet silence of our inspired writers is there to prove it. Paul however has in fact stated this truth in more positive fashion by declaring that Jesus is risen to a completely new, unprecedented life with God. "You know that Christ, risen from death, can no longer die: death possesses no more power over him. The death he died was a death once for all to sin: the life he now lives he lives unto God" (Rom 6:9–10). Paul can state this facet of Jesus' resurrection in another way, when he contrasts the entry into human existence of the first human being with Jesus' entry into his risen life. "Thus it has also been stated in Scripture, 'the first man Adam became a living person'; the last Adam has become life-giving Spirit" (1 Cor 15:45).

There is a particular feature to be noted that is characteristic of the Gospel accounts of Jesus' post-resurrection appearances to his own. Our evangelists appear to be very much aware of a danger inherent in their attempts to describe these ineffable experiences of the disciples. While, on the one hand, they wish to insist upon the reality of Jesus' bodily presence on these occasions, yet, on the other, they wish to avoid any impression that Jesus has simply returned to his old way of life. These writers' concern to make their reader realize that the disciples never regained their former comfortable familiarity with the risen Jesus has already been mentioned earlier. This is the function of the frequent mention of the attitude of doubt which the men, at least, who were confronted with the risen Lord, displayed (Mt 28:19; Lk 24:38; Jn 20:25). Moreover, the thrust of Jesus' warning to Mary Magdalene at Jn 20:17 should not be missed. Mary, upon recognizing her beloved Master, had grasped him about the knees in an ecstasy of loving adoration. "Do not go on clinging to me!" Jesus admonishes her. This peremptory prohibition is really intended to forbid any desire to return to the past, to hanker after the old, human relationships with Jesus, enjoyed by those who knew and loved him in his earthly existence.

A second trait of the post-resurrection narratives merits our attention: the risen Lord is consistently depicted as endowed with a totally new and untrammeled freedom in his dealings with his own. He has by resurrection become the one uniquely free human being. I do not mean that ghost-like attribute which the Scholastic theologians were pleased to predicate of the risen One—*agilitas*, that is, the ability to pass through solid walls or locked doors. I venture to suggest that this imagined characteristic of a risen body is simply based upon questionable inference from a text like Jn 20:19: "When evening came that first day of the week and the doors of the place where the disciples met were locked out of fear of the Jews, Jesus came and stood among them. . . . " The writer does not state, or even necessarily imply, that Jesus came through the locked doors. Surely it is equally possible to conclude that he was already with them but unseen until the moment he willed to manifest his presence to the Eleven. This viewpoint has the advantage of bringing these experiences of the disciples, privileged indeed as they were, closer to our own experiences of "meeting" the risen Jesus through faith in our contacts with other persons in our daily lives.

The evangelists' intention of illustrating this new-found freedom of the risen Christ is to be seen in their silence about how the Lord came to his disciples on these various occasions; or, except possibly for Lk 24:31—"And he vanished from their sight"—how he took leave of them. This same unlimited freedom of action was probably attributed to the risen Jesus in the very ancient *credo*, cited by Paul to the Corinthians (1 Cor 15:5ff). The choice of the Greek term for "he was seen" (*ōphthē*) may well be influenced by the Septuagint, where it was employed to describe an Old Testament theophany and exhibited the meaning "he allowed himself to be seen," thus safeguarding the divine liberty. Thus it is not unlikely that the Pauline passage should read, ". . . and that *he allowed himself to be seen* by Cephas, then by the Twelve. . . . "

Yet another feature of certain of these post-resurrection narratives in the Gospels is to be remarked upon. The evangelists hint strongly that without the new Christian faith which the risen Jesus bestows in these meetings with the disciples, they remained unable to "see," that is, to recognize him in his risen state. This explains why Mary Magdalene (Jn 20:15) mistook her Master at first for the gardener. She had not yet received the gift of faith, until *through the word of Jesus* (which for John is the sure basis of genuine faith), calling her by name, she was able to respond in recognition, "Rabbouni!" Similarly, the two disciples of Emmaus in the Lucan story are described, when Jesus falls in with them on their journey, as failing to recognize the risen One. "Something kept them from seeing who it was" (Lk 24:16). It was only in the course of the meal which these disciples' hospitality offered this stranger that "their eyes were opened, and they recognized him" (v. 31). As they later relate to the Eleven in Jerusalem, he let himself become known to them "at the breaking of the bread" (v. 35). There is however another detail in this narrative which is significant. After their recognition of Jesus and his disappearance, the two disciples reflect upon their earlier experience en route to Emmaus, as Jesus "explained to them the passages which referred to him all through the Scriptures" (v. 27). "And they said to each other, 'Did not our hearts glow when he talked with us along the road, and was explaining the Scriptures to us?' " (v. 32). In retrospect these followers of Jesus were able to perceive the effects of his (as yet unrecognized) presence to them. It was the birth of faith in their hearts that, half-consciously felt through his words to them, eventually gave them the capacity to "see" the risen Jesus. St. Thomas Aquinas, with his extraordinary insight into the Scriptures, observed appositely in the *Summa Theologica,* "After his resurrection the disciples saw the living Christ, whom they knew to have died, *with the eyes of faith (oculata fide).*"[31] This perceptive remark is crucial for the understanding of these post-resurrection narratives, by means of which the evangelists present the genesis of Christian faith in Jesus' chosen disciples. St.

Thomas does not wish to imply that the risen Jesus was not bodily present on these occasions, or that the truth of his resurrection consists merely in a subjective conviction by these disciples that Jesus was somehow again near them, or that by carrying on his work in history, with the help of their persuasion that he did not remain dead, these disciples felt justified in proclaiming, "He is risen!" St. Thomas is obviously convinced that belief in the resurrection demands the admission that "something happened to Jesus"—and not simply to the disciples' attitudes towards their dead leader. St. Thomas, on the contrary, does mean to declare that our natural human organs of perception, unaided by faith, cannot discern the glorified body of Jesus. He also implies that, without the free acquiescence of the risen Lord, it is impossible for any follower of his to see him. St. Thomas intends by his provocative statement to provide an interpretation of the data in the Gospel stories about these meetings with the risen Jesus. He appears to be aware that they describe in very concrete fashion a series of data which almost defy description, yet which adequately explain to the reader how the disciples first became Christians. St. Thomas may well imply moreover that, while these experiences were indeed unique, and so provide the basis for our own faith, yet they were fundamentally of the same quality as our own "meetings" with our Lord through the contemplation of the Gospels, in other persons with whom we deal, and in the vicissitudes of our ordinary daily lives. To "see him with the eyes of faith" was as necessary for these first disciples as it is for us.

In the *second place*, the evangelists, Luke and John, like Paul, lay stress upon the reality of the *bodily* resurrection of Jesus. To some extent indeed, Mark, who has refused to record any appearances of the risen Lord in his Gospel, speaks of him in terms that imply corporeity. The young man relays the message for "the disciples and Peter" to the women: "He has been raised—he is not here! See the spot where they laid him. Now go, tell his disciples and Peter, 'He goes ahead of you leading you into Galilee. It is there you will see him, as he told you'" (16:6–7). Even if, as Norman Perrin asserts in a new book published after his deeply regretted death,[32] Galilee becomes for this evangelist a symbol of the mission to the pagans, it seems implausible that a Semite like Mark could conceive of the risen Jesus as a bodiless shade. Matthew's story of Jesus' confrontation with the two women hurrying away from the empty tomb contains the remark, "But they went up to him and clasped him by the feet, and did obeisance to him" (28:9b). The Lucan accounts of these experiences underscore the reality of the risen Jesus' bodily presence by portraying him as actually eating—in defiance of the Pauline theologoumenon (1 Cor 6:13) to the effect that in the risen state eating will be abolished by God. Thus Luke implies that Jesus ate with the disciples at Emmaus: "Taking bread he blessed and broke and gave it to them" (24:30), while in the scene in which Jesus appears to the Eleven and other disciples, after failing to convince them of the reality of his bodily presence by ordering them to touch him (v. 39), Jesus is represented as taking the piece of broiled fish they offered, "and he ate it before their very eyes" (v. 43). Luke—only he speaks of Jesus eating—refers again in Acts to this action of Jesus, both during what is depicted at Jesus' final leave-taking of the disciples (Acts 1:4) and in Peter's address to Cornelius. "God ... caused him to be plainly seen ... by witnesses God had designated beforehand, that is, by us who ate and drank with him after he had risen from the dead" (Acts 10:41).

We may recall that for the inspired writers, who were Semitic, the body indicates the *unique self* of the human personality, and it expresses both his distinctiveness as an individual, and also the basis of communion with others. Jn 20:20 provides an example of this point of view. "He showed them his hands and his side; and the disciples rejoiced at seeing the Lord!" Throughout the Bible, man does not have a body, he *is* body; and from this point of view it would be inconceivable that someone should be himself without his body.

This is certainly the mentality consistently evinced by Paul. It is significant that he nowhere speaks of the resurrection of the flesh, but only of the body. Moreover, the whole tenor of Paul's argumentation against the Corinthian enthusiasts, which he keeps as the climax of his entire first letter to that community, demands a firm belief in the bodily resurrection of Jesus and, ultimately, of all faithful believers. This is easily seen in the rather convoluted argument (1 Cor 15:35ff) by which he tries to counter the objection of his adversaries: "How will the dead be raised?" As one reads this tortuous demonstration one is tempted to think that Paul might have been well advised to pass over the point in silence. Yet his insistence shows how very crucial for him is this belief in bodily resurrection. At the same time Paul insists upon the transformation of man's present, mortal bodily state (vv. 53--54). Thus when he speaks of a "spiritual" body (v. 46), his meaning is inadequately represented by the notion advocated by certain Protestant liberal theologians that this was a kind of ectoplasm or ethereal body. While it is obvious that we can form no precise idea of the nature of a risen body (much less imagine what it is like!), since the reality transcends our experience, it is of paramount importance to our Christian faith in Jesus' resurrection, as well as to orthodox belief in the sacramental presence of the risen Lord in the Eucharist. A further consequence of this aspect of Jesus' resurrection will be taken up in the next point.

In the *third* place, a complete diagnosis of the faith in Jesus' resurrection, as attested in the New Testament, must take into consideration not only the assurance that our Lord has gone forward into this totally unprecedented existence with God with his glorified humanity, but also that he has taken with him what I can only call his "historicity." That is to say, Jesus' being "raised from death by the glory of the Father" (Rom 6:4) has also affected that sum of human experiences which we call his earthly life—from the Incarnation to the grave. One might restate this truth in another way. Jesus' life among men here upon earth can no longer be regarded as belonging merely to the past, a past that might be reconstructed by the genius of the historiographer or litterateur, in the way in which, for example, Plato's literary and philosophical talents have enabled the dead Socrates to live perpetually in the *Dialogues.* Jesus' earthly life has in him risen been divinely endowed with a new, dynamic contemporaneity. The point requires some demonstration from the New Testament. We may begin with St. Paul.

In his first extant letter to Corinth he writes, "For my part, brothers, when I came to you, I came not with high-flown rhetoric or sophistry proclaiming the mystery of God. For I resolved while I was with you to think of nothing except Jesus Christ—and him as remaining crucified!" (1 Cor 2:1–2). To describe his Gospel of Jesus, Paul deliberately employs the Greek perfect participle, because he knows (and at the moment wishes to emphasize this) that in a very real sense Jesus, even in his risen state, remains the crucified majesty of God. Paul employs the expression of set purpose as he prepares to confront the errors of the "enthusiasts" in the Corinthian community, who have all too easily forgotten or played down the cross—a salient feature of the Gospel. It would appear that, in their view, the glorification of Jesus has wiped out every vestige of his Passion.

We have already adverted to Paul's peculiar manner of referring the words and actions of the earthly Jesus to "the Lord," the risen Christ. He can only think in this fashion because of his conviction that these words and the experiences of Jesus' mortal life have gone forward with him into the new, glorious existence with God. It is to be recalled that, while several of Paul's references to the experiences of Jesus' mortal life have to do with his Passion (1 Thes 2:15; 1 Cor 2:8; 11:26; Gal 6:14), yet Jesus' actions at the Last Supper are also called those of "the Lord Jesus" (1 Cor 11:23). Indeed, there is at least one text which speaks of Jesus' entire earthly career as that of "the Lord Jesus." "You realize the graciousness of our Lord Jesus Christ, how being rich he beggared himself for your sake. . . . " (2 Cor 8:9). As has already been seen earlier in this chapter, Luke frequently speaks of the actions and words of the Jesus of the public ministry as those of "the Lord."

In the Fourth Gospel Jesus is spoken of as "the Lord" in three texts belonging to narratives of the public life (Jn 4:1; 6:23; 11:1). While this reading is questioned in the first two instances by modern textual critics, it is well supported by some of the best Greek witnesses. What is perhaps more significant is the evangelist's presentation of the risen Jesus as recognizable from the wounds in hands and side. "And upon saying this he showed them his hands and his side; and the disciples rejoiced *at seeing the Lord*" (20:20).

Another writer of the school of John, the author of the Apocalypse, portrays the glorified Christ as Master of history by means of a striking symbol, that of "a lamb standing, with the marks of his slaying still upon him" (Apoc 5:6). This image of the risen Jesus appears at one of the most moving moments in the entire book, which itself is a dramatic presentation, in the apocalyptic key, of the Gospel. The seer of Patmos is transported in ecstasy to heaven, represented in this vision as an ancient Near Eastern court (Apoc 4:1–5:14). God, the cosmic Sovereign, sits enthroned in splendor, and he holds in his right hand a scroll sealed with seven seals. The scroll is probably intended to symbolize the Scriptures of Israel, which for this author contain the key to the interpretation of the future history of the world. The question "Who is worthy to open the scroll by breaking its seals?" evokes no response from the heavenly senate. The visionary himself admits that he "went on weeping, because no one was found worthy to open the scroll and read it" (5:4). The right to do so, it would appear, belongs to the one who is empowered by God to direct the course of history—as the events consequent upon the breaking of the seals indicate. One of the heavenly senate intervenes to console the seer. "Do not go on weeping! Bear in mind that the lion of the tribe of Judah, of David's line, has won the right to break open the scroll with its seven seals" (v. 5). It is at this moment, our author states, that "I saw, between the throne and of the four living beings, and in the midst of the elders, a lamb standing, with the marks of his slaying still upon him" (v. 6). As the risen Christ takes the scroll from the enthroned deity, the court of heaven bursts into a joyous "new song" in honor of the Lord of history. As the glorified Christ breaks the seals, he causes a series of happenings in our sublunary world. It is *as the crucified* that Jesus exercises his newly acquired lordship and direction of history. This leads us to a final aspect of the mystery of Jesus' resurrection.

In the *fourth* place it now becomes possible to explain why the evangelists, who, as we have stated, display no nostalgia for the past life of Jesus *as past*, still devote most of their books to the earthly history of Jesus. They do so, I suggest, out of the conviction that the glorified Jesus has become Lord in the way in which he now exists *by virtue of the experiences he has undergone during his human and mortal life*. If the author of the Apocalypse has depicted the Lord of history as eternally adorned with the stigmata of the Passion, he wishes to call attention to this significant truth by selecting the most significant and dramatic moment in Jesus' mortal life, his sufferings and death. For him the resurrection of Jesus has not "papered over" his Passion; rather it is precisely *as crucified* that Jesus conducts the divine direction of whatever happens in our world since his glorification.

Thus our evangelists equivalently tell their readers, "If you wish to know what kind of Lord the glorified Jesus has now become, he is a Lord once nailed to the cross, a Lord who once opened the eyes of the blind, restored to cripples and men deformed the use of their limbs, the kind of Lord who once sat down by a well in Samaria, being exhausted from a journey, and broke every existing convention by speaking with a strange woman, a Samaritan!" It is especially the fourth evangelist, who with the creativeness of genius has radically re-edited the traditions he had received, in order to concentrate attention upon the person and mission of Jesus himself rather than on his principal message, the imminent advent of God's sovereign rule in history. Thus, to John, Jesus' "acts of divine power" (his miracles) are best understood by the believing reader as "signs," pointers to the mystery of Jesus. Yet, as will be seen in the following chapter, each of the Synoptic writers has formed his own distinctive portrait of Jesus, which has influenced the narratives of the public ministry in minute but significant ways. Accordingly, it seems capable of demonstration that all these writers are aware that the stories of Jesus' life, *as they have retold them*, provide so many avenues of approach to the risen Lord, who is otherwise beyond the reach of any reader, being now beyond the range of our present human experience. All the evangelists have written up the earthly life of Jesus as they have because they realize that, by contemplating these narratives, the Christian in any age can be helped to relate in faith to the Lord Jesus.

We are now in a position to tackle a question raised early in the present chapter: "Is it possible to pray to the infant Jesus, or the agonizing Jesus of the Passion?" I believe that, once the important aspect of Jesus' resurrection is grasped, that is, the truth that the entire human life of Jesus (his "historicity") has been given a new, dynamic and ever contemporary reality through his glorification, it is indeed possible (in fact, desirable) to pray to the risen Lord through the reality of these experiences as they now exist in him. Thus, not only is the traditional *instinctus catholicus* inspiring such devotion justified, but it can be shown to be an important factor, for instance, in both Ignatian and Cistercian spirituality. In his suggestions for a colloquy at the conclusion of the contemplation on the Incarnation in the *Spiritual Exercises*, St. Ignatius Loyola remarks, "According to the light I have received, I will beg for grace to follow and imitate more closely our Lord, who *has just become man for me*" (*Spir. Ex.*, #109). The great Cistercian, Bernard of Clairvaux, indicates his awareness of this same, ever contemporary quality of Jesus' birth in his sixth sermon for the vigil of the nativity, as he comments on the joyous announcement proclaimed in the choir from the monastic martyrology: "Jesus Christ, Son of God, *is being born (nascitur)* in Bethlehem of Judah." St. Bernard declares: "That is ever new, which always renews our hearts; nor does he ever become old, who never ceases to bear fruit in us, because for eternity he defies corruption. He is indeed the Holy One, to whom it is given not to see corruption. He is that new man, utterly incapable of ever growing old, who refashions those, whose bones have all become decrepit, to true newness of life. And that is why it is tonight most aptly announced that he is 'being born,' rather than that 'he was born,' as the martyrology asserted, 'Jesus Christ, Son of God, is being born in Bethlehem of Judah.' "

The contemplation with faith of the mysteries of Jesus' earthly life, as narrated for us in the Gospel texts, is not simply a pious exercise of the imagination. These narratives enshrine, in a specially privileged manner (because of the charism of biblical inspiration), that "dynamic power of God leading to salvation" (Rom 1:16), since they symbolize that existential reality, which for Paul is "the Gospel."

Finally, we may add a word about the problems which have been recently raised about the "imitation of Christ." Whatever may be regretted about the exaggerations of medieval piety on this subject, one cannot ignore Paul's repeated insistence upon such imitation, both of Christ and of himself as Christ's apostle. The evangelists never speak of imitation; they do speak of the life of Jesus' disciples with him as the "following of Jesus." This term appears to describe the experiences of those who knew, loved, and lived with Jesus during his public ministry, sharing his triumphs and hardships, the opposition of his adversaries, being privy at times to his personal reactions to men and events. Paul had not known Jesus personally during this period of his own mission to "the lost sheep of the house of Israel" (Mt 10:6). When therefore Paul speaks of imitation, it is not the "historical Jesus" he sets forth as an example. Rather, it is the words and actions preserved in the tradition, which (as has been seen) Paul attributes always to "the Lord." It is the teaching and example of Jesus as experienced by hearing the Gospel with faith. It is, in brief, the earthly history of Jesus experienced as a communication of the risen Christ. This is the reason why Paul frequently speaks of imitation in the context of the adherence in faith to the Gospel. And, moreover, since he speaks always of the Gospel as he himself proclaimed it, it will be noted that he speaks of imitation only to those communities he himself founded and continued to direct. Thus he writes to Thessalonica: "Our Gospel reached you, not as a matter of mere words, but with the power of the Holy Spirit—and that in generous measure. You know, of course, what we meant to you, while we were with you. You in your turn became imitators of us and of the Lord, by having accepted, despite great tribulation, the word with joy, a gift of the Holy Spirit. As a result, you became an example for all the faithful in Macedonia and Achaea. From your community the word of the Lord has re-echoed. . . . " (1 Thes 1:5–8). "In receiving the word of God preached by me, you have accepted not a human word, but, as it truly is, the word of God, which is actively operative in you as believers. You have indeed become imitators, brothers, of the churches of God in Judaea, the Christian communities, since you yourselves have endured the same sufferings from your own countrymen, as they did from the Jews. . . . " (1 Thes 2:13–14). To Corinth also Paul speaks of imitation in the context of the Gospel. "You have not a plurality of fathers, since as regards your union with Christ it was I who fathered you through the Gospel. Consequently, I beg you, become imitators of me" (1 Cor 4:15–16). Paul is conscious that his Gospel, his presentation of the risen Jesus and his earthly history, was created out of his own personal experience of his Lord, chiefly the confrontation on the Damascus road. He insists that he had learned this Gospel not from any human being, or human teaching, "but through a revelation by Jesus Christ" (Gal 1:12), a deeply personal experience. His own converts have had an experience through Paul's Gospel of the risen Jesus that is indeed personal to each of them. At the same time, because it was through Paul's Gospel that they were brought to faith in Christ, they have had a *mediated* experience of Christ. One might say that it was to Paul's Christ that they were attracted and won over to the faith. Hence Paul can summon them to the imitation of Christ, but also to the imitation of himself.

We might pause to remind ourselves of Paul's intense conviction regarding the *sacramental* value of the Gospel, the proclaimed word. This is clear from some of the texts just cited above. For him God's word as preached by him is "not a human word, but as it truly is, the word of God, which is actively operative in you as believers" (1 Thes 2:13). This sacramental efficacy of the word Paul attributes to "the power of the Holy Spirit" (1 Thes 1:5); and the acceptance of "the word—despite great tribulations—with joy," he acknowledges, is "a gift of the Holy Spirit" (v. 6). He voices this same conviction to the Corinthians: "The word I spoke, my Gospel, was not set forth in subtle arguments; it carried conviction through a demonstration of the Spirit and power, so that your faith might be founded not upon mere human wisdom but upon the power of God" (1 Cor 2:4–5). "I shall come shortly, if the Lord will; and then I shall take the measure of these conceited people, not by what they say, but by what power is in them. The kingdom of God is not a matter of human speech, but of power" (1 Cor 4:19–20). And to Rome Paul writes, "I am not ashamed of the Gospel: it is the dynamic power of God leading to salvation for everyone with faith" (Rom 1:16). This sacramental efficacy of Paul's "word," or "Gospel," he well knows, stems from Jesus' resurrection together with his saving death. The risen Jesus is, in fact, "God's power and God's wisdom for those who have a Christian vocation"—that is, the risen "Christ whom we proclaim as having been crucified" (1 Cor 1:23–24).

Now it is (as we have already seen) this Christ, proclaimed in the Gospel of Paul and others, whom Paul proposes for "imitation" by his Christians. Hence, this Pauline imitation is simply the living out by the believer of the experience of "hearing," that is, of submitting oneself with a total, personal, profound assent to the person of the risen Christ, *as he has revealed himself to the man of faith through his earthly history.* But this presupposes a prior, very privileged experience of that history by an apostle like Paul, in consequence of which he has *selected and interpreted* the facts concerning Jesus and his words that he judges relevant to Christian living. Accordingly, I venture to suggest that it is an inadequate view of Pauline imitation to assert that "we could imitate Christ, even if we were totally uncertain about the historical facts."[33] I consider it irrelevant, moreover, to object that "the Gospels, in fact, do not provide enough historically accurate information for us to be able to imitate Christ."[34] That implies our faith is founded upon mere history, not upon the power of the risen Lord. At the same time it is crucial for faith that God has in Jesus Christ uttered his definitive claim upon us, made his ultimate offer of salvation to us, through the historical process. The historicity of this divine imperious summons is of paramount importance, and must in consequence be verifiable. But it is a historicity that has become dynamic for Christian faith by being assumed, together with Jesus' total humanity, into the new "life with God" (Rom 6:10), to which Jesus himself has acceded by his resurrection from death.

NOTES

1. It is important to recall that the preliminary draft of this document was rejected by the intervention of John XXIII. It began with a chapter which declared that Scripture and tradition were "two sources

of revelation." This was replaced by a more biblical and personal concept of revelation: the source is God himself through the incarnate Word—more precisely, through Jesus Christ become Lord by resurrection and dynamically present to history. The privileged recipients of his redeeming and revealing activity transmit this self-disclosure of the Godhead by testimony given either orally (tradition) or by writing (Scripture). Thus the Bible is an historical record of God's manifestation of himself, his plans for mankind, through the historical process; in consequence, Scripture must be said to *contain* revelation. The quotations in this paragraph are drawn from the sixth chapter of the Constitution," Sacred Scripture in the Life of the Church."

2. See the fifth chapter of *Dei Verbum*, nos. 17–18, 20.

3. Pp. 79–80.

4. Heinrich Schlier, *The Relevance of the New Testament* (New York, 1967), "What Is Meant by the Interpretation of Scripture?" p. 60.

5. *Ibid.*, p. 61.

6. George W. MacRae, S.J., "The Gospel and the Church," *Theology Digest* 24 (1976), 348.

7. *Ibid.*, 348.

8. These remarks formed part of George MacRae's comments on my paper, "Revitalizing Our Prayer Through the Gospels," at the International Symposium, "Ignatian Spirituality and Reform," University of San Francisco, July 15–31, 1974. They were subsequently published under the title of the above paper, *Program To Adapt the Spiritual Exercises* (Jersey City, 1973), p. 3.

9. *Ibid.*, p. 3.

10. Pierre Benoit, O.P., "The Holy Eucharist II," *Scripture* 9 (1957), 11.

11. The reader is referred to p. 4 of the study cited in n. 8.

12. It is particularly in the second week of the Exercises that the imitation of Christ is put forward as one of the principal goals. It will be recalled that in the third and fourth weeks, devoted to Jesus' Passion and resurrection respectively, imitation is not spoken of.

13. See David M. Stanley, S.J., *The Apostolic Church in the New Testament* (Westminster, Md., 1965), " 'Become Imitators of Me': Apostolic Tradition in Paul," pp. 371–389.

14. *The Way, Supplement* 16: *Prayer and the Ignatian Exercises, New Directions* (1972); see Edward Yarnold, "The Basics of the Spiritual Exercises," 13; also John Ashton, "The Imitation of Christ," 28–45.

15. R. A. F. MacKenzie, S.J., *Faith and History in the Old Testament* (Minneapolis, 1963), pp. 63–64.

16. H. Schlier, "What Is Meant by the Interpretation of Scripture?", where the "second guiding-principle" is stated thus, "Scripture must fundamentally be understood as documenting a claim expressed in God's self-utterance in Jesus Christ, a claim now expressed in Scripture."

17. *Ibid.*, p. 62.

18. *Ibid.*, p. 63.

19. *Ibid.*, p. 67.

20. See the thorough discussion and the interesting hypothesis proposed by Raymond E. Brown, *The Gospel According to John I–XII* (Garden City, 1966), pp. xxxiv–xxxix.

21. For the Latin and official English versions of the text, see *Catholic Biblical Quarterly* 26 (1964), 305–12. A highly informative commentary by Joseph A. Fitzmyer, S.J. will repay careful reading: see *Theological Studies* 25 (1964), 386–408. We have made use of the excellent translation appended to his article by the author.

22. Joseph Fitzmyer's comments upon this last statement are worth citing: "This leaves no doubt that the Commission has in mind the use of the Form-critical method. However, the forms which are mentioned specifically ('catecheses, stories, testimonia, hymns, doxologies, prayers') are indeed found in the New Testament, but it is another question whether they are all used in the Gospels. . . . But still more important is the admission by the Commission that there are other forms not specifically mentioned . . . such as were used by men of that time. As far as the Gospels are concerned, one thinks readily of genealogies, parables, miracle stories, midrash, etc."

23. These are Mt 1:22–23 (Is 7:10); 2:15 (Hos 11:1); 2:17 (Jer 31:5); 3:3 (Is 40:3); 4:14–16 (Is 9:1–2); 8:17 (Is 53:4); 12:17–21 (Is 42:1–4); 13:14–15 (Is 6:9–10); 13:35 (Ps 78:2); 21:4–5 (Is 62:11; Zech 9:4). For a useful discussion of the similarities of these quotations with those found in the Qumran literature, see Joseph A. Fitzmyer, S.J., *Essays on the Semitic Background of the New Testament* (London, 1971), "The Use of the Old Testament," pp. 3–89.

24. See Guenther Bornkamm, "The Stilling of the Storm in Matthew," *Tradition and Interpretation in Matthew* (London, 1963), pp. 52–57.

25. See *Dei Verbum,* #11.

26. Pp. 64–65.

27. Harald Riesenfeld, "Observations on the Question of the Self-Consciousness of Jesus," *Svensk Exegetisk Arsbok* 25 (1960), 32.

28. *Ibid.*, 34–35.

29. "Instruction Concerning the Historical Truth of the Gospels," Paragraph V, "As occasion warrants, the interpreter may examine what reasonable elements are contained in the 'Form-critical method' that can be used for a fuller understanding of the Gospels." The Pontifical Biblical Commission rejects six presuppositions, "which not infrequently have vitiated the method itself as well as the conclusions in the literary area." Three stem from rationalism: the denial of the supernatural, the denial of the divine intervention in history as God's self-revelation, and the denial of the possibility of the miraculous. In addition, there are the incompatibility of faith with historical truth, rejection of the historical value of the sacred books, and undervaluing of the apostolic testimony with overemphasis on the creative powers of the community.

30. Edgar V. McKnight, *What Is Form Criticism?* (Philadelphia, 1973), p. 33.

31. *Summa Theologica*, III, 55, 2 *ad* 1.

32. Norman Perrin, *The Resurrection According to Matthew, Mark, and Luke* (Philadelphia, 1977, p. 26. The really crucial question as regards Jesus' resurrection remains one that Dr. Perrin does not answer (at least with his usual clarity): "Did anything happen to Jesus?" On p. 83 he remarks on the experiences of those whom the risen Lord confronted: "In some way they were granted a vision of Jesus which convinced them that God had vindicated Jesus out of his death and that therefore the death of Jesus was by no means the end of Jesus' impact upon their lives and upon the world in which they lived."

33. Edward Yarnold, "The Basics of the Spiritual Exercises," p. 13. See the comments on this point by John Ashton, "The Imitation of Christ," pp. 31–33.

34. Edward Yarnold, "The Basics of the Spiritual Exercises," p. 13.

II
FOUR INDIVIDUAL
APPROACHES
TO CHRISTIAN FAITH

One of the most significant developments in recent New Testament scholarship has been the creation of a new method of looking at the four Gospels, called in German *Redaktionsgeschichte*.[1] The object of this enterprise is to discover the theological, more specifically the Christological, conceptions which have presided over the composition of the books of Mark, Matthew, Luke, and John. One might perhaps express the insight that has prompted this type of criticism very simply: Mark's Jesus is not John's Jesus, and the Jesus of Luke or of Matthew is again distinctly different from either. The idea may well appear novel to not a few readers. Yet it is a valid approach to the one Christ, who nonetheless makes his perennial appeal to contemporary believers in every age through the fourfold presentation of our evangelists.

It is moreover an approach that has an especial attraction to Christians in our day, who have come, particularly since Vatican II, to realize more thoroughly perhaps than their predecessors in the faith that the Jesus of India is not the same as the Japanese or American Jesus, that the twentieth-century Jesus is very different from that of the Middle Ages, or even of the nineteenth century. No Christian will of course deny the truth of the statement by the author of Hebrews, "Jesus Christ, yesterday and today the same—and so forever!" (Heb 13:8). Still, the modern mind, in contrast with what has been called the "classical mentality," has become more aware, more intrigued by and attracted to what is changeable in man (his historicity) as in the world around us (its contingency). Indeed, it may still come as a surprise to many Catholics, accustomed for so long to accepting the immutability of dogmatic enunciations by the Church of its Christian faith, to read in *Mysterium Ecclesiae*, a declaration issued in 1973 by the Congregation for the Doctrine of the Faith, acknowledgment of the historical relativism that inevitably attaches to all credal formulae, even "definitions *de fide*" from the highest magisterium of the Church.[2]

What we are attempting to discover in this present chapter is the distinctive, personal character, if that be possible, of the conception of Christian faith entertained by each of our four evangelists. By the fact that each, as we believe, wrote his Gospel under the special inspiration of the Holy Spirit, each of these men enjoyed a privileged experience of Jesus' earthly history. And yet, as has already been noted, none of them actually followed Jesus "in the days of his flesh" (Heb 5:7); they were not acquainted with the historical Jesus. It was through their acceptance by faith of the traditions handed on to them by one or two generations of Christians that they reacted to him and to his history. That personal reaction of faith was conditioned by everything that had gone into the making of each one's personality, as well as by the needs and interests of the varied audiences for which they wrote their Gospels. Accordingly, it should be possible, from an examination of each Gospel, to pick out the salient features of the notion of faith entertained by each of the four evangelists and how he conceived its role in the life of the believer. So far as I have been able to discover, this precise kind of investigation has not been attempted. Most discussions of the various modalities of faith found in the New Testament simply contrast the view of the Synoptics with that of Paul and the author of the Fourth Gospel.[3]

The Marcan Conception of Faith

"Christology is essentially the Church's response to the history of Jesus," as Dr. R. H. Fuller has shrewdly observed.[4] Now the significance of Mark's view of Christian faith lies in this: (1) Mark's originality in creating the first Gospel has its immediate source in his personal reaction of faith to Jesus' earthly history; (2) because he is the first writer to set out *as a book* the Gospel of the earliest Church, Mark's notion of faith must in many ways be very close to that primordial response to Jesus' history on the part of the first disciples, once they were gifted with the unprecedented grace, by the Spirit, of Christian faith after, and as a consequence of, Jesus' resurrection to a totally new existence; (3) finally, Mark's notion of faith has left its stamp indelibly upon the other two Synoptic evangelists, Matthew and Luke. While, as we hope to show, each of these very different personalities possesses his own distinctive concept of what faith means to him, yet their use of the Marcan Gospel to create their own books means their concurrence with Mark in what the authentic response of faith ought to be for any Christian.

It is not surprising then that Mark first discloses to the reader what faith means to him at the moment he presents Jesus inaugurating his public ministry in Galilee. We shall find in this initial description *three elements:* conversion, response to the Gospel, following of Jesus. "Now once John had been handed over, Jesus came into Galilee heralding the good news from God. He announced, 'The time [set by God] has found fulfillment and God's sovereign rule has drawn near: be converted and believe in the good news" (1:14–15).

At his first appearance in public life Jesus is depicted as a herald of the Gospel or "good news" that emanates from God himself. The Gospel, as Rudolf Schnackenburg remarks,[5] is not teaching, but an announcement of a momentous happening, the imminent realization of God's definitive presence to history as king. Indeed, this proclamation in the mouth of Jesus is itself an *event:* it is Jesus' presence as preacher that makes God's new presence to history palpable, credible, imperative. Thus to "believe in the good news" connotes a profoundly personal and total response to this God-made happening. Yet this response is a tripartite one: first, an about-face is demanded, a complete "turn-around," "conversion." A man must come back to the God he has rejected with a sincere "change of heart" and "repentance" for past infidelities. In the second place, a man must open his heart to the incredibly "good news" from God, viz. that history is at a turning point, because God has, in his own good time, decreed to make his sovereignty an historical reality. To believe involves a response to God on man's part which is total involvement with the message-happening announced by Jesus. Yet, as Mark indicates in the double vocation-story he appends to the announcement (1:16–20), it is not enough to look to Jesus simply as the mouthpiece of this divinely ordained transformation of our human history. A wholehearted acceptance of his proclamation inevitably includes "following Jesus." "And Jesus said to them, 'Follow me . . .' and immediately they left their nets and *followed him.* . . . And immediately he called them; and they left their father . . . and *followed him*" (vv. 17-20). Without this deeply personal relationship with Jesus there can be no authentic response of faith. Nothing less than this, in Mark's view, is an adequate expression of "belief in the good news." And by the very fact that Mark was the first to put together these three elements and *wrote them into his book,* we have his own testimony to his conviction that his reader in any age is being summoned now to this same kind of faith.[6] Through the Marcan Gospel God's sovereign reign continually "draws near" to each successive generation of believers.

Yet this summons to faith, in Mark's eyes, does not go uncontroverted: it meets with implacable opposition, as the brief history of the young Church has already shown to Jesus' disciples. Jesus, announced by the Baptist as "the stronger one" (1:7), must prove himself stronger than "the strong one" (3:27), Satan. Thus Mark, at the outset of his account of Jesus' ministry, narrates five "controversy stories" (2:1—3:6). To make "the good news" credible, to create the very possibility of Christian faith, Jesus must conduct the battle *in history* against the "strong one" who holds all humanity in fee; and Jesus does this on various fronts—against the incredulity of the "establishment," the Jewish religious leaders, against Satan's "possession" of men's hearts, especially through disease and deformities, even ultimately against the obtuseness, cowardice, and brashness of his own followers. And this vivacious, fast-moving narrative is orientated by our author to the dramatic confession of faith by Peter at Caesarea Philippi, "You are the Messiah"—the Lord's anointed! (8:29). In the course of leading up to this "watershed" of Jesus' Galilean ministry Mark shows Jesus consistently seeking to elicit faith from those for whom he works miracles (2:5; 4:40; 5:34–35). To "follow Jesus" as a mere worker of "wonders" is not enough without a personal self-surrender to the person of Jesus, however obscurely perceived.

Indeed, as Mark wishes to remind the Church of his day, so constantly involved in controversy about its Christian faith with the "teachers of the Law" (9:14), it is only faith expressed *through prayer* that can enable the Christian to win the victory in the ongoing struggle against the powers of evil. This is the thrust of the dramatic scene in which, as he descends from the mountain of the transfiguration, Jesus delivers an epileptic boy from an "evil spirit" (9:14–29). Faith, Mark insists, alone makes everything possible of accomplishment by the believer (9:23b). That Mark intends the reader to take the remark, "Everything is possible for the person who has faith," with utmost seriousness may be gauged by Jesus' later observation, "Everything is possible for God!" (9:27). Also to be noted in this episode is Jesus' response to the frustration of the disciples who had been impotent in their attempts to cure the epileptic. They appear to seek some secret technique by which to work miracles, "Why couldn't we expel it?" (9:28). Jesus' answer is remarkable in its utter simplicity, "This kind can be driven out by nothing except prayer!" (v. 29). Eduard Schweizer's comment is worth quoting: "Perhaps the truth that all power is found in God and not in the inner being of the believer is stressed more emphatically by Jesus' call to prayer than by his call to faith. There is no room whatever for human achievement; all that man can do is be receptive to the action of God."[7]

Actually, until he comes to his narrative of Jesus' struggle and prayer in Gethsemane, Mark has devoted little space to the topic of Christian prayer. Apart from two brief allusions to the place of prayer in Jesus' own life (1:35; 6:46), the evangelist, in addition to the saying just cited, gives but a single instance of Jesus' teaching on prayer. He presents it, however, most emphatically as an articulation of faith. Here we undoubtedly come very close to an aspect of Christian faith that gives it much of its value for Mark.

The sayings of Jesus regarding faith/prayer (11:22–25) occur in different contexts in other Gospels: v. 22 is echoed by Jn 14:1b; v. 23 is found at Mt 17:20, probably in its original form (see Lk 17:6; 1 Cor 13:2); v. 24 (see Mt 21:22 as possibly a variant form) is restated by Jn 14:13–14 as prayer "in Jesus' name"; and v. 25 can be seen in a slightly different formulation at Mt 6:14. The context for these sayings in the Marcan Gospel is the mysterious incident of Jesus' cursing of the barren fig tree, a narrative whose historicity presents commentators with serious problems. Whatever be the proper assessment of its provenance, the story was preserved in the period of oral tradition prior to Mark, where it was given its point as an illustration of the power of prayer by being joined with these sayings we are considering.[8] The creative way in which Mark has framed Jesus' symbolic action in cleansing the temple area by means of the fig tree incident (see 11:12–14; 11:20–25) shows that he means the latter as a lesson for the Church, which is summoned to become a "house of prayer" (11:17) and, indeed, "for all the nations." This theme of an evolution from a place of worship reserved to Judaism to one that is supranational will play a significant role in the Marcan Passion narrative (see 14:58; 15:29–30).[9]

What then do we learn about Mark's attitude to Christian faith from 11:22–25? The evangelist notes that Jesus' response to Peter's exclamation over the withered fig tree is addressed "to them"—all the disciples present—and hence, in this Gospel, to the Church. "Have faith in God!" The Greek reads literally, "Have God's faith!"—that is, faith which is a totally free gift by God to the Christian, which, moreover, receives its entire significance from the believer's new relationship with God through Jesus. Faith in this sense, as Rudolf Schnackenburg observes, is "an absolutely radical and unshakable trust in God. . . . It means saying Amen to God, taking one's stand and building on the firm ground of God and his word."[10]

Jesus continues, "Amen, I tell you: if anyone says to this mountain, 'Off with you and be hurled into the sea!', without doubting in his heart of hearts, but continuing to believe that what he says is actually happening, it will be done for him" (v. 23). The original form of this saying is seen in Mt 17:20, which speaks of faith tiny as the mustard seed. Not indeed that faith is "quantifiable," or is even to be of a certain quality: it is a trusting faith "to which everything has been promised, just because it expects everything from God and nothing from itself."[11] What appears to be the dominant quality of this faith for Mark may be judged from the term he uses for "without doubting," that is, without duplicity—hence, with utter *simplicity*. Nothing of self remains in such naked faith!

With v. 24 Mark adds a saying of Jesus not found in the other Synoptic Gospels. "As a consequence I tell you: everything whatsoever you pray for and petition for, keep believing that you have received, and it will happen for you." Prayer of petition is prominent in the teaching of Jesus (see Mt 7:7–11), and indeed it must be concluded that it is a type of prayer characteristic of the Christian. The reason most likely is that no other kind of prayer so clearly and adequately sets forth that attitude of utter openness to God that is demanded by the Christian view of God's graciousness and of grace itself. Rudolf Schnackenburg states that Mark "wants the Church to realize it is a 'house of prayer.' Because it is God's eschatological community, it has God's promise of a hearing."[12]

"And whenever you stand up to pray, if you hold anything against anyone, forgive him, in order that your Father in heaven may forgive you your trespasses" (v. 25). The communitarian aspect of the prayer of the Church demands that we display this "community-building" attitude through forgiveness of those who have wronged us. We must, in the very act of praying, do what we can to accept these persons as members of our community. The paramount importance of this function of Christian prayer may be seen from its inclusion in both the Matthean (Mt 6:12) and the Lucan (Lk 11:4) formulations of the *Pater noster* (see also Mt 5:23–24; 6:14–15). The presence in Mark of this verse indicates his familiarity with the dominical prayer, even if he has omitted it from his Gospel.

Christian faith to be genuine must be radically orientated to the saving death of Jesus, and Mark has shown in his Passion story that he is not unaware of this important aspect. We see this in Mark's presentation of the mockery by the priests and scribes of the Crucified: "Let the Messiah, the king of Israel, come down off that cross, in order that we may see and may believe!" (15:32). Mark calls these words "derision," a term which for him connotes blasphemy.[13] "King of Israel" was a divine title, jealously guarded throughout Old Testament history and used in Israel's traditional articulation of her faith in the one God. "What appears most crude is the misunderstanding revealed by the demand that he display his power in order that they might believe. This is the very thing which would destroy the possibility of belief...."[14] Without the twin events of Jesus' death and resurrection, faith would indeed be a delusion.

Mark will shortly bring his account of Jesus' sufferings to a peak with his concise but dramatic description of Jesus' death. "Jesus however uttered a loud shout and expired" (15:37). Mark, I venture to suggest, interprets this unarticulated, final cry of Jesus as a shout of victory by appending two events as a consequence of this momentous happening of Jesus' saving death. "And the curtain in the sanctuary was torn in two from top even to bottom" (v. 38): Jesus' death, with his resurrection (announced proleptically by this final shout), has inaugurated that "sanctuary erected not with human hands" (14:58), thus terminating the function of the old holy of holies as symbol of the divine presence to Israel. A second result of Jesus' death-resurrection Mark reserves as the climax of his entire narrative: a pagan Roman is portrayed as making the first act of Christian faith in the Crucified. "Now the centurion, who had taken his stand opposite him and had observed that he expired crying out in this fashion, asserted, 'Truly this man was God's Son!'" (v. 39). We have already drawn attention to the Petrine profession of faith as the high point of the first section of Mark's Gospel (8:29). It was however an act of Jewish faith, made by Peter in acknowledgment of Jesus as the God-given answer to the messianic expectations of Israel. This *credo* by a pagan soldier, Mark desires the reader to understand, expresses an act of justifying faith such as any Christian must make; and therewith Mark brings the second part of his Gospel to a speedy conclusion.

The Marcan conception of faith is dominated by, and centered in, the Marcan Jesus. It is enough to remind oneself that Mark's Jesus is distinctively different from the Matthean or Lucan or Johannine Jesus to appreciate how personal this evangelist's approach to the reality of Christian faith actually is. At the same time, it remains authentically Christian, even as Mark's Jesus remains very truly that of Mark's colleagues, the other evangelists. Consequently, it will cause no surprise, as we turn to Matthew's and Luke's presentation of faith, to discover that this Marcan view of it has profoundly affected their notions of faith—which however exhibit, each in its turn, an unmistakable individuality.

Faith for Matthew

To page through the Gospel of Matthew is to feel oneself ushered into the presence of the Church of the last decade or two of the first century. This is at once to sense a considerable distance from the Marcan Gospel, and still more from the time of the first reactions of Christian faith by the earliest Christians to Jesus' earthly history. Here one meets much more Christological sophistication: the Christ of this evangelist is Emmanuel (1:23), who is not thought of as in heaven, but "with you every day until the consummation of the age" (28:20)—a Christ who is forevermore "Lord" to all his disciples. It will be noted that, with the exception of Judas (26:25, 49), none of Jesus' disciples ever call him Rabbi or Teacher; they consistently address him (and this is a peculiarity of this Gospel) as Lord. Moreover, the celebrated Marcan messianic secret, on which the second Gospel has made its fortune, is an open secret from the beginning of Matthew. From the Infancy narratives to the Passion inclusive, Jesus is denominated "the Messiah" (1:16, 17, 18; 2:4; 11:2; 16:16, 20; 26:63; 27:17, 22). And having taken care to explain the name Jesus as denoting him "who will save his people from their sins" (1:21), our evangelist never tires of inserting the holy name into passages he has taken over from Mark. Further, the continuing presence of Jesus to his Church is above all, for Matthew, a *teaching presence*. More than any of his colleagues, our evangelist is concerned to cite sayings of Jesus. And throughout this book, particularly in the Passion account, Jesus speaks to the disciples to dispel the ambiguities of the historical situation. Thus it is uniquely the Matthean Jesus who, with the first prediction of his own Passion, "from then on began to *make clear* to his disciples that it was necessary that he go off to Jerusalem and suffer greatly.... " (16:21). In fact, for Matthew, Jesus' "mighty acts of power," his miracles, like his other actions, were intended to teach the believing community. And it is not implausible that for this reason the Matthean miracle-stories contain some explicit reference to faith (as will shortly be seen) more consistently than in either Mark or Luke. For Matthew the risen Jesus continues to communicate his teaching to the community of faith in every age. This is the force of the constant refrain, "Jesus *says*," and "I *say* to you."

It may be helpful to recall that Matthew's characteristic phrase, "the disciples," holds special significance for him: it becomes a symbol for the future community of believers. "Disciple" connotes in a special way for Matthew the Christian in his enduring relationship by faith to the "one Master." By way of contrast with Judaism, in Christianity the disciple-relationship is regarded as permanent. Our evangelist manifests his concern to make this truth perspicuous: "For your part, you must not be given the title Rabbi, since but one of you is the teacher, while you are all brothers.... You must not be called Teacher, because you have but a single teacher, the Messiah" (23:8–10).

One might expect, in view of these characteristics of the Matthean Gospel, to find its author speaking continuously about faith. Yet surprisingly such is not the case. Here no parallel is found to the imperative which the Marcan Jesus issues from the inception of his public ministry, "Believe in the good news!" (Mk 1:15). The word faith (or any of its cognates) does not appear on the pages of this Gospel until Matthew recounts a series of miracles by Jesus (see 8:10). However there is a single exception to this: in his exhortation to the disciples to avoid undue anxiety about temporal concerns, Jesus calls them "men of little faith" (6:30). The term is distinctive of Matthew among the evangelists (8:26; 14:31; 16:8; 17:20); it constitutes an indicator of his great interest in the development of faith among the followers of Jesus.

As already noted, Matthew, far more frequently than either Mark or Luke, makes explicit mention of faith in his stories of Jesus' miracles: the leper comes to Jesus with a cry of faith (8:2); a pagan soldier's faith is praised (8:10)[15] and rewarded (8:13) by Jesus; the prayer for rescue by the terrified disciples in the storm (8:25) is answered, but Jesus upbraids them for lack of faith (8:26). Jesus intuits the faith of the paralytic's friends (9:2); he answers the confident request of Jairus for his dead child (9:18) and points to the faith of the woman afflicted with hemorrhaging (9:22); he catechizes two blind men[16] on the subject of their faith in his power (9:28–29); and later he rewards the faith of a Canaanite woman near Tyre (15:28), as on the other hand, he informs the disciples that it was on account of their "little faith" (17:20) that they were unable to cure the "lunatic" child. The divergence of this admonition from the Marcan response, "by nothing except prayer" (Mk 9:29), will be noted.

While the Johannine Jesus demands faith in himself (Jn 14:1), it is sometimes queried whether the Synoptic Gospels represent such a demand by Jesus. In fact, Rudolf Schnackenburg asserts emphatically that in these Gospels "no such explicit demand can be found in anything he said."[17] I suggest that the Matthean Jesus at least does expressly require faith in himself when he asks the two blind men, "Do you believe that I can do this?" (9:29). Moreover, only Matthew among the Synoptics employs the Johannine expression "believe *into* me" in the saying about scandalizing "little ones" (18:6).

One important feature of Matthew's conception of faith is disclosed in a saying concerning John the Baptist which is not found in any other Gospel. "Amen, I tell you, tax-collectors and harlots are preceding you into the kingdom of heaven. For John came to you with a way of uprightness, yet you would not put faith in him, whereas the tax-collectors and harlots did believe him. As for yourselves, even after seeing that, you displayed no regret, nor did you later put faith in him" (21:31–32). One of Matthew's most characteristic descriptions of the thrust of Jesus' public ministry centers in a term, thoroughly Pauline, but rare in every other Gospel—uprightness. Missing entirely from Mark, the word occurs once only in Luke (Lk 1:75) and in but a single passage of the Fourth Gospel (Jn 16:8, 10). Our evangelist uses it seven times (3:15; 5:6, 10, 20; 6:1, 33; 21:32).

Matthew delineates Jesus as the fulfillment of the authentic religious spirit of the Mosaic religion: he comes to bring the new justice, or uprightness—and this by way of the fulfillment, not the destruction of the ideals of the Old Testament (5:17). In Matthew's eyes, however, Jesus is not the first to proclaim this good news: it is the Baptist.[18] In this Gospel Jesus takes up the message first announced by John, "Repent, the kingdom of heaven has drawn near" (3:2; see 4:17). Yet, paradoxically, it is John who must learn from Jesus the nature of the new justice. Hence, to John's objection that he needs baptism from Jesus, Matthew has Jesus reply, "Permit it for the moment: this is the proper way for us to bring justice to its fullest realization" (3:15). This is the new justice which Jesus inaugurates here, which he describes in detail through the Sermon on the Mount. Various facets of this new justice are set forth in the Beatitudes (5:3–11) which describe what is required of those who submit to the supreme sovereignty of God, "the kingdom of heaven." This programmatic discourse in chapters 5–7 presents God consistently as "Father"; accordingly, the new justice proclaimed by Jesus is summed up in the saying, "Be perfect as your heavenly Father is perfect" (5:48). This totally new filial relationship is maintained by (1) bringing the Torah, divine revelation, back to its original intent, (2) displaying utter sincerity in the practice of religion and exhibiting complete confidence in the Father's providential care, and (3) developing one's consciousness of one's true self-identity as brother/sister to the entire human family.

Now it is surely obvious that the heart of this new justice—this unprecedented filial attitude toward God as Father—is Christian faith; and for Matthew that means faith in Jesus *as the Son of God.* We have already remarked upon the expression "believe *into me*" (18:6), so characteristic of the Fourth Gospel, which Matthew alone of the Synoptics employs. An exact parallel to it has been created by the evangelist in his redaction of the mockery of the Crucified: "King of Israel he is! Let him come down now off that cross and we will believe *into him*" (27:42b).[19] And Matthew adds here a verse which specified this "believing into him": "He has put his faith in God! Let him rescue him now if he wants him—for he declared, 'I am God's Son'!" (v. 43). Already in his introduction to the mockery Matthew had inserted the all-important phrase, missing in Mark, into his text, "You would tear down the sanctuary and erect one in three days, would you! Save yourself! If you *are the Son of God*, come down off that cross!" (27:40).

Indeed, throughout his Gospel Matthew has continually alerted the believing reader to Jesus' identity as Son of God through his studied redaction of the Marcan text and by certain additions of his own. The heavenly voice at Jesus' baptism (3:17) and transfiguration (17:5) addresses, not Jesus (as in Mark), but the believer, "This is my well-beloved Son!" Two of the messianic temptations by the devil focus on the question, "If you are the Son of God . . . " (4:3, 6). In his narrative of the Sanhedrin trial Matthew has dramatized the significance of the high priest's question to Jesus: "I charge you by the living God: tell us on your oath if you are the Messiah, the Son of God!" (26:63). Finally, Matthew has created three great confession-scenes in which the credal formula has been rendered expressly Christian. At the end of his second account (see 8:23–27) of the storm on the lake, after Peter and Jesus enter the boat, Matthew tells how "the men in the boat fell down to adore him, declaring, 'You are indeed God's Son!' " (14:33). The Petrine confession at Caesarea Philippi has been likewise turned proleptically into an act of Christian faith, "You are the Messiah, the Son of the living God!" (16:16). A similar transformation has been wrought in the Marcan report of the centurion's exclamation after Jesus' death by Matthew's omission of the word "man": "Truly this was God's Son!" (27:54b).

With consummate artistry our evangelist has created the scene with which he closes his entire book, the appearance of the risen Lord upon a mountain in Galilee, where the reader is given a concrete picture of what his Christian faith means to Matthew. Here, in contrast with the post-resurrection narratives of Luke or John, Jesus performs no action. He simply *speaks*, issuing instructions to the Eleven as he commissions them to found his Church. "The disciples" here, as throughout this Gospel, constitute a group, without any individual being singled out, as in the other evangelists' accounts of appearances of the risen Lord. As a group they adore the exalted Christ, yet "some doubted" (28:17). Within the community of faith some are still in process of attaining full belief in Jesus. Matthew has earlier indicated in the parable, peculiar to himself, of the dragnet (13:47–50), his conviction that the Church is not merely a group of "the elect," but a mixture of "sheep and goats" (25:31–46) between which only the final judgment will discriminate.

In the scene before us attention is focused, as is customary with Matthew, upon Jesus, now imbued with cosmic authority as a consequence of his death and resurrection. The Matthean Jesus acts in character here as he issues "injunctions," after commissioning the Eleven to "make disciples of all the nations," and not merely from Israel. Employing in all probability the baptismal formula current in the community to which our author belonged, the risen Jesus points to the trinitarian character of Christian faith. It is a triple, deeply personal relationship with the person of the Father, of the Son, and of the Holy Spirit (28:19). To become a disciple, however, means that this new-found faith must be expressed through wholehearted acceptance of "everything I have enjoined upon you" (v. 20a). This teaching of Jesus, issued as imperatives (it will have been seen from this Gospel), is the entire Law of God once given to Israel, but now "fulfilled," without being "destroyed," by Jesus (5:17). It is from Jesus risen that the Christian then receives the authoritative interpretation of Israel's Scriptures. This is indicated concretely, in the instance of our evangelist, by his ten "formula-citations," a uniquely Matthean feature in the New Testament.

The concluding promise of consolation is typical of Matthew's Jesus: he is *Christus praesens.* "And remember, I am with you every day until the consummation of the age!" (28:20b). He is the Jesus who, through the pages of this Gospel, issues his "injunctions" anew to each succeeding generation of believers.

The Lucan Conception of Faith

In turning to the Lucan writings, the Third Gospel and Acts, one has the distinct impression of entering a very different world from that of either Mark or Matthew. In fact, with Luke's literary effort (and his achievement is of high quality), the type of literature we call a Gospel may be justly said to have made an impressive bid to introduce the Christian message into the field of Greek letters and to solicit the interest of the Hellenistic reading public in the person of Jesus of Nazareth. Unlike the ingenuous Mark, so devoid of any literary pretensions, Luke is a self-conscious litterateur, a writer intensely proud of that Hellenistic culture to which he owes his gift of expression. It is worthwhile recalling this author's own statement of purpose, deliberately composed in the classical grand manner as an impressive periodic sentence. "Since many have tried their hand at drawing up an account of the events, which have been fulfilled in our times, relying upon traditions which the original eye-witnesses, who also become ministers of the word, passed on to us, I, in my turn, noble Theophilus, after thorough and complete research into their origins, have resolved to write an ordered narrative for you, in order that you may possess a deeper knowledge of the solid basis for what you heard in the catechesis" (1:1–4).

Yet one should not be deceived. Luke is no "secular" historian. He remains ever an evangelist—but one for whom the "good news" extends from the period of the Baptist's ministry, through that of Jesus, culminating in his death and resurrection, into the kaleidoscopic experiences of certain prominent personages in apostolic Christianity, among whom Paul appears as the most heroic figure. For all that, in Luke's view, the twelve "apostles," as he calls them by preference, even during Jesus' earthly career (6:13; 9:10; 17:5; 22:14; 24:10), occupy always the place of privilege as "the original eye-witnesses," upon whose

testimony the apostolic preaching is firmly based. It is this proclamation, or kerygma, of which Luke gives (often in his own
language and marked by his own theology) several precious sam-
ples, which is seen as the normative means of spreading "the
faith"—the word has frequently in Acts become a synonym for
the content of Christian belief, in fact, for Christianity itself
(Acts 6:7; 13:8; 14:22; 16:5). Thus for Luke "the twelve apostles,"
as that specially favored group that had personally and collec-
tively experienced Jesus' entire earthly life from the inception
of his public ministry until his ascension (Acts 1:21–22), alone
merit the title "apostle." Luke, despite his obvious admiration,
even preference for Paul, has refused his hero this privileged
rank—in contradiction to Paul himself (1 Cor 9:1). This peculiarly Lucan theological principle will be seen to govern our
evangelist's view of faith, enabling him to distinguish, probably
more clearly than Matthew, Christian from Jewish faith.

A second theological *prise de position* on Luke's part is manifest in his desire to provide a satisfactory explanation for the delay of the parousia, which before the end of the first Christian
century had become an acute problem, it would appear, for the
Church. Part of Luke's response to primitive Christian disillusionment on this score is perceptible in his reiterated emphasis
on the contemporary availability of *salvation*. In what Hans
Conzelmann[20] has felicitously called "the time of the Church,"
salvation is available for all men of good will—through faith.
This optic will be seen to govern the Lucan redaction of Jesus'
earthly history, received by him through Mark from "the original eye-witnesses." Thus "salvation" becomes a more prominent
motif in the Third Gospel than in any other.

There is a third feature, this time of Lucan Christology,
which reveals a significant aspect of Luke's view of faith. This
evangelist has by anticipation conferred on Jesus during his
earthly existence the resurrection-title, "the Lord." Matthew, as
has been seen, depicts the disciples as consistently calling Jesus
"Lord" during his public ministry. Beginning with his narrative
of the raising of the widow's son (7:13) through the momentous
confrontation of Peter by Jesus as he is led to the Sanhedrin
(22:61), there are possibly sixteen instances of this Lucan tech-

nique. Not implausibly the evangelist wishes to remind the reader that the presence, even of the earthly Jesus, had an important influence upon the disciples' growth into Christian faith, which they receive only from the risen Lord.

There remains to mention, in the fourth place, the special meaning Luke has given to the term "temptation" in his Gospel, as Dr. Schuyler Brown, S.J. has brilliantly demonstrated.[21] This will be important, not only for understanding the Lucan presentation of Gethsemane, but also Luke's approach to the reality of faith.

In his Infancy narratives Luke mentions faith twice. The beatitude Elizabeth pronounces on Mary is, strangely enough in the course of what passes as reported conversation, put into the third person. "Happy the woman who made an act of faith in the perfect accomplishment of the Lord's promises to her!" (1:45). Thus Mary is presented as the genuine disciple, a model for future Christian faith. By contrast, Zachary's incredulity in the angelic message is punished with enforced silence: "Now you will remain silent, unable to speak, until the day when this happens, in return for your refusal to put faith in my words, which will find their fulfillment in their own proper time" (1:20).

Three notable peculiarities of Luke's redaction of the traditional materials concerned with the topic of faith deserve mention. He has turned the logion, "Your faith has saved you," recorded twice by Mark and only once by Matthew, into a kind of refrain in the healing narratives (7:50; 8:48; 17:19; 18:42). Of the Synoptics Luke alone speaks of Jesus as Savior (1:69, 71; 2:11, 30; 3:6; 19:9). The contemporary Hellenistic world displayed great interest in "health-healing-salvation" (the one term signifies all three), and it is part of Lucan strategy to present Jesus as the divinely-given answer to these aspirations. Accordingly, this evangelist underlines the vital connection between "salvation" and faith. A second feature of Luke's redactive activity discloses his high concept of faith, its essential connection with "the Lord" Jesus, as also how crucial it is for "the apostles." "And the apostles said *to the Lord*, 'Give us more faith!' And *the Lord* said, 'If your faith is no bigger than a mustard seed, you could have said to this mulberry tree, "Be pulled up by the roots and be planted in the sea!", and it would have obeyed you!' " (17:5). In the third place, as already noted, Luke attaches a special meaning of his own to the term "temptation." This is wholly diabolical in its origins, as Luke's carefully worded account of Jesus' desert experiences indicates. Jesus is not (as in Matthew 4:1) "led by the Spirit into the desert to be tempted by the devil"; rather, it was while "he was being led by the Spirit around the desert" that "through forty days he was tempted by the devil" (4:1–2).[22] When our author sets out the explanation of the parable of the sower, he modifies the Marcan text in consistency with his own view of faith as essential for salvation and with his use of "temptation" as leading to apostasy. "Those by the road are they who heard [the word of God]; then the devil comes along and snatches the word from their hearts, *lest having put faith in it they might be saved*. Those on the rock are they who whenever they hear it receive the word with joy; yet they have no root and so keep faith only temporarily, while *in time of temptation they apostatize*" (8:12–13). Luke does not, as does Mark 4:17, ascribe loss of faith to "tribulation or persecution," but to the devil. Accordingly, in the Lucan version of the dominical prayer, the final petition, "but deliver us from the evil one" (Mt 6:13b), is omitted, since it is present by implication in the prayer, "and do not lead us into *temptation*" (Lk 11:4b).

From the Lucan presentation of Jesus' teaching during his ministry one may gather certain indications of the evangelist's attitude toward faith. It is the capacity for insight into the significance of Jesus' exorcisms as a means of making God's sovereignty present to history: "But if it is with the finger of God that I drive demons out, then the kingdom of God has overtaken you" (11:20). This saying is paralleled by Mt 12:28. Another saying appears however only in Luke. It was occasioned by a question put to Jesus by the Pharisees as to when the kingdom of God would come. "The coming of the kingdom of God is no mere matter of observation. There will be no saying, 'See, here it is—or there!' Remember, the kingdom of God is among you" (17:20–21). Luke alone records two occasions when Jesus apostrophizes Jerusalem, rebuking that city for its inability to recognize in his exorcisms and cures an invitation to accept him as a prophet. Jesus is represented on this occasion as replying to the warning of the Pharisees that Herod has decided to kill him. "Go and tell that fox, 'Listen! I am driving out demons and performing cures today and tomorrow; and on the third day my mission will be consummated.' Now it is God's will that I continue on today, tomorrow, and the day after, since it is unthinkable for a prophet to meet his death outside Jerusalem.— Jerusalem! Jerusalem! murderess of prophets, stoning those that have been sent to her! How many times have I longed to gather your children around me, as a hen gathers her brood under her wings, yet you refused!" (13:32–34). On the second occasion, during Jesus' messianic entry into the city itself, Luke records that "he wept over it. 'If only on this day of days you recognized, yes you!, the road to peace—at the moment however it has been hidden from your eyes!' " (19:41–42).

There are a number of the parables in Luke, particularly those found nowhere else, which—to adopt a suggestion of Dr. R. H. Fuller[23]—are better regarded as comments on Jesus' own experiences during his ministry, rather than illustrations of timeless truths. If this is an accurate observation, then it is possible to see in several of them allusions to the need to accepting Jesus with faith. The Good Samaritan (10:30–37), found only in Luke, does not seem to answer the lawyer's query, "Who is my neighbor?" (v. 29). Rather it is better understood as a picture of Jesus' redemptive mission in history; hence it becomes an invitation to put faith in Jesus himself. Similarly, the three parables, proposed to counter the criticism of the Pharisees and doctors of the Law in Chapter 15—the lost sheep, the silver piece, and the prodigal son—illustrate what Paul has called "the folly of God" (1 Cor 1:25) in his loving offer of redemption, and the terrible scandal of God's "sending his Son in the likeness of sinful flesh" (Rom 8:3).

Luke has indeed preserved certain values already characteristic of Old Testament faith. One of these is faithfulness that springs from the believer's response to the divine fidelity manifest in God's historical self-revelation. A saying of Jesus preserved only in this Gospel exemplifies this attitude: "If then you have not proven yourself reliable with regard to ill-gotten wealth, who will put faith in you so far as genuine riches are concerned?" (16:11). Mary, the mother of Jesus, selected earlier (1:45) as the perfect example of this fidelity, is praised by Jesus when to a woman who has extolled his mother: "Happy the womb that bore you, the breasts that nourished you!" he replies: "Rather happy are they who keep hearing the word of God and guarding it!" (11:27–28).

Luke is careful to distinguish, particularly in the case of Jesus' close disciples, their earlier Jewish faith from that Christian faith which comes only through the intervention of the risen Lord and the Spirit. Thus Luke will excuse the disciples' lack of comprehension of Jesus and his mission during the public life. Accordingly, at Jesus' transfiguration, Luke comments on Peter's suggestion about building three booths, "He did not understand what he said" (9:33b), a less critical comment than that in Mk 9:6. The reaction of the disciples to Jesus' second prediction of his "being handed over into the power of men" is presented thus: "But they did not understand what he meant. It had been hidden from them, so that they might not comprehend it, and they were too frightened to ask him about its meaning" (9:45). A similar observation is made concerning the disciples' attitude at the third prediction: "Yet they understood nothing of all this; its meaning had been hidden from them, and they did not grasp what was being said" (18:34).

And yet, in Luke's view, the disciples do not lose faith in Jesus or desert him during his sufferings. They do not run away (as in Mark and Matthew), but are present on Calvary (23:49) as spectators of Jesus' martyrdom. As for Peter, since Jesus has prayed for him specifically that his "faith may not fail" (22:32)— and Jesus' prayer must always be efficacious—this disciple does not "deny Jesus," as in Mark and Matthew; he denies "knowing Jesus" (see 22:34, 57). In fact, Peter remains a disciple: he is still following Jesus (22:54b) after his arrest. Thus Jesus is pictured as "turning round to look at Peter," who is thought of as following "the Lord" (v. 61).

This persevering loyalty to Jesus is however based upon Jewish faith, Luke well knows. Hence in his post-resurrection scenes he keeps reminding the reader that this earlier faith of the disciples has suffered eclipse through their Master's death. They react with utter incredulity to the women's announcement of the resurrection (24:11), while Peter's only reaction to the empty tomb is "wonder" (24:12). The pair of disciples en route home to Emmaus exhibit "faces full of gloom" (24:17); they had obviously given up "hoping he was the one to liberate Israel" (v. 21): they remain "dull of heart and slow to believe all the prophets had said" (v. 25). Earlier in this narrative Luke had observed, as these disciples meet the risen Jesus, that "something kept them from recognizing who it was" (v. 16). It is only as they eat a meal with him that "their eyes were opened, and they recognized him" (v. 31) as he vanished from their sight. Our evangelist is careful however to note the gradual development of this new-found Christian faith. In retrospect the disciples recall that even before their recognition of the risen Jesus, "our hearts were on fire as he talked with us on the road and explained the Scriptures to us" (v. 32).

In his picture of Jesus' confrontation of the Eleven, Luke dwells again upon this evolution to full faith. The two newly returned from Emmaus learn that "the Lord is in fact risen and has let himself be seen by Peter" (24:34); yet when the risen One appears to them all, they "were startled and panic-stricken, thinking to see a ghost" (v. 37); they "were filled with terror," while "doubts arose in their minds" (v. 38); "they doubted for very joy" (v. 41) and, like Peter earlier, "kept wondering." It is only when "he opened their minds to the understanding of the Scriptures" (v. 45) that these disciples finally attain Christian faith. No other evangelist has been as painstaking as Luke to make his readers aware of the vast distance that separates the disciples' old faith from the new.

In Acts, "the believers" (22:19), "those who had become believers" (2:44; 4:32), are simply synonyms for "Christians." Likewise, "the faith" means the Christian beliefs (13:8; 14:22; 16:5), perhaps the Christian community. This may be the meaning of the difficult, uniquely Lucan saying at 18:8, "However when the Son of Man comes, is he then going to find *the faith* upon earth?" Faith in Christ effects "remission of sins" (28:18), purifies pagan hearts (15:9), leads to salvation (14:9). It is belief *"into* the Lord Jesus Christ" (14:23; 20:21: 24:24) or *"unto"* him (11:17; 16:31). Such expressions, reminiscent of Paul or of the Fourth Gospel, appear to indicate that, in Acts, Luke or his sources have reached common early Christian usage.

Faith for the Fourth Evangelist

Pierre Benoit, the distinguished New Testament scholar of the École Biblique in Jerusalem, has pointed out the contrast between the fourth evangelist's notion of faith and that found in Paul. "With our two theologians," he writes, faith is basically "adherence of man's whole being, heart as well as mind, for otherwise it would be neither authentic nor Christian; nonetheless, faith appears more contemplative in John, more creative in Paul. John associates faith closely with seeing. 'He saw and he became a believer' (Jn xx.8). Even when recast in the form, 'Happy those who have not seen yet have believed' (xx.29), this dialectic of 'seeing' and 'believing' ... reveals the horizon of light against which Johannine faith is situated.—Pauline faith cannot but be also a welcoming of the Word (Rom x.14–17), adherence to a teaching (Rom vi. 17; Col ii.6–7); but it quickly descends to the depths of a being rooted in Christ (Gal ii.20; Eph iii.17), of a gift of salvation by pure graciousness (Rom ii.8–9), of a stage in the plan of salvation, which replaces the [Mosaic] Law and introduces the new era of the new man in Christ (Gal iii. 23–28."[24] Some years ago I myself characterized Paul's as a theology of "discontinuity" in contrast with the Johannine theology of "continuity."[25] The statement, like all generalizations, may well admit of certain exceptions; for example, Paul certainly stresses the continuity and consistency of God's dealings with man under the old and the new covenants, as his conception of the faith that justified Abraham and the Christian illustrates (see Rom 4:1–25). The characteristically Pauline doctrine of man's justification by faith (Rom 3:28) might appear to be missing from the Fourth Gospel; however, as Pierre Benoit has pointed out,[26] it is discoverable in the ambivalent nature of the Johannine "judgment," which the historical appearance of the incarnate Son precipitates (3:18–21). In this Gospel Jesus utters statements that seemingly contradict one another. "God did not send his Son into the world to judge the world, but rather that the world might be saved through him" (3:17). "It is for judgment that I am come into this world, in order that those who do not see may see, while those who see may become blind" (9:39).

The term "faith" does not occur in the Fourth Gospel; its author however employs the verb "to believe" three times as often as the Synoptics taken together.[27] In addition, there are instances where "knowing" appears to be interchangeable with "believing" (17:8; 14:7–10),[28] and with "seeing" (1:14b; 6:40; 12:45) and "hearing" (5:24; 6:45; 12:47).[29] We note that by far the most frequent expression used by this evangelist is "believe into" Jesus (a single exception is 14:1, "believe into God"). Thus, as Rudolf Schnackenburg observes, "We are justified, therefore, in speaking of a personal allegiance to Jesus Christ, a dedication of oneself. . . . "[30] The Johannine predilection for "believe into" would appear to imply (1) a conviction of the profound *reality* of the believer's personal commitment to Jesus, and (2) a most dynamic view of faith, which moves the believer into a life-giving communion with the *person* of the risen Jesus ("that everyone who believes might *in him* possess eternal life"—3:15).

In this Gospel "to believe" is also found with the dative, where it is question of faith in Jesus' words (2:22; 4:50) at least by implication (4:21; 6:30), which are actually the Father's words (5:24). In addition, this construction is also used with other testimony than that of Jesus, that of Moses (5:46) or his writings (5:47), or that of "the works of my Father" (10:38). John uses "believe that" when introducing credal formulae (6:69; 8:24; 11:27), thus denoting Jesus as the entire content of Christian faith, its object. As H. Braun remarks, "It is Jesus' earthly history *(das Jesusgeschehen)* which has created the content of faith" for John.[31]

To appreciate this single-minded concentration of our evangelist upon Jesus it will help to recall here the very radical manner in which John has revamped the Jesus-tradition, which he inherited (toward the end of the first century) from some apostolic source that appears to be independent from that behind the Synoptic Gospels.

First, John the Baptist's chief function is that of "witness" to Jesus, not that of "baptizer" (he does not baptize Jesus in this Gospel), and hence John is assimilated to Jesus who has entered history precisely "to give testimony to the truth" (19:37c).

Second, the dominant theme of the Synoptic Jesus' proclamation, the near advent of "the kingdom of God," is not heard. Instead John's Jesus speaks mainly of himself, endeavoring through symbols to reveal the mystery of his person and mission to his hearers. His miracles, "acts of power" in the other Gospels, are denominated as "signs," pointers to Jesus himself. It is a large part of this author's genius to make all Jesus says and does (including especially his death) serve his principal theme of *revelation*. Jesus remains throughout "the Word of God," the perfect expression of the Father through a human life.

Third, John (who almost certainly knew Mark's Gospel) has transposed the "caesura," as I venture to call it, that occurs in Mark (it does not go unnoticed in Matthew and Luke) after Peter's profession of faith in Jesus as Messiah (Mk 8:29), which represents a significant turning point in Jesus' public life. Thereafter, Jesus makes no further attempt to win the crowds back to himself, but concentrates upon the instruction of the Twelve. The period of his miracles is all but concluded, and with the exception of certain controversial episodes in Jerusalem Jesus works with his few faithful disciples until his arrest. The caesura occurs in the Fourth Gospel at the termination of the entire public ministry; thus John's book is divided into two easily recognizable sections. The first twelve chapters are nowadays commonly designated "The Book of Signs," while the balance, which begins with the narrative of the Last Supper, is known as "The Book of Glory." As a conclusion to The Book of Signs, our evangelist dwells, even more emphatically than Mark, upon the net result of Jesus' sustained efforts to disclose his own identity to "the Jews," the religious leaders of Jerusalem (12:37–50), pronouncing it to have been an utter failure. The discerning reader will have noted the inconsistency of this negative judgment by the evangelist with the words of Jesus cited at 6:63: "The Spirit is the life-giver: the flesh is useless; *the words that I have spoken to you are Spirit and they are life.*" Why then did

Jesus' words fail to win allegiance and faith from "the Jews"? Indeed, as late as the Last Supper, Jesus' own disciples—Peter (13:36), Thomas (14:5), Philip (14:8–10), Jude (14:22–23)—are still incapable of grasping Jesus' meaning.

To find the answer to this problem, a fourth point of John's redaction must be mentioned. The disciples become capable of what this writer calls "remembering" only when they have received the gift of Christian faith through the operation of the Holy Spirit. John's gloss on the conundrum with which Jesus confronts "the Jews," who seek an explanation for his symbolic action in clearing out the temple area ("Destroy this sanctuary, and within three days I will raise it up again"—2:19), is noteworthy: "When therefore he had been raised from death, his disciples *remembered* that he had said this, *and they believed* the Scriptures and the word Jesus had spoken" (2:22). John makes a similar comment upon the significance of Jesus' messianic entry into Jerusalem: "These things his disciples did not understand at first, but when Jesus had been glorified, then they *remembered* that these things had been written concerning him, and that they had done these things to him" (12:16). The crucial importance, for our evangelist, of this remembering is made clear through the discourse at the Last Supper. It is only "the Paraclete, the Spirit of truth . . . who will teach you everything and *make you remember all I have told you*" (14:26). John returns to this activity of the Spirit and illustrates its paramount value for the Christian understanding of Jesus' history by what is probably a reference to the trial of Jesus.[32] "When he comes he will convict the world of sin and convince it about justice and about judgment. He will convict them of sin, because they do not believe in me; he will convince them about the judgment, that the prince of this world has been judged" (16:8–11). The play on the word "convict/convince" makes translation difficult, but the sense is abundantly clear. Only the intervention by the Spirit can effectively communicate the message contained for faith in Jesus' words and actions. This would seem to be the thrust of the final beatitude, put into the mouth of the risen Jesus, toward the close of this Gospel: "Happy those who have come to the faith without having seen me" (20:29).

Fifth, we must note here a characteristically Johannine theme, which I can only designate "the poverty of the Son" (see 5:19, 30, 36; 7:15b; 8:28b; 12:44–50). All Jesus says, all that he does, all that he *is* as the Word, he has received as gift from the Father. As a consequence, it is not enough to regard Jesus as bearer of a message from God, empowered like the Old Testament prophets to act and speak in God's name. When Jesus acts, it is the Father who performs his "works"; when Jesus speaks, it is truly the Father who speaks through Jesus' words. Hence to see Jesus with Christian faith as "the Son" (6:40) is to see the Father in very truth (14:9). Here we find the explanation of a passage in the Last Supper discourse which may have puzzled the reader. It is actually an attempt by our evangelist to explain more profoundly the intimate relationship of the Spirit to the words and actions of Jesus, that is, his necessary intervention in "unveiling" these words and actions as those of the Father. "I have still much to tell you, but you cannot bear it now. However, when *he* comes, the Spirit of truth, he will guide you into the fullness of truth; for he will not speak on his own, but he will utter whatever he hears, and he will unveil the future for you. It is he *who will glorify me*, because he will take what is mine and unveil its meaning for you. Everything the Father has is mine; for this reason I said, 'He will take what is mine and unveil its meaning for you' " (16:12–15). It will be recalled that, in John, "glory" and "glorify" indicate (as in the Old Testament) the divine self-revelation. Throughout the public ministry John has portrayed Jesus as making every effort to disclose his true identity. Yet, as has been seen, the evangelist records the failure of all this effort—until Jesus "has been glorified" and has disclosed who he truly is through his death on the cross. Only then, through "the other Paraclete" (14:16), will real faith become a possibility.

Lastly, in order to grasp the very simple, yet profound message of this writer, it will help to assemble a series of texts which will show the relation of Jesus' "glorification" to Christian faith. To appreciate our evangelist's creativeness in dealing with the Jesus-tradition he himself received, we begin with the astonishingly paradoxical character of the all too familiar words,

"The Word became flesh and pitched his tent among us; and we have beheld his glory" (1:14). Jesus Christ is first presented in this ode, which John has prefixed to his Gospel, as the Word of God, pre-existing the created universe and dwelling in personal relationship with God. As the Word, he is the perfect expression of the Father, while being himself "God" (1:1). His eternal, divine existence stands in marked contrast with the "becoming" of all that is created "through him" (1:3). Consequently, that "the Word *became flesh*" comes as a twofold shock. "Flesh" for our evangelist is a symbol of man's creatureliness and impotence vis à-vis the divine power: "The Spirit is the life-giver; the flesh is useless" (6:63). To "become" is what has characterized the created universe. How dare John assert that the Word, "through whom all things became" (1:3), himself "became"? Yet, as the balance of v. 14 declares, in terms that appear to be part of a primitive Christian *credo*, "We have beheld his glory!" As already noted, "glory" in this Gospel retains its traditional biblical sense of God's self-revelation *in power*, constantly associated in the Bible with the divine Spirit. Here then in a single verse John has actually stated the problematic, to the solution of which his entire book will be devoted.

After stating through Jesus' discourse on the bread of life that "the bread I will give—it is my flesh [given] for the life of the world" (6:51b), John admits that "the flesh is useless." The entire context makes it clear that the evangelist intends to include even the flesh of God's Word. But if so, how can this flesh impart life? A first clue is provided through Jesus' announcement during the feast of Sukkoth. "If anyone thirsts, he must come to me; and he must drink—I mean, the man with faith in me! As Scripture says, 'From his heart will flow rivers of living water'" (7:37f.). John's comment here is significant. "He [Jesus] said this concerning the Spirit, which those who found faith in him were destined to receive. For the Spirit did not yet exist, since Jesus was not yet glorified" (7:39). When in the view of our author did Jesus' glorification occur?

Here we recall one of John's most innovative departures from the traditional approach to the Passion. In that earliest tradition, accepted first by Paul, then by the Synoptics, the Passion and death of Jesus, indeed his entire earthly career, as can be seen from a primitive liturgical hymn cited in Phil 2:6–11, were qualified as a "self-emptying," a "self-humiliation" (vv. 7–8). By contrast, the Passion and death are viewed in the Fourth Gospel as "the glory" of Jesus. His mounting the cross constitutes his "lifting-up" (3:14; 8:28; 12:32, 34), or his "glorification" (12:16, 23; 13:31–32).

This remarkably untraditional conception dominates the entire Johannine Passion narrative, particularly the presentation of Jesus' death, a picture utterly divergent from those found in either Mark or Matthew. "When he had taken the dry wine, Jesus declared, 'It has been brought to perfect fulfilment' " (19:30a). As commonly in the New Testament, this passive indicates the divine activity: God has brought Jesus' entire historical mission, which is his definitive self-revelation to mankind, to its consummation at the very moment of Jesus' death, which has been presented as the supreme proof of his love for "his friends" (15:13–14). It will be recalled that The Book of Glory begins with the observation that Jesus, "having loved his own who were in the world, loved them to *the end*" (13:1b), to his dying breath *and* to perfection. If then one asks how God has brought Jesus' earthly life to its "perfect fulfillment," John provides the answer with the second part of the verse which describes Jesus' death: "And bowing his head *he handed over the Spirit*" (19:30b). The dying breath of Jesus has become a symbol of the Spirit promised by Jesus to his disciples at the Last Supper. Thus John provides his solution to the puzzle he created at the outset of his Gospel (1:14). It is for John at this very moment, when Jesus reveals his own identity as "God's only Son" (3:16), whose "flesh" is given "for the life of the world" (6:51b) through the supreme act of love, that he "handed over the Spirit," that "other Paraclete" and "life-giver," the cause of the apostolic "remembering."

We are now in a position to ask what is peculiar to John's conception of Christian faith. Because for this writer Jesus is the Word of God, genuine faith is the response of the whole man to the word of Jesus. In the first four chapters of this Gospel particular emphasis is laid upon the acceptance of Jesus' word as the true basis for faith. The mother of Jesus, symbol in this book of the perfect disciple, gives the reader the salutary admonition, "*Whatever he says* to you, you must do" (2:5). The mysterious response of Jesus to "the Jews," "Destroy this sanctuary and within three days I will raise it up" (2:19), is explained fully. "He was however speaking of the sanctuary of his own body. When consequently he had been raised from death, his disciples remembered he had said this, and they put faith in the Scripture and *in the word* Jesus had spoken" (2:21–22). Jesus addresses Nicodemus with the paradox, "Amen, amen, I tell you: unless anyone be born again, he cannot see the kingdom of God" (3:3; see v. 5). This enigmatic statement is underlined by repetition, the implication being that this word of Jesus will ultimately elicit faith from this learned Pharisee once Jesus would be glorified through death (19:39). It is perhaps not fanciful to see Jesus' word at work in Nicodemus from his intervention in the gathering of the Pharisees, "Surely our Law does not pass judgment on the man without first *hearing from him* and ascertaining what he is doing" (7:51).

John's commentary upon the witness of Jesus points to the Spirit as the source of the effectiveness of Jesus' word: "The one God has sent utters *the words of God*; for he imparts the Spirit unstintingly" (3:34). It is Jesus' word that reveals to the woman in Samaria his identity as Messiah. "I know," she confesses, "that when Messiah comes—the one called Christ—he will unveil everything for us" (4:25). Jesus' reply is to be noted, "I am he—*the one speaking* to you!" (v.26). In the sequel, the woman leads her fellow villagers to Jesus. They come at first to him "because of the woman's word" (v. 39), but later they say to her, "No longer do we believe on your say-so; we have ourselves heard and we know that this man is indeed the Savior of the world" (v. 42). This disclaimer John introduces with the observation, "And many more of them found faith *because of his word*" (v. 41). The ruler from Cana, with the dying son, "believed *the word* Jesus had spoken to him, and went off home" (v. 50).

For our evangelist indeed signs can be an important element in the genesis of faith, since through them "Jesus revealed his glory and his disciples began to put faith in him" (2:11). The ruler from Cana is pictured as inquiring from his slaves "the hour at which [his son] took a turn for the better" (4:52a). And as a result, "he himself became a believer and so did his entire household" (v. 53). Yet for John it is the word of Jesus that constitutes the radical foundation for authentic belief. However this word does not operate in any magical manner. There are two provisos. It is only after Jesus has been glorified through death that his words become "spirit and life" (6:63b). Moreover, since faith is most truly an interpersonal relationship between Jesus and the believer, it is necessary that Jesus freely communicate himself through his word or his "signs." This is the force of John's terse observation on events connected with Jesus' first visit to Jerusalem. "While he was in Jerusalem at Passover in the festival throng, many found faith in his name, on seeing the signs he kept working. However Jesus himself did not let himself be believed in by them because he knew them all" (2:23–24).[33] This all-important element of divine predilection John can also state in terms of the Father, who speaks in Jesus. Thus to the Jews at Capharnaum who take umbrage at his words, "I have come down out of heaven" (6:42b), Jesus asserts: "No one can come to me except the Father who has sent me draw him" (v. 44). He reaffirms this a little later, adding a significant clarification, "It is for this reason I told you, 'No one can come to me unless *the gift has been given* him by the Father' " (v. 65). John's repeated use of the verb "give" is one of the features of his discourse on the bread of life. The Father not only gives his Son, incarnate wisdom, to mankind, and the eucharistic bread; it is also by his gracious giving of faith that the believer is readied to respond receptively to these divine benefactions.

For the Christian experience of faith to be fully realized in the believer, another word of Jesus must be hearkened to and obeyed: the "new commandment" of love for the entire believing community. Paul indeed has not neglected this necessary complement to faith; he presents to the Galatians his picture of the Christian community. "By the Spirit we look with anticipation to the hope of uprightness through faith; for in union with Christ Jesus circumcision has no force at all, neither has the lack of circumcision, but only faith given dynamism through love"

(Gal 5:6–7). Thus he can conclude that "the entire Law has been brought to its fulfillment with the commandment, 'You must love your neighbor as yourself' " (v. 14). He had already written to the Corinthians, "There is nothing love cannot face; love believes everything, puts its hope in everything, endures everything" (1 Cor 13:7).

For John this second word of Jesus can only be grasped in the revealing light of his death, through which his love for the Father stands disclosed (14:31), as it also demonstrates the Father's love for Jesus (10:17–18), as well as Jesus' love for "his friends" (15:13). With admirable restraint our evangelist reserves mention of this "word" for the second section of his Gospel. Through his narrative of the Last Supper, beginning with his twofold explanation of the foot-washing,[34] John repeatedly dwells on the utterly novel character of this word of Jesus, which, when obediently carried out, brings to its completion each genuinely Christian experience of the new life first imparted to the believer through faith. "You must love one another, by virtue of the fact I have loved you" (13:34; 15:12, 17). The unprecedented novelty of this characteristically Johannine word of Jesus should escape no one. In the first place, it is designated paradoxically as a "commandment," imperiously demanding love. Moreover, John nowhere alludes to that "greatest commandment," recorded in the Synoptic tradition, regarding love for God (Mk 12:29–41). In fact, our evangelist is even silent about Jesus' teaching on love for one's enemies (Mt 5:44). Nor does the Johannine Jesus appear to require love for himself from his disciples; instead, he interprets this "love for one another" as a manifestation of love for himself (14:23).

Two reasons are assigned for this strangely innovative doctrine. First, it is uniquely this Christian experience of love, given and received within the Christian community, that creates the essential milieu for the gift to each believer of "another Paraclete" (15:16). And, in its turn, it is this abiding which brings to each a true experience of Jesus' relationship to the Father, together with the mutual abiding of Jesus and the disciple (15:20). This giving and receiving of love within the Church

alone wins the Father's love and his abiding in any genuine follower of Jesus (15:23).

In the second place, fidelity to this "new commandment" or
word of Jesus realizes that communion among believers which
is the hallmark of real discipleship (13:35). Over and above that,
moreover, it constitutes the specifically Christian call to assure
the on-going challenge to "the world" through "their word"
(17:30), the apostolic preaching. Just as during his earthly career
Jesus had flung down the gauntlet to "the Jews" by proclaiming
"I and the Father are one!" (10:30), so also this communion with
one another through love given and accepted in the community
can alone provide the persevering and intrepid prolongation in
every succeeding age of that challenge issued by Jesus himself.

NOTES

1. Norman Perrin, *What Is Redaction Criticism?* (Philadelphia, 1969).

2. *Acta Apostolicae Sedis* 65 (1973), 396–408; for some relevant citations in English, see George W. MacRae, S.J., "The Gospel and the
Church," *Theology Digest* 24 (1976), 347.

3. For instance, R. Bultmann, art. *"pisteuo,"* in G. Kittel, *Theological
Dictionary of the New Testament,* Vol. VI, pp. 217ff.; H. Braun, art.
"Glaube im NT," in *Die Religion in Geschichte und Gegenwart* (3rd ed.),
Vol. II, col. 1590–1597; C. H. Pickar, art. "Faith in the Bible," in *New
Catholic Encyclopedia,* Vol. V. pp. 794–796; Jean Duplacy, art. "Faith," in
Dictionary of Biblical Theology (X. Léon-Dufour, S.J., ed.), pp. 138–140.

4. Reginald H. Fuller, *The Foundations of New Testament Christology*
(London/Glasgow, 1965), p. 102. The author had earlier remarked:
"Thus Christology is essentially a response to a particular history. It is
a confessional response. . . . It is a kerygmatic response" (p. 15).

5. Rudolf Schnackenburg, *The Gospel According to St. Mark,* Vol. I
(New York, 1971), pp. 21–22.

6. Eduard Schweizer, *The Good News According to Mark* (Richmond,
Va., 1970), p. 48.

7. *Ibid.,* p. 189.

8. *Ibid.,* p. 232.

9. *Ibid.,* p. 236.

10. R. Schnackenburg, *The Gospel According to St. Mark*, Vol. II, p. 71.

11. E. Schweizer, *The Good News According to Mark*, p. 234.

12. R. Schnackenburg, *The Gospel According to St. Mark*, Vol. II, p. 72.

13. *Ibid.*, p. 153.

14. E. Schweizer, *The Good News According to Mark*, p. 350.

15. Wolfgang Trilling, *The Gospel According to St. Matthew*, Vol. I (New York, 1969), p. 147: "The narrative supposes that Jesus has already been at work for some time and has found little response among his fellow countrymen. At least he did not encounter what the heathen attests here: that great and worthy picture which he has of Jesus and such unlimited confidence in his power. The two together ... Jesus calls 'faith.' "

16. *Ibid.*, p. 171.

17. Rudolf Schnackenburg, *The Moral Teaching of the New Testament* (New York, 1965), p. 35.

18. Guenther Bornkamm, "End-Expectation and Church in Matthew," in *Tradition and Interpretation in Matthew* (London, 1963), p. 15: "Thus the Baptist becomes also a preacher of the Christian congregation."

19. *Ibid.*, p. 27.

20. Hans Conzelmann, *Die Mitte der Zeit* (Tübingen, 1965).

21. Schuyler Brown, S.J., *Apostasy and Perseverance in the Theology of Luke*, Analecta Biblica 36 (Rome, 1969).

22. *Ibid.*, pp. 16–19.

23. Reginald H. Fuller, *Preaching the New Lectionary: The Word of God for the Church Today* (Collegeville, 1976), p. 514: "But the Jesus of the parables is never promulgating timeless truths of religion and ethics. He is always commenting on what is happening concretely in his own ministry."

24. Pierre Benoit, "Paulinisme et Johannisme," *New Testament Studies*, 9 (1962–63), 204f.

25. "Lo! I make all things new (Apoc 21, 5)," *The Way* 9 (1969), 278–291.

26. Pierre Benoit, "Paulinisme et Johannisme," 202.

27. See Raymond E. Brown, *The Gospel According to John I—XII* (Garden City, N.Y., 1966), p. 512.

28. *Ibid.*, p. 513.

29. Rudolf Schnackenburg, *The Gospel According to St. John*, Vol. I (New York, 1968), pp. 563–567.

30. *Ibid.*, p. 560.

31. H. Braun, "Glaube im NT," col. 1596.

32. Raymond E. Brown, *The Gospel According to John XIII—XXI* (Garden City, N.Y., 1970), p. 712: "Moreover, the trial is only indirectly a trial of the world. It is properly a rerun of the trial of Jesus in which the Paraclete makes the truth emerge for the disciples to see."

33. George W. MacRae, S.J., *Faith in the Word: The Fourth Gospel* (Chicago, 1973), p. 37: "The point is that the 'many' regarded his signs the same way as the Jews who 'demanded signs' did, and this kind of belief in Jesus is not the faith that leads to life. Faith that rests on the miraculous, in other words, is not good enough."

34. This symbolic action, like those charades executed by the Old Testament prophets, is meant by John to refer to Jesus' death in the first place (and probably also to the Eucharist); only secondarily is it "an example" (13:15), closely related to Jesus' death. See Raymond E. Brown, *The Gospel According to John XIII—XXI*, pp. 558–562.

III

EARLIEST INTERPRETATIONS OF GETHSEMANE BY THREE ANONYMOUS CHRISTIANS

The profoundly mysterious character of Jesus' reactions to his Passion, presented in such dramatic fashion by the evangelist Mark and located by him, as also by Matthew, near Jerusalem in Gethsemane, constituted an enigma for the believers in the primitive Christian Church, who had accepted the Jesus-tradition from the first disciples. It was not simply the paradoxical nature of Jesus' struggle in the face of suffering and death which was a problem. There was, in addition, the question of the tenor of Jesus' prayer, associated in the tradition with the conflict that went on within him: For what did Jesus pray when confronted with the terrible prospect of the consummation of his earthly mission? Moreover, it would appear that the collective memory of the earliest Church retained the conviction that it was thanks to his persevering prayer to God his Father that Jesus emerged from this "testing," not only resigned to an inevitable destiny but filled with the courage and calm assurance enabling him to go forward spontaneously to meet the death which, he was fully conscious, formed an integral part of his divinely given charge as the eschatological prophet, through whose words and actions God's definitive, imperious bid for man's acceptance of his final offer of salvation entered our human history.[1]

Accordingly, very early in the life of the young Church, Christians came to see in this pain-filled episode, the very thought of which was painful for them, a dark, yet powerful lesson in prayer, and its dynamic, crucial role for the living of the Christian life. For if Jesus had been enabled by prayer to win through to victory in the prosecution of his mandate from the Father for man's salvation, then surely prayer would empower the Christian to attain that salvation—and that not despite, but actually through the myriad slings and arrows that accompany man's life in this world. And yet the answer to the great conundrum of Jesus' struggle and prayer on the eve of his death was not found readily, nor all at once by the inquiring eyes of Christian faith. Nor indeed was a single answer to the mystery, it would seem, the total solution to the problem. The answers given by the later inspired writers would depend on several factors: each one's conception of Jesus in his relationship with the individual believer, with the community of the faithful, with the world; the precise cause of Jesus' revulsion from the demands God was making upon him at the climax of his earthly existence; the concrete nature of this "testing" (if indeed it was testing) of Jesus by the Father; the part played by his close followers in this drama; and, finally, the significance of this awesome combat, in which prayer played such a paramount role, for the Christian comprehension of God's reconciliation of the world to himself through Christ.

The present chapter is devoted to the consideration of three very early attempts to express the meaning of the incident in the life of Jesus prior to composition of our Gospels. It is indeed an impoverishment that we possess no reflections by Paul upon this august mystery. It is not implausible that it is included in the celebrated passage in Philippians which speaks of Jesus' self-emptying, self-humiliation, and obedience during his earthly career (Phil 2:7–8). However, the passage is not original with Paul, but the citation of an earlier liturgical hymn, one no doubt familiar to the community in Philippi. We are fortunate enough to recover with some assurance, based on a fairly wide consensus of modern scholarly opinion, two written sources which form the basis of the Marcan construction of the scene in Gethsemane (Mk 14:26–42). These two primitive narratives will be designated simply "Source A" and "Source B"; and after reconstructing them as accurately as possible, their Christological and theological viewpoints will be investigated. A third interpretation of Jesus' sufferings and prayer to God for deliverance is found in what appears to be an early hymn, adapted by the author of Hebrews and incorporated into his learned and moving exhortation (Heb 5:7–10). We shall begin with this last text without, however, implying that it is older than the two brief essays recoverable from the Marcan Gethsemane scene, but as a simple matter of expediency. Our discussion of the Marcan sources will lead logically into the next chapter, where Mark's narrative will be considered. It may be helpful to begin the investigation of the meaning of this hymnic passage enshrined in Hebrews by recalling that writer's attitude toward the earthly history of Jesus. In this way we shall be able to evaluate the new meaning with which he has invested the tiny scrap of poetry he cites, and to judge the great value he has set upon it.

A Highly Original Hellenistic Transposition of the Gospel

We begin by remarking that there is probably no other piece of New Testament literature so misnamed and (what is much graver) so misinterpreted as the book which passes by the name of the Epistle to the Hebrews. We shall omit here all reference to the erroneous, if very ancient, ascription of the document to Paul, since this problem may be considered settled by the almost unanimous consensus of present day critical scholarship. Hebrews is in the first place not an epistle (even in the sense in which James may be so denominated); much less is it a letter, like those of Paul. It seems best to categorize it as a sermon or homily, or to employ the author's own designation, "a word of exhortation" (13.22), as he describes it in the closing lines (13:22–25) he added to his text when dispatching it to the community he hopes eventually to visit. To ask "What community?" leads to a second mistaken, early conjecture. It is not "to the Hebrews," if by that term he meant some group of Jewish-

Christians, whether within or outside Palestine. In fact, such a designation probably arose from the incorrect assumption, not yet expunged from a number of modern commentaries, that the addressees were a group of converts from Judaism (indeed, even converted priests!) filled with nostalgia for the gorgeous ceremonial of the Herodian temple, and so in grave danger of apostatizing from the Christian religion. Actually our author makes no reference to any of the successive temples in Jerusalem, but only to "the tent of testimony," the portable shrine that accompanied the Israelites during the wandering in the desert. Another false and equally unfounded presupposition may have contributed to this wrong identification of those for whom the document was intended, namely, the misapprehension that the writer was concerned, particularly in parenetic passages, to engage in polemic against the Old Testament or the religion which created it.

There are, on the other hand, positive indications that the addressees were of Hellenistic culture, and hence also of Gentile provenance. The citations from Scripture are all from the Septuagint, the Greek version of the Hebrew Bible. Moreover, the author appears to be speaking to people who he knew took for granted, no less than he did himself, the peculiar *Weltanschauung* known today as Neoplatonism. This heritage from the influential Greek philosopher Plato had won widespread acceptance in the Hellenistic world. One of its salient features was the persuasion that the only true reality behind the "appearances" (*ta phainomena*) in our sublunary world was to be found in the heavenly sphere, where the immutable "ideas" of the things seen subsisted. The philosopher-theologian Philo, an Alexandrian Jew, had put this popular world-view under tribute in order to present Judaism with her sacred books (now translated by Alexandrian Jews into Greek) as the one true "wisdom" or "philosophy," in an attempt to win acceptance from Greek-speaking peoples for the ancient religion of Israel. Our preacher (for so we ought to designate him), the author of Hebrews, appears to have adapted certain Neoplatonic viewpoints to his audience-addressees, in order to help them overcome certain problems with which they were confronted.

It is to the credit of F. J. Schierse that he has, in a brilliant doctoral dissertation[2] and through a small, popular commentary on Hebrews,[3] created a quite new, eminently satisfactory approach to the understanding of our document. Dr. Schierse finds that the author tries to solve *three* problems, with which his audience is faced. "These are: (1) The fact that salvation was not yet a visible reality (2) Moral weakness; and (3) The hostility of the world."[4] The Neoplatonist outlook, no doubt familiar and congenial to his constituency as it was to himself, presents the author with the framework within which he can tackle these difficulties. "Consequently, the author, who was an accomplished philosopher, chooses instead the spatial and metaphysical idea of an earthly and a heavenly world. Like the Jewish religious thinker and philosopher, Philo of Alexandria (*c.* 20 B.C. to *c.* A.D. 50), he divides reality into two spheres, an earthly, shadowy, and ephemeral world, and a heavenly, real, and eternal world. The earthly world is only an image of the heavenly reality which is its prototype. This Platonist idea proved to be of real value in explaining the meaning of the saving events of the New Testament. This meaning is quite independent of the time when these events will be fully accomplished. With its law, its cult, and its priesthood, the Old Testament is inextricably bound up with the visible, earthly, and transitory world."[5]

Thus the right key, which unlocks the door to the satisfactory interpretation of Hebrews, is the insight that the opposition between "the world to come" (2:5) and "the [present] world" (1:6) or "cosmos" (10:5) is *not to be conceived in temporal,* but in *spatial* terms. This viewpoint, which today we find less comfortable than the Pauline linear, temporal one (past, present, future), is undoubtedly part of the legacy of the Johannine school of thought, to which our author fell heir. The thought patterns of the Fourth Gospel are also constructed with spatial rather than temporal coordinates: Jesus is "the one coming from above" in contrast with man "who is of the earth" (Jn 3:31). In opposition to the Jews, who "are from below," or "from this world," Jesus insists, "I am from above," and "I am not from this world" (Jn 8:31). The author of Hebrews is fond of using the verb which means "to be coming" (*mellein*); yet one must be on one's guard against thinking of this as future. In the mind of our preacher it signifies rather "heavenly," and so invisible reality. Accordingly, the Christians have already "been enlightened, have tasted the *heavenly* gift, and become participants in the Holy Spirit, have savored the beauty of God's word as well as the dynamism of *the age to come*" (6:4–5), for these are *not* future, but celestial realities. Thus when, at 1:14, they are denominated as "those who are the coming heirs of salvation" (*tous mellontas klēronomein sōtērian*) the writer understands that all believers already have inherited this *heavenly* salvation, if they only realized it. The contrast elaborated between the purificatory rites and religious accessories of the Mosaic religion and that created by Christ's saving work is also worked out in spatial terms. The sanctuary erected by Moses was "this-worldly" (*kosmikos*), or "a symbol related to the present time" (9:1, 9), "only a model and a shadow of the heavenly" (8:5), that is, "the real tent that the Lord [Jesus], not any human being, has made" (8:2). Consequently, the ritual performed in this imperfect, shadowy sanctuary "was powerless to qualify the worshiper in conscience to approach God" (9:9). "But Christ, come as high priest of the good things *to come*, has entered once for all into the sanctuary through that greater, more perfect tent, not made by human hands, that is, not of this creation . . . and so has secured our eternal redemption" (9:11–12). Like the expiatory rites of Judaism, the Mosaic Law itself "constitutes but a shadow, and not the true image, of the good things to come" (10:1). Again by contrast, we Christians, by Christ's accomplishing "the will [of God], have been consecrated once for all by the offering of the body of Jesus Christ" (10:10).

Now it is crucial to a satisfactory interpretation of this very creative, yet not readily comprehensible, picture of Jesus' redemptive activity to see that through this spatial imagery of our Lord's priestly traversing the "real" and "perfect" and "heavenly" tent, the author is in fact referring to *Jesus' entire earthly life*, consummated by his saving death on Calvary. F. J. Schierse's comment on the passage referred to above on Christ's entry into the celestial holy of holies is incisive and illuminating. "The present passage also makes it clear that Jesus has already 'come,' 'appeared,' or 'made his début,' as our high priest. The author is obviously not speaking only of the ascension; he is giving a theological interpretation of Jesus' entire life. . . . The metaphorical idea of a space which we get from Leviticus 16 does not have to have any parallel in the case of Christ, in the form of some region which is sacred. Therefore, it is certainly wrong to start thinking about the 'lower regions of heaven' or any other 'suprasensible region.' The daring figure of a 'tent which was not made with hands and does not belong to this creation,' which seems so strange to us, is intended to be a theological description of Christ's entire historical existence."[6]

If, as I believe it does, this interpretation rests upon a correct assessment of the meaning of this sophisticated piece of Christian literature, it provides an exciting illustration of how the believing biblicist can avoid the footfalls of fundamentalism, eschewing every literalistic acceptation of a text that has resisted the efforts of so many commentators, in order to seize its proper thrust by questioning it (and the commonly accepted view that our author speaks only of Jesus' celestial exaltation). Moreover, this successful hermeneutical presentation of the principal theme of Hebrews also illustrates the truth of what was stated in an earlier chapter, that is, that orthodox belief in Jesus' bodily resurrection also involves faith in the truth that he has also carried with him into the new life with God his "historicity."[7]

Indeed, the message our preacher addresses to his audience is basically a very simple one: through the sum of his own human experiences (his earthly, mortal life) Jesus has "learned obedience in the school of suffering and, having been made perfect [attained priestly consecration], has become source of eternal salvation for all who obey him, being appointed by God high priest in the likeness of Melchizedek" (5:8–9). It is in truth his whole earthly life that abides in him risen and exalted, making him the kind of priest he *now* is for eternity. The author never tires of repeating this conviction of his. "Since therefore we possess a great high priest, who has transcended the heavens, Jesus the Son of God, let us hold fast to our profession of faith. . . . Let us therefore approach with confidence the throne of grace, that we may obtain mercy and discover the graciousness of his timely aid" (4:14–16). The preacher in fact insists: "This is my main point: just such a high priest we possess, and he has taken his seat at the right hand of the throne of God's majesty in the heavens, a liturgical minister in the real sanctuary...." (8:1–2). "But Christ, come as high priest of the good things to come, has entered once for all into the sanctuary ... and so secured our eternal redemption" (9:11–12). The reassuring consequence of this consummation of Jesus' earthly life, carried with him into the very presence of God, provides the answer to the threefold fear which has been haunting this writer's addressees: salvation is in very truth an actual, if not a visible, reality; moral weakness can be overcome by confidence and hope/faith in Jesus' present high priestly status; the experience of death (whether by violence or not) is a *condicio sine qua non* of reaching Jesus "through the veil," hiding the contemporary reality of "the sanctuary" from our eyes. "So now, brothers, since we possess the freedom to enter the sanctuary by Jesus' blood, by that new and living way he has opened for us through the veil, I mean, his flesh ... let us approach with a sincere heart and full assurance of faith.... Let us be firm and unswerving in the profession of our hope" (10:19–23).

The last phrase, which we, accustomed to speak of the profession of *faith*, may find curious, expresses a point of view characteristic of our author. He can speak indifferently of "the full certainty of hope" (6:11) or "the full certainty of faith" (10:22). Indeed, he regards faith as containing a preponderant admixture of hope. This is evident from his lengthy list of illustrations of what *faith* ought to mean to us, and by his marshaling "a cloud of witnesses" (12:1) from the saints of the Old Testament, who displayed *hope* in the divine promise on such an heroic scale. "Faith," he says simply, "provides the underpinnings for what we hope for, and makes us certain of those realities we do not see" (11:1).

While our author is well aware that it is only through the experience of Christian death that the faithful can finally enter the heavenly sanctuary to share with the glorified Lord Jesus in the celestial worship (9:24–27), yet one may ask whether he evinces the conviction that the Christian can, even in this life, in some sense lay hold of that future salvation and liberation from sin, won for all by Jesus through his earthly life and death. Sufficient data may be discovered in this sermon to make it abundantly clear that the believer can and ought to have such an experience by his participation in the liturgical life of the community, that is, by the reception of baptism and especially by taking part regularly in the central act of Christian worship, the eucharistic cult. The preacher defines a Christian as one "who has tasted the heavenly gift and become a sharer of the Holy Spirit, and tasted the beautiful utterance of God and the dynamic powers of the world to come" (6:4–5). His exhortation to "hold fast to our profession of faith," which is made in the liturgical assembly (4:14), is founded in the persuasion that the faithful can, in the here and now, "approach with confidence the throne of grace, that we may obtain mercy and discover the graciousness of his timely aid" (4:16). A later passage, which by its vocabulary intentionally recalls that just referred to, contains, in the opinion of James Swetnam,[8] a veiled allusion to the celebration of the Eucharist through its reference to participation in the glorified redeemer's flesh and blood and the assertion that access to "the real tent" (8:2), in which the risen Jesus officiates now as high priest, is already open to all. "Since then we possess the freedom to enter the sanctuary through the blood of Jesus, by that new and living way he has opened for us through the veil, I mean his flesh . . . let us approach with a sincere heart and full assurance of faith . . ." (10:19–22). When the preacher sounds an ominous warning to anyone "who tramples the Son of God underfoot, and regards as profane the blood of the testament by which he was made holy, and outrages the Spirit of graciousness" (10:29), he has in mind the profanation of the Eucharist. Indeed, his urgent plea in this context "not to neglect our coming together, as some do" provides a motivation reminiscent of the Pauline insight into the meaning of the Lord's supper: ". . . the more so, as you observe the Day approaching" (10:25). In his gloss on the words of eucharistic institution, Paul had said, "As often as you eat this bread and drink from the cup, you proclaim the death of the Lord, until he comes" (1 Cor 11:26).

It is then this deep concern of the preacher to instruct his audience about the meaning of the community's central act of

worship which has produced his highly innovative interpretation of Jesus' earthly history as priestly activity, and caused him
to present its saving significance symbolically by laying under
tribute the levitical cultus, especially that connected with the
Day of Atonement. While the conception of Jesus' self-offering
as a sacrificial and priestly oblation was not entirely absent in
primitive Christianity, as the various formulations of the words
of eucharistic institution attest (1 Cor 11:24–25; Mt 26:28; Lk
22:19–20; Jn 6:51) and as Paul (1 Cor 5:7) and John (Jn 17:19) also
indicate, Hebrews' thoroughgoing, creative presentation of Jesus' life and death as a priestly, liturgical action is without parallel in the New Testament. The question which consequently
must be posed is this: Where did our author derive his inspiration for his conception of Jesus as "the great high priest"? A
large part of the answer to this problem may be discovered in a
passage (5:7–10) which appears to contain a hymn-fragment not
composed by our writer, but taken over by him from an earlier
source.

The Hymn in Hebrews 5:7-10

In the opinion of some contemporary scholars,[9] the basis of
this pericope is an early Christian hymn-fragment into which
the author of Hebrews interpolated certain themes characteristic of his personal conception of Jesus' high priestly activity. We
begin by citing the passage as it stands in the sermon; then we
shall attempt a reconstruction of the underlying hymn, in order
to uncover its original meaning, which will turn out to be relevant to our general investigation. "[Christ] in the days of his
flesh offered in sacrifice pleas from need and supplications to
him, who had power to save him from death's thrall, with a
mighty cry and tears. And God heard his prayer.[10] Through his
piety (Son though he was), he learned obedience in the school of
suffering; and having been made perfect, he has become the
source of eternal salvation for all who obey him, proclaimed by
God high priest 'in the likeness of Melchizedek.' "

The context is one one of exhortation to courage and confidence in "Jesus, the Son of God" as "a great high priest," who

despite his exaltation "is not one who is incapable of sympathiz-
ing with our weaknesses, since he has been tested in every way
like us apart from sin" (4:14–16). This is indeed a characteristic
of "every high priest," although all others are "able to bear patiently with the ignorant and misguided" because they are sinners themselves (5:1–3). The principal resemblance of these
human, sinful priests to Jesus is that their vocation is a God-giv-
en one (5:4–6). Since the preacher feels that his audience is in
need of confidence in the glorified Christ's compassion, he adds
the passage under consideration, adapting a hymn, familiar to
his listeners.

To recover the fragmentary hymn contained within 5:7–10,
so far as is feasible,[11] we must first single out such vocabulary as
is not otherwise employed by the preacher, some of it in fact not
occurring elsewhere in the New Testament. Other words, while
not of unique occurrence, appear exceptional by reason of their
meaning or usage. All these words may with reason be assumed
to form part of the hymn. The following are found only here in
Hebrews: pleas from need (*deēseis*), supplications, mighty cry, he
was heard, he learned, obedience, source, proclaimed. Words
used here with a meaning not found elsewhere in the sermon
are death (that is, the realm of the dead) and save (in the sense of
rescue from death's power). The use of a term to describe Jesus'
prayer, which means a plea springing from a felt need (*deēsis*), is
nowhere else found in the New Testament. Likewise, the verb
"offer in sacrifice," frequently employed by our author to describe Jesus' self-offering through death, appears in a most
unusual combination with "pleas and supplications." Extraordinary also is the description of Jesus' attitude to God as "piety," a
term originally meaning "fear."

On the other hand, there are four phrases which reflect certain themes prominent in the preacher's own theology; these
consequently may plausibly be considered to have been introduced by him into the original hymn. "In the days of his flesh,"
an expression which sums up Jesus' entire earthly history, appears to be an addition by our author. He frequently alludes to
Jesus' life and mission as a unity, as we have seen. It is moreover
the meaning of this history, taken as a whole, which he seeks to

explain to his audience, since it is the reality which imparts a sacramentally efficacious significance to Christian public worship. A second interpolation is the clause "Son though he was": this motif of Jesus' divine sonship dominated especially the first four chapters of Hebrews. With some hesitation we suggest that the adjective "eternal" ("eternal salvation"), by which our author frequently designates Jesus' achievement, is an insertion of his. Also somewhat dubiously, "for all who obey him" may be considered an addition by the preacher. It is, seemingly, prompted by the mention of Jesus' obedience. Finally, the allusion to Psalm 110:4, which becomes a refrain in Hebrews, "according to the likeness of Melchizedek," has been joined to the end of the hymn, in order to lead into the subsequent comparison between Jesus' priesthood and that of this non-levitical priest. In the light of these considerations, it is now possible to propose a reconstruction of the hymn. While the tentative nature of such a project cannot be emphasized enough, the following version is sufficiently plausible to provide an insight into one early Christian interpretation of Jesus' prayer.

> Who pleas from need and supplications,
> To him who had power to save him from death,
> With a mighty cry and tears
> Offered in sacrifice; and God heard his prayer.
>
> Through his piety he learned
> Obedience from what he suffered;
> And being perfected he became [for all] cause of salvation,
> Proclaimed by God high priest.

In its Greek form the hymn gives a consistent impression of an intention to celebrate a single occasion on which Jesus prayed with great fervor and perseverance,[12] and to relate that prayer to his successful attaining of the goal (the fundamental sense of "being perfected") that had been set out for him. It was moreover an occasion of prayer that preceded and was directly connected with his own death. For it was addressed to God,

who is depicted as "the one who could save him from death."
Obviously the early Church was very much aware that Jesus actually died and that his death was "for our sins according to the
Scriptures" (1 Cor 15:3). The Church also believed that "he was
raised on the third day according to the Scriptures" (1 Cor 15:4).
Indeed, the Lucan sermons in Acts, which critics admit preserve
elements of a very early tradition, indicate the use of Psalm 16
especially to exhibit the conviction that, though he died, Jesus
was freed from the power of death by being raised to new life,
and so "he did not see corruption" (Acts 13:35; see Acts 2:24–31).

   This use of "the Scriptures," in which the primitive
Church found the declared will of God with regard to Jesus'
death and resurrection, was one of the most important hermeneutical aids in the Christian presentation of the saving significance of Jesus' sufferings, death, and resurrection. As the
Passion narratives in our Gospels attest, the psalms were particularly helpful in early attempts to present concretely the meaning of the Passion and to articulate the attitudes and sentiments
of Jesus himself.[13] The author of our hymn exemplifies the influence of the Psalter by his choice of terms to describe this very
important prayer of Jesus. August Strobel has drawn attention
to the vocabulary of Pss 114 and 115 (LXX) as source for much of
the language of the hymn.[14] The importance of recognizing such
borrowings from the Greek Psalter may be seen especially with
regard to the word "a mighty cry," which indicates an intense
cry to God for help in prayer (Ps 17:7; 101:2). "Tears" likewise is
employed often in the psalms as a symbol of the fervent prayer
of the suffering just man (Ps 114:8), as is also "plea from need"
(deēsis) (Ps 114:1). And the same is true of the verb which has
been rendered "God heard his prayer" (Ps 114:1).[15]

   Once the influence of the Psalter particularly upon the vocabulary of our hymn is appreciated, it becomes possible to see
clearly that it is unnecessary (and unhelpful) to try to relate
these references to "tears" and "a loud cry" to the various traditions enshrined in our Gospels.[16] They are simply drawn from
the classical descriptions of the prayer of the just man in the face
of persecution found repeatedly in the psalms. Hence they cannot be construed as an argument against the otherwise strong

impression given by the poetic author that his hymn celebrates a specific prayer of Jesus at a point in his earthly life when he came face to face with death.

Perhaps the most striking point in this description of the prayer of Jesus is the interpretation that it was "offered" as a sacrifice to God. The hymnist views this intensely fervent prayer as a priestly act by Jesus. This insight, I suggest, has had a strong influence upon the author of Hebrews, who by generalizing what is a particular instance (by his interpolation, "in the days of his flesh") had succeeded in presenting Jesus' entire earthly history as priestly activity. In addition, this view of Jesus' prayer as a sacrificial offering implies that this prayer was offered not for himself, but "for us and for our salvation," or (to use the expression of our preacher) "for all who obey him."

That "God heard his prayer" should cause no difficulty (as it appears to cause some commentators),[17] once it is seen that the prayer is a priestly offering on behalf of all men. Through it indeed, as is seen from the second strophe, Jesus "reached perfection," attained his goal as heavenly intercessor for mankind (7:25; 9:24). Actually, the second strophe is devoted to drawing out the consequences of this sacerdotal prayer of Jesus. It was his "piety," reverent, filial fear which made him accept the Father's will for himself in all the concrete historical circumstances of his death, which helped him "learn obedience," that is, experience personally God's will for himself.[18] Jesus' obedience to his Father is also singled out as a salient feature of his redemptive mission by the author of the hymn in Philippians (Phil 2:8). We shall see that this filial submission to God is highlighted by all the Gospel narratives of Jesus' prayer on the eve of his death. In this way our hymn provides an answer to the agonizing question, "Why the Passion?" It is possible that the author of Hebrews inserted the clause "Although he was Son" where he did in order to explain how he himself understood the ambiguous word "piety."[19] It was, for him, God's way of revealing Jesus' divine sonship. In his exhortation to his audience to accept suffering (12:4–11), which he bases upon a recall of Jesus' sufferings (12:2–3), he asserts that such divine treatment demonstrated for these Christians, who had experienced suffering in their own lives, the genuine quality of their divine adoptive son-ship.

It may appear strange, on the assumption that the above in-terpretation of the hymn be correct, that a hymn of praise for use at public worship by the Christian community should be composed in honor, *not* (at least explicitly) of Jesus' saving death and exaltation, like that in Phil 2:6–11, but rather of Jesus' prayer before his death—and, moreover, that such a prayer should be presented as a priestly act of sacrifice. To this objection it may be answered, in the first place, that such an act of self-obla-tion by Jesus lies at the heart of his redeeming death. That already in the early Church there was an awareness of this will become ev-ident from our examination of the various Gospel narratives of Jesus' final prayer before his Passion. The author of Hebrews indicates his appreciation of the truth that it was essentially by an act of willing acceptance of God's decision determining the part he was to play in man's salvation that Jesus had redeemed us, that the external historical circumstances of his mission were simply the execution of his attitude of obedience to the Father. Thus our author puts the words of Ps 40:6–8 into the mouth of Jesus to express his acquiescence in the divine will, "that will by which we have been made holy, through the offering of the body of Jesus Christ once-for-all" (Heb 10:5–10). In the second place, a little reflection upon the function of hymnody at public worship in the early Church will reveal how appropriate was the liturgical commemoration of Jesus' final prayer of self-obla-tion to God before his death. For the Church from its very ori-gins took with utmost seriousness Jesus' command to repeat his words and gestures at the Last Supper, at least on "the Lord's day." It was understood that the celebration of "the Lord's sup-per" entailed the gathering together of the community to unite itself as a body with Jesus' self-offering by offering itself to God. Indeed, one of the principal aims of our preacher, it would seem, was to teach his audience the meaning of a sincere partici-pation in the Eucharist. To his mind such participation could only be genuine if it were a true symbol of a continuous, earnest effort to live the Gospel.[20]

Discerning the Two Pre-Gospel Narratives

Mention was made earlier of a fairly wide consensus of scholarly opinion that in all probability two earlier written accounts of Jesus' struggle in prayer before his Passion can be detected by an analysis of the Marcan Gethsemane narrative. It will however be necessary to introduce the results of such research by some preliminary considerations.

First, there is general agreement among New Testament critics that the first continuous written accounts of any part of Jesus' earthly life were concerned with his Passion, death, and resurrection. It is also generally agreed that these primitive Passion narratives, created for use in the public worship of the community, began only with the arrest of Jesus; they included, after recounting his suffering and death, at least one episode from the post-resurrection period. If consequently we assume Mark to have been the first Gospel-writer, it was he who prefixed an account of Jesus' struggle in prayer in Gethsemane to the story of his arrest. It is further conjectured that Mark's purpose in this was to forge a link between the capture of Jesus by his enemies and an account of the Last Supper with the institution of the Eucharist, which he determined to include in his own Passion narrative.

Second, in the Fourth Gospel the story of the Passion properly so-called begins with the scene of Jesus' apprehension by the soldiery (thereby furnishing evidence concerning the inception of the earliest Passion accounts). There are however some indications that John knew the tradition regarding Jesus' acceptance of "the cup." While he does not include any account of a struggle to accept it on Jesus' part in his story of the arrest in "a garden," the evangelist does record the saying, "The cup my Father has given me—shall I not drink it?" (Jn 18:11). Moreover, it should be noted that, immediately prior to this scene, the Fourth Gospel contains a lengthy prayer by Jesus, the theme of which is his "hour" (Jn 17:1–26). This procedure may be construed as evidence that the evangelist was aware that Jesus did pray when confronted with the immediate prospect of his own death, a prayer in which he offered himself to God for his followers. "And for their sake I consecrate myself, that they in their turn may be sanctified by truth" (Jn 17:19). In addition, as is frequently remarked, one finds a series of sayings by Jesus scattered through this Gospel, which parallels most of the elements in the Marcan Gethsemane narrative. Jesus prophesies the dispersal of his disciples, "each to his own home" (Jn 16:32); he foretells Peter's triple denial (Jn 13:36–38). In the scene with the Greeks there is a brief prayer by Jesus, which (as will be seen later) reflects his struggle in the face of "the hour" (Jn 12:27–28). Twice Jesus announces "the hour has come" (Jn 12:23; 17:1; see 13:31). The remark which brings the scene (Mk 14:42) to a conclusion, "Get up! Let us go from here" (Jn 14:31), is also recorded. Thus, while the Fourth Gospel has no reference to the "testing," to the sleep of the disciples, or to Jesus' command to "remain awake," its author provides impressive evidence that the tradition he received attested the essential elements of the Gethsemane scene, however one wishes to explain their scattered, piecemeal arrangement.[21]

Third, the very manner in which the fourth evangelist has disseminated these various items of tradition as *disjecta membra* throughout his Gospel would seem to imply his acceptance of their basic historical character. And indeed little support has been given by other scholars to the radical suggestion of Martin Dibelius that behind the Gethsemane story lies no concrete historical event, but simply a conviction of the early community "that such an agony and such a prayer belonged to the passion motifs which had been taken from the Psalms in order to understand the suffering of Jesus."[22] Although the argument in defense of the fundamental historicity of Jesus' struggle through prayer to accept the divine will as regards his death is certainly not new (it appears as far back as Origen), still it retains a certain validity. The argument runs thus: it is inconceivable that any Christian should have invented such a story that Jesus recoiled in the face of death, if there were nothing to substantiate such a tale beyond a kerygmatic exposition of the meaning of the Passion.

Finally, the notable differences between the Marcan and

Matthean narratives and the Lucan version obviously demand some explanation. Luke, omitting any hint of Jesus' highly emotional reactions as depicted by the other two evangelists, records but a single prayer by Jesus, while all the disciples in a group are within seeing and hearing distance of him. Such divergences remind us that if, on the one hand, our Gospel-writers intend to recount an actual incident which occurred shortly before Jesus' death, they are chiefly concerned to portray its significance for Christian living and Christian belief. In this instance the way they have chosen to tell the story is determined by their presentation of Jesus in his role as redeemer and also by their attitude toward his disciples who figure in the scene. In particular, while it can be plausibly demonstrated that Mark has employed two earlier written sources as the basis of his account, it must not be forgotten that he has dealt with these sources in a highly creative way, editing or "redacting" the traditions he received so as to put them at the service of the various themes which preside over the composition of his entire book. Precisely how much Mark manipulated the narrative structure of his predecessors and to what extent he refurbished their vocabulary and phraseology is to some degree conjectural. That he actually did so can be shown in the important transformation he wrought in order to depict Jesus' prayer as happening in three phases, as will be noted when we come to consider the Marcan account for itself.

For the moment we turn our attention to the two earlier written stories which appear to underlie the Marcan narrative of Gethsemane. We accept the overall validity of a convincing source-analysis of the Marcan text published by a German scholar, K. G. Kuhn, while differing from his conclusion in several details.[23] In fact, as a general criticism of this perceptive piece of work, it may be stated that Kuhn has perhaps been too much influenced by one of the tenets of the form-critical method to allow any great scope for the role of Mark as a real author, not a mere collector of various traditions. The more recent technique in the study of the Gospels, Redaction criticism, has tended (while relying on the achievements of Form criticism) to correct this one-sided view.[24] It would be out of place here to sketch even in summary fashion the steps taken by Kuhn in discerning the two sources, since our concern is with the success and limitations of these very early essays in exposing the mysterious experience of Jesus preserved in the memory of the primitive community. Suffice it to say that Kuhn, like other critics, has been struck by the observation that each element in Mark's story has been told over twice: Jesus leaves his disciples for prayer (Mk 14:35 and 39); the tenor of Jesus' prayer is given both in vv. 35 and 36; the concluding point of the story, expressed in a saying of Jesus, is seen in vv. 37–38 and also in v. 41. Kuhn finds this final feature particularly revelatory of a twofold source, since it is a canon of Form criticism that such Gospel stories end with a single saying by Jesus.

One observation is fitting before presenting the text of the two sources as we suggest they might be recovered. Kuhn has not sufficiently attended to the fact that there are two introductions to this narrative which parallel each other. Mk 14:26 reads, "And having sung the hymn they went out to the mount of Olives"; and another beginning of the scene occurs at Mk 14:32, "And they came to a place, Gethsemane by name." The intervening verses 27–31 are the result of Mark's editorial work on traditional materials, as will be seen later. Consequently, we conclude that source "B" probably began with the observation that "they went out to the mount of Olives." It is Mark who introduced the reference to the singing of the psalm, probably to suggest that the Last Supper was a Passover meal.

SOURCE "A"

32 And they came to a place, Gethsemane by name; and he said to his disciples, "Sit down here while I pray." 33b And he became filled with terrified surprise and distressed from shock. 35 And he went forward a little and fell upon the ground. And he was praying that, if it were possible, his hour might pass him by. 40 And coming back he discovered them sleeping: their eyes seemed to have heavy weights upon them. 41 And he said to them, "Are you sleeping? Are you taking your rest? Enough of that! The hour has come! See, the Son

of Man is being handed over into the power of sinful men." 42a "Get up! Let us be on our way!"

We propose this version as a reasonable approximation to Mark's first source, without taking the time to justify it.[25] Instead we turn to the study of the significance which its author has seen in the episode.

The anonymous composer of this story of Jesus' painful trial has obviously sought to concentrate attention upon Jesus himself.[26] The disciples are mentioned only with reference to Jesus. Their sleep is significant because it is Jesus who finds them in this pitiful state; and thus, since they play no active part in the scene (they say nothing, do nothing) except for sleeping, the point of their presence is to form a contrast with the wakeful, praying, agonizing Jesus. In failing to stay awake, they are however not disobedient, for they receive no command to "watch"; they simply fail Jesus in his time of trial. Indeed they exhibit the utter powerlessness of human nature left to its own resources. Still, the author's main purpose, seemingly, in introducing the disciples is to emphasize the utter solitariness of Jesus.

That Jesus is left completely alone is the most salient feature of this picture of him. God is nowhere mentioned explicitly, and his action in the "handing over of the Son of Man" is only hinted at obliquely by the use of the passive. Whether or not God has heard the plea of the sufferer likewise is left unstated. That Jesus has in fact been heard by God is disclosed at the climax of the scene by his spontaneous going forward to meet his "hour."

There is one symbol which dominates the narrative to the extent that it appears to reveal the chief significance of the entire scene: "the hour." What it symbolizes is made clear by Jesus' words to the wakened disciples, "The Son of Man is being handed over into the power of sinful men." "The hour" then clearly symbolizes God's action, at the moment of his own choosing, in offering Jesus, as "the Son of Man," into the hands of sinful mankind to accept as Redeemer or to destroy to their own destruction. That "his hour might pass him by" is presented as the dominant note in Jesus' prayer, and this serves to explain the awful reaction experienced by Jesus as he comes to prayer. It is made clear that this repugnance to accept "his hour" is precisely what Jesus brings to prayer. At the same time his request to God is presented conditionally: "if it were possible." Despite his reluctance then, Jesus remains open to the divine decree. And there the author leaves the prayer of Jesus without attempting to unveil its secret. He is content to depict this struggle through prayer as surrounded in mystery. He does not presume to ask why such suffering was inflicted upon Jesus, nor does he offer any explanation for the transformation in Jesus' attitude by the end of the scene where he fully accepts God's design to "hand him over" to his death and voluntarily moves toward the tragic denouement of his life.

In fact one of the striking features of this entire narrative is that nowhere is any recourse had, even implicitly, to "the Scriptures" of Israel in order to explain Jesus' isolation in his sufferings as a sign of their vicarious character. Thus no allusion is made, for instance, to the Deutero-Isaian Suffering Servant of God (Is 53:12). By their drowsiness and their incomprehension of what Jesus undergoes the disciples become a symbol of the awesome mystery surrounding Jesus' relationship to God.

Moreover, no light is thrown upon the relation of the disciples to Jesus. He does not ask them to pray, nor even invite them to "watch." They are evidently not meant to have any part, even a supportive role, in this event in Jesus' life. Nor does the writer give any reason why Jesus takes them with him as he goes to meet the hour. Is it to protect them as long as he can? Is it that they may witness the tragedy of his seizure by his enemies? The question is left unresolved.

All this appears to indicate a very early origin for this narrative, and this impression is heightened by form of the saying concerning Jesus as "the Son of Man." In the view of the critics it is like that found in Mk 9:31, the simplest and earliest type of statement regarding the sufferings of the Son of Man, and hence is thought to be of Palestinian Christian origin.[27] If this opinion is correct, this source is one of the most ancient, and consequently most precious, traditions we possess regarding the prayer of Jesus in Gethsemane. Perhaps a further indication of its antiquity is to be seen in the presence of the puzzling term, preserved by Mark but eliminated by Matthew, which is used by Jesus in rousing the disciples: "Enough of that!" In thus translating *apechei* we have simply followed the Latin Vulgate, which makes as good sense as any. Its omission by Matthew may indicate that by his day the sense of the word had been lost.

The very incompleteness and tantalizing features of source "A" that reveal it as a representative of an archaic tradition also indicate its great potential for exploitation through the subsequent reflection upon its cryptic character by the evangelists. One example of this may be perceived in the evolution in the meaning of "the hour" in the Lucan Passion, followed by the fully orchestrated treatment the conception receives in the Fourth Gospel.

SOURCE "B"

26b He went out to the Mount of Olives, 33a and he took Peter, and James and John with him. 34 And he said to them, "My heart is filled with sorrow to the point of death. Stay here and watch. " 36 And he began to say, "*Abba*, dear Father! Take this cup away from me. Still, not what I will, but what you. . . . " 37 And he discovered them sleeping; and he said to Peter, "Simon! Are you sleeping? Were you not able to watch for one hour? 38 Remain watching, all of you! And keep praying that you may be spared the testing. The spirit is willing, but the flesh is weak."

The distinctive, parenetic (or hortatory) character of this narrative which impresses the reader from the outset is the result of certain prominent features. One notable trait is the consistent use of direct discourse by Jesus, which has the effect, from at least halfway through the account, of deflecting attention from Jesus himself to the disciples, so that the climax is reached when the spotlight is turned fully upon them. The focal point is no longer the mystery of Jesus' relationship with God, or of his prayer, or of his final destiny. As has been noted,[28] Jesus here appears as a model for the disciples and as the Master, who by his injunctions and warnings imparts principles of guidance for Christian living.

The key word which surely dominates this entire presentation is the command, "Watch!" It is the initial command of Jesus as he intimates to his disciples his own extreme suffering. It appears a second time as a reproach to the sleeping Peter for his disobedient failure to "watch one hour." It occurs finally in conjunction with the exhortation to persevering prayer, directed to all the disciples, as the means of avoiding exposure to the "testing" which Jesus himself has already been undergoing. This insistence upon watching suggests a strong eschatological orientation in this second account of Jesus' final prayer. The letters of Paul (1 Thes 5:6, 10; 1 Cor 16:13; Col 4:2) and the Synoptic Gospels (Mt 24:42; 25:13; Mk 13:34–37; Lk 12:37–39) all attest the importance attached by the early Church to this imperative in the teaching of Jesus. To remain vigilant was a paramount concern to a community of believers who looked for the coming in glory of the risen Jesus as an imminent happening. Thus what may be called the "contemplative" element in Christian living was regarded as one of the deepest values in the new religion. By his exhortation to watch, Jesus here appears as a model of fidelity to contemplation. For this reason he is not depicted as withdrawing from the disciples for prayer, but as praying to the Father in their hearing, and his prayer is set forth in direct discourse. His prayer is to be understood as an example for the Christian community, as may be inferred from the bilingual form (Aramaic and Greek) of his address to God. That this double address to God early became a liturgical usage in Hellenistic Christian churches may be taken for granted from its appearance in the letters of Paul (Gal 4:6; Rom 8:15). Accordingly Jesus' prayer, while addressed to God, is also directed to the instruction and encouragement of his followers.

The presence of two symbols in the narrative serves to highlight the eschatological aspect: the "cup" and the "testing." In the Old Testament the cup appears as a variable symbol: of the divine wrath bringing destruction (Is 51:17; Jer 25:15–18; Ez 23:32–34), of God's consolations (Jer 16:7), or of the destiny of the individual, whether happy or unhappy (Ps 16:5). However, none of these meanings is appropriate for the cup of which Jesus speaks. Certainly no Christian could have conceived of God's punishing Jesus. That the cup might stand for Jesus' destiny, which he desires to have changed, is not impossible; in the Hebraic milieu it would not be readily comprehensible as a symbol of his sufferings and death. The cup as symbol of death is indeed found in extra-biblical Jewish writings, although such usage is rare.[29] However, to any Christian from the earliest period of the Church a symbolic use of the cup would immediately evoke the words of eucharistic institution, and it will be remembered that the most ancient written form in which we have them is that of Paul: "This cup is the new testament in my blood" (1 Cor 11:25). In this formula the cup symbolizes the saving blood of Jesus as instrument of the new covenant. Yet if one accepts this signification (and it seems to be the most probable), one is left with a further difficulty. Did the unknown author mean that Jesus prayed to be excused from acquiescing in his redemptive death, which was to crown his entire earthly mission? I suggest that the narrative offers no explanation for the problem. Yet it is important to keep in mind this unsolved mystery, which (as will be seen in the next chapter) Mark in his turn appreciated, and to which he gave a solution.

The "testing" is a symbol with which the early Christian would be familiar from one of the last petitions in the dominical prayer, "Lead us not into the testing." And its presence in this source is interesting as it will be found to recur in all the Gospel narratives of Gethsemane. As Raymond Brown has pointed out,[30] this petition is not for delivery from the daily round of temptations, but rather from the final onslaught of the forces of evil, so dramatically portrayed in Rev. 19:11–21. Perhaps the author of source "B" is suggesting that Jesus himself is now undergoing such a "testing"—a theme that is dwelt on by the author of Hebrews (Heb 2:18; 4:15)—to show the exalted Jesus' capacity for compassion with sinners. The climax of our narrative however suggests that the writer has chiefly in mind the testing of the Christian, whom he wishes to arm with the weapons of vigilance and prayer.

The final words of Jesus, "The spirit is willing, but the flesh is weak," while reflecting compassion for the disciples' failure to obey his command to watch, are probably meant as a warning to the Christian against presuming on his own strength when faced with the "testing" throughout life. The thrust of this axiomatic saying seems clear enough, but the world of ideas out of which it comes remains shrouded in obscurity. The biblical antithesis, flesh and spirit, declares the impotence of man vis-à-vis the divine power of God's Spirit. The psalmist who composed the *Miserere* prays, "Grant me a willing spirit to uphold me" (Ps 51:12b). It is not impossible that our author alludes to this text in order to underscore the gravity of Jesus' warning: even that "willing spirit" which is a gracious gift of God is not impervious to the downward pull of man's weakness. However, to date no totally satisfactory suggestion for the background of this saying has been put forward.[31]

To conclude, the orientation of source "B" is frankly toward the perilous business of Christian living, by contrast with "A" with its attention to the mystery surrounding Jesus' prayer. In consequence "B" has employed the exhortations by Jesus to his disciples for his own parenetic or hortatory message to his Christian contemporaries. Given this concern of the author, Jesus is delineated as the exemplar for Christian conduct in the face of the "testing." Jesus here displays that watchfulness and constant prayer, combined with a profound mistrust of one's own strength, which constitute for the Christian the chief means of ultimate salvation.

Reflections Upon the Results of Our Investigation

At the end of our "archeological" investigations in the present chapter through which we have been able to recover three early documents underlying the text of Hebrews and Mark, it may be useful to reflect upon some of the values that have been disclosed.

First, the richness and the variation in these interpretations of Jesus' struggle and prayer indicate the high regard in which this mysterious event was held in early Christianity. The author of the hymn cited in Hebrew saw in Jesus' agonizing, yet prayerful acceptance of his own death an act of priestly intercession for sinners. This poet-theologian had recourse to the Psalter in order to present the fruit of his personal reflections on this precious incident. The composer of the "A" source, whose essay was useful to the evangelist Mark, was struck by the mystery of God's decree in handing over the Son of Man, and by the mystery inherent in the prayer of Jesus. The Christian who composed the "B" source found in this episode significant lessons for the Christian living of the Gospel.

Second, the very incompleteness of these ancient attempts to plumb the meaning of Jesus' prayer to God on the eve of his death appears to have been an aid to the author of Hebrews and to Mark in their turn. In Hebrews we see the preacher developing the initial insight of his predecessor by presenting Jesus' entire earthly history, "the days of his flesh," as priestly activity. This sacerdotal action was prolonged and immeasurably enhanced by Jesus' exaltation "at the right hand of Majesty on high," becoming the celestial intercession on man's behalf, already affirmed by Christian faith (Rom 8:34). The manner in which Mark was inspired by the efforts of his sources will be seen in the next chapter.

Third, however tentative our recovery of these earlier written sources may be—and the disagreements by various scholars about the concrete details in each case warn that any such reconstruction remains open to question—yet the very attempt to make contact with the unknown authors upon whose shoulders our sacred writers have stood in writing their own accounts possesses a real value for our own faith. For all these very believers' testimony, the fruit of their own contemplation of Jesus' experience, forms the basis upon which our own faith reposes. Moreover, we come to appreciate more deeply the sacred texts of the New Testament once we have learned, by such an exercise, to regard them not merely as two-dimensional, but multi-dimensional in form.

Finally, as we learn to estimate the indebtedness of, for example, Hebrews and Mark to their predecessors, we value more highly their creative, yet reverent editorial manipulation of the tradition they themselves received. In this way we are taught the profound significance of the reality we call "living tradition." It is an open-ended process by which the memory of what Jesus did and said is kept green by each successive Christian generation. It is "living" because it comes to the next generation augmented by the prayerful insights into the Christian Gospel of those whose care is to hand it on to the believers who come after them. And hand it on they did, not after the fashion of the timorous, over-cautious slave in Matthew's parable of the talents who buried his master's talent in the earth, but with something of the flair displayed by the other pair of slaves, who incremented the money entrusted to them by venturesome investments (Mt 25:14–30). The tension we have glimpsed here in the interplay between respect for the tradition and boldness in risking an innovative redaction of that tradition will be perceived again and again as we study the narratives of Gethsemane in the works of the four evangelists.

NOTES

1. Reginald H. Fuller, *The Foundations of New Testament Christology* (London, 1965), p. 130: "It is the unexpressed, implicit figure of the eschatological prophet which gives a unity to all of Jesus' historical activity, his proclamation, his teaching ... and finally his death in the fulfilment of his prophetic mission. Take the implied self-understanding of his role in terms of the eschatological prophet away, and the whole ministry falls into a series of unrelated, if not meaningless fragments."

2. Franz Joseph Schierse, *Verheissung und Heilsvollendung: zur theologischen Grundfrage des Hebräerbriefes* (München, 1955).

3. F. J. Schierse, *The Epistle to the Hebrews* (New York, 1969), which appeared in the series *New Testament for Spiritual Reading*, edited by John L. McKenzie.

4. *Ibid.*, p. xii.

5. *Ibid.*, pp. xiiif.

6. *Ibid.*, pp. 55f.

7. See pp. 45–47.

8. James Swetnam, S.J., " 'The Greater and More Perfect Tent': A

Contribution to the Discussion of Hebrews 9, 11," *Biblica* 47 (1966), 91–106.

9. See especially Gerhard Friedrich, "Das Lied vom Hohenpriester in Zusammenhang von Hebr. 4, 14–5, 10," *Theologische Zeitschrift* 18 (1962), 95–115, who refers to G. Schille. Friedrich's view is cited by Myles M. Bourke in his commentary on our book in *The Jerome Biblical Commentary*, p. 390.

10. Literally, "he was heard," where the passive is to be understood as representing God's activity, as frequently in the New Testament.

11. While there is good evidence of the hymn-character of parts at least of these verses, there will be differences of opinion on concrete details. Thus Friedrich differs with Schille as to the extent of the cited hymn, and my own analysis has led to still further variations.

12. "In its Greek form," because especially of the consistent use of the aorist tense (which designates a single occurrence of a past action), with all the participles and finite verbs found in the original hymn.

13. Especially Pss 22 and 69; also Pss 31 and 42–43.

14. August Strobel, "Die Psalmengrundlage der Gethsemane-Parallele Hbr 5:7 ff.," *Zeitschrift für die neutestamentliche Wissenschaft* 45 (1954), 252–266.

15. *Eisakouein* (to hear) is frequently found in combination with deēsis in the Psalter.

16. Jesus is reported to have wept at Lazarus' grave (Jn 11:35), over Jerusalem (Lk 19:41); in Mk 15:34, 37 (Mt 27:46, 50) the dying Jesus is reported as uttering a loud shout, articulated the first time through Ps 22. Jn 11:43 describes Jesus as shouting to Lazarus after his prayer to the Father.

17. They object that, as Jesus actually died, God did not hear his plea "to save him from death." However, Jesus' priestly prayer is that of the mediator of man's redemption; a similar presentation will be seen in the prayer at Jn 12:27.

18. Since the word "obedience" occurs only here in Hebrews (a fact to which Friedrich, "Das Lied," n. 9, has not adverted), it is to be considered part of the early hymn.

19. This interpolation has caused the debate about the translation of *eulabeia*. Should it be rendered "He was heard [and delivered] from fear" or "He was heard for his piety"? More probable is the version given in our text "through his piety he learned obedience": see Robert W. Funk, *A Greek Grammar of the New Testament* (Chicago, 1961), #211.

20. Thus our author cites the invitatory Psalm 95, where the psalmist on issuing the invitation to appear at public worship made the same

point, viz. that such cult is only genuine when it reflects fidelity to the divine commands: see the long hortatory passage, Heb 3:7—4:3.

21. Raymond E. Brown, "Incidents That Are Units in the Synoptic Gospels But Dispersed in St. John," *Catholic Biblical Quarterly* 23 (1961), 143–152.

22. Martin Dibelius, "Gethsemane," *Crozer Quarterly* 12 (1935), 254–265; for the above citation, see p. 265.

23. Karl Georg Kuhn, "Jesus in Gethsemane," *Evangelische Theologie* 12 (1952–53), 260–285.

24. An example of this may be found in the unpublished doctoral dissertation presented to the Toronto School of Theology by Terrence Prendergast, S.J. *"Without Understanding" (Mark 7:18): A Redaction Critical Study of the References to the Disciples' Lack of Understanding in Mark's Gospel.*

25. I wish to acknowledge my indebtedness to J. Warren Holleran, *The Synoptic Gethsemane: A Critical Study,* a doctoral dissertation published in *Analecta Gregoriana* (Rome, 1973), for drawing attention to a suggestion made by M. Dibelius that v. 33b is a doublet of v. 34: see p. 143.

26. For a helpful series of reflections on the theology of this source, see J. W. Holleran, *The Synoptic Gethsemane,* pp. 201–206.

27. For a review of various opinions on the point, see Reginald H. Fuller, *The Foundations of New Testament Christology* (London and Glasgow, 1965), p. 151.

28. J. W. Holleran, *The Synoptic Gethsemane,* p. 205, finds that "what is of principal importance here is the behavior of the disciples in response to the demand and example of Jesus."

29. See R. Le Déaut, "Goûter le calice de la mort," *Biblica* 43 (1962), 82–86.

30. Raymond E. Brown, S.S., "The Pater Noster as an Eschatological Prayer," *Theological Studies* 22 (1961), 205.

31. For a discussion of the antithesis in Paul and its background, see W. D. Davies, "Paul and the Dead Sea Scrolls: Flesh and Spirit," *The Scrolls and the New Testament,* ed. K. Stendahl (New York, 1957), 157–182.

IV
MARK'S NARRATIVE
(MK 14: 26–42)

We have assumed that Mark was the first Gospel-writer, and it is of paramount importance to appreciate the magnitude of his achievement. It may be gauged by the fact that the form of literature we call a Gospel stands without parallel outside the New Testament itself. Even when we realize that Mark had certain predecessors who created primitive Passion narratives, or set forth in writing certain episodes from Jesus' life, or even composed written records of his sayings, yet the person who first put together an entire book, however little structured it may appear to modern students of the Marcan Gospel, however lacunary (Mark's successors would fill in from other sources what was felt to be missing), must be acknowledged as a creative writer. And indeed one may say that, particularly with the advent of Redaction criticism, Mark's Gospel has at last come into its own.[1] For it is to be confessed that, in the patristic age, much more attention was paid to Matthew, considered the first in time of all evangelists (whose work it was often thought Mark had abbreviated).

This twentieth-century preoccupation with the Gospel of Mark has greatly enhanced our esteem of this work. At the same time it has also made it more difficult to answer certain basic questions concerning it. What plan, if any, did this writer follow: What themes dominate his exposition? For what kind of audience did he produce his narrative of Jesus' earthly history? What considerations led Mark to enlarge the scope of earlier Passion narratives, prefixing to the hitherto traditional beginning with Jesus' arrest by his enemies a series of episodes, of which undoubtedly the Last Supper with its inclusion of the eucharistic institution is by far the most significant? Without attempting to allude to the swelling chorus of opinions, we venture to suggest some answers to these problems here by way of introduction to the Marcan narrative of Jesus' struggle and prayer in Gethsemane, in order to provide some background for solving issues which arise in our efforts to understand its meaning.

The Marcan Gospel, unlike the others, exhibits a title, "The beginning of the Gospel concerning Jesus Christ, Son of God" (Mk 1:1). The much-quoted remark by Martin Kähler, "One might call the Gospels Passion-stories with a detailed introduction,"[2] retains its validity. Mark gives his reader the impression that Jesus moves rapidly and unhesitatingly through his public ministry toward his death and resurrection.[3] If, as I have asserted, the first verse is in fact a title for the entire book, why has the evangelist named it "*the beginning* of the Gospel"? It would seem, to me at least, because one of his concerns was to explain the origin of a notable phenomenon in the very beginning of the life of the Church, namely, the creation of the apostolic preaching, in which, as Rudolf Bultmann has observed, "the proclaimer became the proclaimed."[4] By placing in the mouth of a pagan centurion standing beneath Jesus' cross the declaration of Christian faith, "Truly this man was God's Son!" (Mk 15:39), Mark unambiguously demonstrates his own awareness that it was only through his death and resurrection that the mystery surrounding Jesus, his divine sonship, was effectively revealed to his disciples.

During the period of Jesus' public life, indeed, Mark dwells more emphatically than any other Gospel-writer upon the disciples' lack of understanding of Jesus, of his message, and of the meaning of his mission. This is the celebrated Marcan "messianic secret," the theme that provided the title for a book by Wilhelm Wrede over seventy-five years ago.[5] Actually, the real messianic secret is of course the mystery of Christian faith that Jesus is the Son of God; and this theme is one of the principal *leitmotivs* of Mark's Gospel. One may say that the entire first section of this book (Mk 1:1—8:30) is orientated to the Petrine confession, "You are the Messiah" (Mk 8:29). In this section, the evangelist recounts Jesus' teaching and miracles during his Galilean ministry, which for him becomes a symbol of Jesus' entire earthly mission. Thereafter, Mark carefully structures his story by means of the triple prediction by Jesus of his death and resurrection (Mk 8:31; 9:31; 10:33—34). Here a definite pattern imposed on his materials by Mark is clearly perceptible: Jesus prophesies his own suffering to teach his followers that suffering is to be an essential part of their own Christian lives; they repeatedly fail to comprehend, and Jesus is forced each time to repeat and clarify his lesson to them. Only through his Passion narrative does Mark present the disclosure to his reader of the "good news" that for every follower of Jesus it is the Christian experience of suffering that guarantees the genuine nature of discipleship.

One might restate this discussion of Mark's intent in terms of the Marcan picture of Jesus which has undoubtedly guided the evangelist in the selection, structuring and redaction of the data he received from tradition. In his eyes Jesus is above all the teacher. This may strike one familiar with this Gospel as strange, for Mark gives more attention to what Jesus does than what he says, and in contrast with Matthew, Mark devotes relatively little space to the sayings of Jesus. This has been done deliberately, however, in order to make the reader understand that it is chiefly by what he does that Jesus demonstrates his "teaching with authority" (Mk 1:27). His miracles are "acts of power," not the exhibitionism of a wonder-worker like the legendary "divine man" whose marvels were propagated in Hellenistic literature. Jesus exorcises demons and heals the sick and crippled to elicit a response of faith, not astonishment, from his audiences. He mostly fails to achieve this purpose, except with his own disciples; yet even they are, during most of the public ministry, slow of comprehension.

A second dominant feature in Mark's portrait of Jesus is

that of the suffering Son of Man. Jesus is indeed the Suffering Servant of God, celebrated in the Servant songs of Deutero-Isaiah. And it is this Old Testament prophecy, together with certain psalms which speak of the just man persecuted by his enemies, which colors the Marcan Passion narrative. Actually, this theme was announced to the reader by the heavenly voice at Jesus' baptism (Mk 1:11), and it is reiterated in the triple prediction of his Passion.

One final observation, without which any discussion of Mark's purpose would be incomplete. This evangelist was moved to write his Gospel for a particular Christian community, of which he himself may have been a member. This community was either confronted with the prospect of suffering and persecution, or it was actually undergoing some such terrible trial. Through his reporting of Jesus' teaching, and still more by recounting Jesus' own experience of suffering, Mark seeks to comfort and hearten this group of Christians, summoned to share in the Passion of their Lord.

Mark's Teaching on Christian Prayer

In order to assist our understanding of the particular thrust of the Gethsemane narrative in this Gospel, it will be helpful to review briefly the several references made by Mark to Jesus' own prayer, as well as his own instructions about the nature of prayer in Christianity.

Our evangelist alludes only twice, in his account of the public ministry, to the place of prayer in Jesus' own life. The first occasion occurs after the first day of Jesus' activity in Capernaum. Despite the fact that that day was a Sabbath, it is depicted as filled with ceaseless labor, teaching in the synagogue, exorcising a demoniac, curing Peter's mother-in-law, and healing many sick people. The next day "rising early in the morning, long before daylight, he was out and off to an isolated spot, and there he was at prayer" (Mk 1:35). Despite its brevity this notice contains some significant insights into Jesus' life of prayer. Prayer is obviously an integral element in Jesus' ministry, and he consecrates to it those hours during which he can reasonably expect to be free from interruption. Mark discreetly draws a veil over the content of Jesus' prayer. Indeed that he expects his readers to respect the mystery enshrouding it may be deduced from his drawing attention, in the two verses immediately following, to the interruption of Jesus' prayer by the disciples, who, in their enthusiasm over his popularity, display for the first time in this Gospel that lack of understanding which Mark considers characteristic of them. The writer hints that this incomprehension of his followers with respect to the necessity of prayer for ministry is one of the reasons he had gone off to a place of solitude. Eduard Schweizer comments that, in Mark's eyes, "prayer was an essential part of his [Jesus'] service and continually guarded that service from over-activity as well as from indolence."[6] Father Rudolf Schnackenburg sees in the earliness of the hour a possible indication of "an inner struggle, similar to the temptation of Satan, from which Jesus as man is not free. But his union with God, quickened and strengthened *in prayer*, leads him to find the right way with inner assurance."[7]

The second recorded instance when Jesus prays follows upon the feeding of a crowd of five thousand. After first making the disciples embark in their boat, Jesus then dismisses the crowd. "And after taking leave of them he went off to the mountain to pray" (Mk 6:45). This prayer, which as Mark suggests is prolonged into the night (v. 47), is the prelude to a revelation by Jesus to his disciples of his divine glory. As Schnackenburg observes, "This seeking of the hills which indicated the proximity of God (cf. 9:2) and his remaining in prayer (cf. 1:35) already point to a special plan."[8] Mark may be suggesting here that the purpose of Jesus' prayer was to win divine assistance, so that his deliberate self-revelation to them might be efficacious. However the evangelist is forced to admit the incomprehension of the disciples, who "had not understood about the loaves" (v. 52). Consequently, their response to the Christophany is not faith; they were simply "utterly beside themselves with astonishment" (v. 51).

It is scarcely accidental that in both these brief references to Jesus' prayer Mark alludes to the total lack of understanding of him by his disciples. Throughout his book Mark insists, either directly or by insinuation, on the necessity of faith for a right relationship with Jesus. We observe the evangelist doing this in two passages containing teaching about Christian prayer. The first saying is a reply to the frustrated disciples, chagrined at their inability to exorcise the epileptic boy. When alone with Jesus they ask, "Why could we not drive it out?" (Mk 9:28), and Jesus tells them, "This kind can be driven out by nothing except prayer" (v. 29). The categorical character of the saying may cause surprise. Is not faith surely necessary? This lesson on prayer, which Mark desires to teach the community,[9] indicates that faith must be expressed and so nourished by humble petition to God for what is beyond any human means to remedy. Such prayer, springing from faith, augments faith in turn. Negatively, what the evangelist here teaches is that prayer is not magic. This may well be why he does not mention any prayer on Jesus' part in performing the exorcism. It is not a question of acquiring a technique for exorcism, which would imply reliance upon one's own powers. It is only "for God that all things are possible" (Mk 10:27). Prayer then means total openness to God's action in and through us; the solution to human frustration is ceasing to look to oneself. This has been well named the prayer of faith.

Mark again employs the convention of a conversation between Jesus and the disciples (this time about the withered fig-tree) in order to teach the community the place of privilege accorded to petitionary prayer by Jesus. First, the absolute necessity for faith in God is mentioned, and the blighted tree becomes a kind of parable of the efficacy of such faith. "Amen I tell you: whoever says to this mountain, 'Off with you and throw yourself in the sea!' and does not doubt in his heart, but believes that what he is saying will be done, it shall happen for him" (Mk 11:23). The "not doubting" within the most authentic part of oneself describes minimal, but genuine faith, without which prayer is a travesty.

Mark now makes the application to prayer by connecting what was originally an independent saying with the foregoing statement. "On this account I tell you, everything you petition and ask for, believe you have received, and it will happen for you" (v. 24). The strange turn of phrase, "believe you have received," was already perceived as a difficulty by some ancient copyists of the Greek manuscript; however, it is to be preferred as the correct reading. It is readily comprehensible as a graphic way of restating the "not doubting" alluded to above. Truly Christian prayer is redolent with a deep, trusting confidence in the God who desires to reveal himself through response to the petitioner. Father Schnackenburg shrewdly notes that Mark "wants the Church to realize it is a 'house of prayer'" (the Marcan formulation of Jesus' utterance at the cleansing of the temple area, the incident immediately preceding).[10]

Mark has not preserved any formula of the *Pater noster* in his Gospel, as have Matthew and Luke. Yet he indicates his awareness of this precious prayer given his disciples by Jesus in adding here a further observation. "And when you stand up to pray, if you hold anything against someone, be forgiving, in order that your Father in heaven may also forgive you your trespasses" (v. 25). The evangelist extends his instruction on the necessity of receptiveness to God's action, which is faith, to include openness to those we know, those with whom we seek to form the community which Jesus had designated as a "house of prayer for all the nations" (Mk 11:17). The spirit of forgiveness toward those who offend us is the yardstick of our love for the Father in heaven. "Without it, prayer to the Father is dishonest and ineffectual."[11] This teaching will be repeated by a member of the school of John: "God no man has ever seen. If we love one another, God abides in us and his love has been realized to perfection in us" (1 Jn 4:12).

It remains to take cognizance of the final prayer of Jesus as he hangs on the cross, before turning to consider the Gethsemane incident. To express the attitudes of the dying Jesus, the evangelists (and the tradition behind them) borrowed from the psalms. By the mysterious "I thirst" John may allude to Ps 22:15; Luke, Ps 31:5, "Father into your hands I commend my spirit!" Mark, followed by Matthew, puts the ominous opening words of Ps 22 upon the lips of Jesus. "And at the ninth hour Jesus with a mighty cry shouted, 'Eloi, Eloi, lama sabachthani?' which means, 'My God, my God, why have you forsaken me?'" (Mk

15:34). The presence of the Aramaic version of these words indicates an interpretation of Jesus' sentiments, his agonizing sense of abandonment by God as he realizes the awful nature of the supreme risk he has taken, which is very ancient. It would appear to go back to the early Jewish-Christian community of Palestine. Thus we should beware of trying to neutralize the terrible realism expressed by these words, as some commentators do, by imagining that the dying Jesus is pictured as intoning a psalm in which the sufferer moves from a feeling of dereliction to a joyful attitude of thankfulness to God for deliverance. Father Schnackenburg is unquestionably right when he observes, "The fact that the early community transmitted Jesus' words in the Aramaic language, with which it was familiar, suggests that it not only wanted to show Jesus using that psalm as his prayer, but also took the content of this introductory verse of the psalm very seriously.... No one can know what Jesus' state of soul really was; but the early Church's intention in quoting this psalm verse was to express deep distress of soul and abandonment by God."[12]

This review of Mark's teaching on Christian prayer reveals that this evangelist has not devoted much space to this theme, and in this he stands in contrast with Matthew or Luke. I venture to suggest that Mark has done this of set purpose, because in his view it is the episode of Jesus' struggle and prayer, in the hour preceding his arrest, which is to be considered *the* school of prayer for all believers.

The Marcan Context of the Gethsemane Narrative

Before we examine in detail the evangelist's account of Jesus' awful experience prior to his arrest in Gethsemane, we shall more readily grasp Mark's insights into its meaning for Christian prayer that he intends to communicate to his reader by first recalling briefly the context in his Passion narrative into which he has inserted the episode.

Mark evidently found too abrupt the traditional accounts of Jesus' Passion, which as we have seen began with his arrest in the garden. Accordingly he has thought it necessary to create an atmosphere which will put the reader in the proper state of mind to appreciate both the terrible nature of Jesus' violent death and the divine plan by which he is led through suffering to victory. Hence Mark has arranged his introductory materials in such fashion as to alternate between light and darkness, the human tragedy and the divine triumph. Thus in contrast with the secretive plotting of the religious leaders to kidnap Jesus and destroy him stands the loyalty to Jesus of the people who might be expected to riot to save him (Mk 14:1–2). Before alerting the reader to the black treachery of Judas, which perhaps originally formed a pendant to the priestly conspiracy (as Luke 22:1–6 suggests), Mark inserts the beautiful episode (originally an independent, ancient Palestinian story) of Jesus' anointing by a woman of Bethany (Mk 14:3–9). Jesus, speaking in defense of the loving action of the woman, displays his divine knowledge of his death and predicts that his anointing will form part of the universal Gospel (Mk 14:8–9).

Mark's story of Jesus' Last Supper with his disciples (Mk 14:12–25) is easily the most important narrative in this introductory part of his account of Jesus' Passion. Jesus again displays his supernatural knowledge by dispatching two of the disciples to prepare the Passover supper, in a manner reminiscent of the arrangements for his messianic entry into Jerusalem (vv. 13–15; see 11:1–4). Into his description of this meal Mark has interpolated a liturgical formulation, probably familiar to his original audience from the eucharistic celebration in the community (vv. 22–25).[13]

Twice in this opening movement of his Passion narrative, it should be observed, Mark has drawn attention to the later liturgical veneration of their crucified and risen Lord by the earliest Church. Apropos of the story of the anointing, Father Schnackenburg remarks: "For the Christian community, the woman had paid Jesus an honor which, after Easter, Christians too wanted to show him. . . . It is, we may say, the foundation of a ritual veneration of Jesus. . . . History shows that the early Church, notwithstanding the duty of charitable service of the poor . . . did not neglect liturgical worship of its Lord . . . as an expression of union with its crucified and risen Lord. . . . "[14] And, as will presently become evident, the words of eucharistic institution will throw light upon the prayer of Jesus in Gethsemane, to which we now direct our attention.

JESUS' PRAYER IN GETHSEMANE (Mk 14:26–42)

26 And having sung the hymn they went out to the Mount of Olives. 27 And Jesus says to them, "You will all lose your faith, since Scripture has it, 'I will strike the shepherd and the sheep will be scattered.' 28 But after my resurrection I will go ahead of you to Galilee." 29 But Peter said to him, "even though they all lose faith, still I will not!" 30 Jesus said to him, "Amen I tell you: today, this very night before the cock twice crows, you will deny me thrice." 31 But he kept declaring extravagantly, "Though it were God's will that I die together with you, never will I deny you!" And they all kept speaking in the same vein.

32 And they come to a farmstead, Gethsemane by name; and he says to his disciples, "Sit down here while I pray." 33 And he takes along with him Peter and James and John; and he became filled with surprise and terror, and distressed from shock. 34 And he says to them, "My heart is bursting with sorrow to the point of death. Stay here and watch!" 35 And he went forward a little, and there he was collapsing upon the ground. And he kept praying over and over that, if it were possible, his hour might pass him by. 36 And he was saying "*Abba!* (dear Father), all things are possible for you. Take this cup away from me; yet, not what I desire, but what you." 37 And he returns to discover them asleep; and he says to Peter, "Simon, are you asleep? Did you not have the strength to watch one (short) hour? 38 Watch, all of you, and pray that you may not encounter the testing. The spirit indeed is willing, yet the flesh is weak." 39 And going off again he began to pray, employing the same words. 40 And again he returns to discover them asleep: their eyes

seemed to have heavy weights upon them. And they did not know what reply they were to make to him. 41 And he returns a third time and says to them, "So you are still sleeping and taking your rest? Enough of that! The hour has come; see, the Son of Man is being handed over into the power of the pagans. 42 Get up! Let us be on our way. See, he who is handing me over has drawn near."

The passage bears the imprint of Mark's editorial hand at various points. There is, for example, the evangelist's characteristic use of the historical present, which makes for a graphic recital, involving the reader in the event as if he were seeing it happening before his eyes. Also perceptible is a certain penchant for employing pairs of words, as well as the (to us) tiresome habit of repeating the same expressions with unvarying monotony. The most striking redactional feature, however, of Mark's handling of traditional materials is undoubtedly the way he has managed, with imaginative boldness, to create, from his sources, three distinct moments in the prayer of Jesus, interrupted by three visits to his disciples. The Lucan account (Lk 22:39–46) presents but a single prayer, even as did the two written sources of Mark. The question as to why Mark has tripled the prayer is a significant one, which is insufficiently explained by the suggestion frequently made that in Jewish tradition a threefold prayer was an indication of fervent petition in time of trial.[15] After our discussion of the passage we shall be in a position to see a more profound reason in this procedure by Mark (in which he is followed by Matthew). We can then ask why this writer had made such creative use of the two earlier sources and combined them in precisely the way he did.

Mark joins the celebration of Jesus' final meal, scene of the institution of the Eucharist, with a notice of the journey to the Mount of Olives as he introduces his story of Gethsemane. *And having sung the hymn* refers to the singing of the second part of the Hallel which concluded the Passover meal. It may be recalled that, in the view of A. Strobel, the vocabulary of the Greek version of some of these psalms (Pss 115–118) was employed by the author of the hymn in Hebrews.[16] *They went out to the Mount of Olives:* this topographical reference comes from the early tradition which had situated Jesus' arrest in this locale. In the prophet Zechariah, whom Mark will quote in the following verse, it is on the Mount of Olives that the Lord takes his stand in the eschatological battle where he gains the victory over his people's enemies (Zech 14:4).

And Jesus says to them, "You will all lose your faith, for Scripture says, 'I will strike the shepherd, and the sheep will be scattered.'" Jesus makes a twofold prediction concerning the little band of disciples who thus far have remained loyal to him. They will be "scandalized," that is, in the idiom of the Septuagint, lose their faith, presumably in him, although Mark does not make that explicit as in Mt 26:31. Secondly, God had already made known the break-up of the community of disciples through Zechariah's Song of the Sword (Zech 13:7). There "the shepherd," a royal figure, possibly symbolic of the sufferings in the messianic age, is celebrated. For Mark, Jesus is the shepherd who, although stricken by God, will show concern for his flock to the very moment of his capture. The evangelist, toward the end of the Gethsemane scene, notes the fulfillment of this prophecy. At Jesus' cry, "But let the Scriptures be fulfilled!" Mark adds immediately, "And abandoning him they all ran away" (Mk 14:49–50). In this way the reader is made aware of the theme which presides over the entire Marcan Gethsemane narrative. It is the ironical truth that the very sufferings Jesus undergoes from the moment of his arrest cause his few faithful followers to abandon him and lose their faith. This highly valuable insight of Mark will be crucial in finding a solution to the symbolism of "the cup" (v. 36).

But after my resurrection I will go ahead of you to Galilee: this allusion to Jesus' final triumph is obviously inserted by Mark to alert his reader to recall what his faith tells him, that Jesus' resurrection forms, with his death, an integral part of the saving event. The fact that these words, put here in the mouth of Jesus, evoke no reaction from the disciples is an indication that they have been borrowed from the Christian kerygma. Peter's rejoinder at this point totally ignores this part of Jesus' prophecy. It is

Mark's way of introducing the traditional data concerning Peter's denials of his Master.

But Peter said to him, 'Even though they all lose faith, still I will not!' Jesus said to him, 'Amen I tell you: today, this very night before the cock twice crows, you will deny me thrice.' But he kept declaring extravagantly, 'Though it were God's will[17] *that I die together with you, never will I deny you!' And they all kept speaking in the same vein.* While all the Gospel-writers advert to Jesus' prediction of this triple denial of himself by Peter, Mark has introduced it into his Gethsemane narrative of set purpose. As will be noted later, Mark is the sole evangelist to relate to Peter alone Jesus' strong rebuke (v. 37). The irony of Peter's self-confident boast is heightened by the use of a term of Pauline coinage, "die together with," which denotes the Christian's participation in the saving death of Jesus (2 Cor 7:3; 2 Tm 2:11). Its appearance here is the more notable as one of the rare indications of Pauline influence upon Mark.

And they came to a farmstead, Gethsemane by name. The impersonal third plural "they" is a characteristic of Marcan style; it may stand for a "we" in the original narrative.[18] The name Gethsemane, which is from early tradition, is retained perhaps for its symbolic value by Mark (as in Mt 26:36). Since it means a press for crushing olives, it becomes appropriate as the place of Jesus' terrible anguish. *And he says to his disciples, 'Sit down here while I pray.'* For the moment the eleven disciples remain in a group. From the following verse it becomes clear that eight of them are simply told to sit in a spot designated by Jesus. They receive no command to pray, nor even to remain awake. While the evangelist remarks upon Jesus' selection of his three favored followers, he forgets to tell the reader at what point all the disciples come together again. That they do so only becomes clear after Jesus' arrest, when "they *all* ran away" (v. 50).

And he takes Peter and James and John with him. Jesus' choice falls upon the specially privileged three who had witnessed the raising to life of Jairus' daughter (Mk 5:37) and Jesus' transfiguration (Mk 9:2–8), and had, together with Andrew, heard the prediction by Jesus of the destruction of the temple (Mk 13:3ff.).

Moreover, James and John had occasioned Jesus' remarks about his "cup" and "baptism" (Mk 10:35–40). While the three names come to Mark from early tradition, he would appear to have reasons of his own for reporting them here. The Marcan references to the "messianic secret," both in connection with the recovery of the little girl (Mk 5:43) and after the transfiguration (Mk 9:9–10), suggest that the scene these disciples are about to witness contains an aspect of Jesus' messianic revelation, of which Peter (Mk 8:32–33), as well as James and John (Mk 10:35–40), has not yet learned.

And he became filled with surprise and terror, and distressed from shock. It is to be noted that the strong colors in which Jesus' agony of soul is painted are more probably the result of Mark's editorial work in the combining of two verbs, however it may have been expressed in the tradition. One indication of this is the modification introduced in Mt 26:37. The first word *(ekthambeisthai)* is found only in this Gospel; it expresses surprise and something akin to fear (Mk 9:15; 16:5), particularly when, as here, it occurs in tandem with a term signifying a state of disorientation *(adēmonein)* almost equivalent to being in a state of shock. Such a display of violent emotions by Jesus is unique in our Gospels, the nearest being Jn 11:33–38. This cruelly realistic picture attests the reality that Jesus is a human being. The puzzling lack of any expression of sympathy, indeed of any reaction by the disciples, reminds us that, as the Suffering Servant of God, Jesus' vicarious Passion must be endured in total isolation. This emotional outburst from Jesus is the more astonishing, since earlier in Mark when he foretold his death only his disciples evinced any horror (Mk 8:32) or fear and terror (Mk 10:32).

And he says to them, "My heart is bursting with sorrow to the point of death: stay here and watch!" Jesus' inner feelings are now externalized with the help of allusions to the Old Testament. The vocabulary seems in part to be inspired by the refrain in Pss 42–43: "Why are you so grievously sad, my soul, and why do you harass me?" A remark by Jonah as he makes the death-wish (found only in the Greek of the Septuagint) may also lie behind the present saying. "I am overcome with excessive grief so as to die of it" (Jon 4:9). Is Mark implying that Jesus here makes the death wish?[19] In view of the prayer in vv. 35–36, this seems implausible, for it is a confident prayer for deliverance. Moreover, it is to be borne in mind that nowhere in the entire scene does Mark (or any other evangelist) give the slightest hint that Jesus' reaction is caused by the prospect of his physical sufferings; these are never mentioned, in contrast with the earlier Passion predictions. It seems more likely that Mark wishes to impress his reader with the terrible paradox of Jesus' reaction at this moment in his career. He has, especially in the Marcan Gospel, been hurrying through the public ministry in order to reach the dénouement of his mission as willed by God. But now he recoils—from what? Only an investigation of the symbolism of "the cup" will reveal this.

"Stay here and watch!" The command issued to the three disciples asks more than was asked of the eight; however, they are not ordered (as yet) to pray. If we are to grasp the orientation by Mark of this painful episode, it is necessary to bear in mind the chief concern of the evangelist, which is pedagogical. He endeavours, as will become clearer by the end of the scene, to teach the community a fundamental lesson in Christian prayer. The difference in the tenses of the two imperatives is noteworthy: the first, *"Stay here,"* is a complexive aorist equivalent to "Don't go away!" As Paul points out (Rom 8:27), our inability to pray must not be allowed to discourage us, since it provides the occasion for the intervention of the Holy Spirit. The present imperative "Watch!" suggests duration, thus demanding perseverance. The view that Jesus wishes these disciples to continue the Passover watch as sequel to the past paschal meal[20] appears less likely than a reference by Mark to the eschatological orientation of Christian prayer.

In the context of this Gospel the Passion narrative opened immediately after the conclusion of the eschatological discourse. The termination of this long instruction by Jesus is relevant here. "Look out! Stay awake! for you do not know when God's time occurs. It is like the case of a man going on a journey, who leaves his household, giving his slaves authority, each over his own work. He enjoins upon the doorkeeper that he watch. So watch! You do not know when the master of the household is coming back, whether by late evening, or midnight, at cockcrow or at dawn. Do not let him come suddenly and find you asleep! What I am saying to you, I say to all: Watch!" (Mk 13:33–37). A Pauline exhortation to perseverance in prayer reflects this same eschatological concern: "Keep persevering with prayer, remaining awake at it through thankfulness!" (Col 4:2).

And he went forward a little, and there he was collapsing upon the ground. As he had earlier, Mark depicts Jesus as going off by himself (Mk 1:35; 6:46), even apart from the specially favored three. By noting this action of Jesus, a symbol of entering the divine presence in preparation for addressing God, Mark discloses his chief preoccupation in composing this scene. The evangelist intends to use this painful episode from the tradition as a lesson to the suffering community for which he writes, on the effectiveness of prayer. Moreover, Mark portrays Jesus as falling to the earth from exhaustion,[21] where Matthew and Luke will present him as much more in command of himself.

And he kept praying over and over that, if it were possible, his hour might pass him by. Only in the Marcan narrative is the tenor of Jesus' prayer, in its initial stages, reported. Indeed, Matthew omits any mention of the hour in the prayers he puts in the mouth of Jesus, while Luke speaks of the hour, to which he assigns a new meaning (Lk 22:53b), only in connection with Jesus' apprehension. The effect upon Mark's reader of this summary of Jesus' petition to God is to cause the heart to stop with dread. What if such a desire had been heard, and the Father had allowed the hour to pass? While Jesus' anguished petition is, even now, contingent upon God's designs for him, yet in the context of the Marcan Gospel the words, *if it were possible,* strike dire forebodings into the attentive reader who recalls Jesus' previous remark to the disciples, "All things are possible for God" (Mk 10:27).

What meaning does Mark assign to the symbol, *his hour?* As will become clear at the close of the episode, it is (like any symbol) ambivalent: it signifies the moment in the divine plan when God hands over the Son of Man into the power of the Romans (v. 41)—this is the theological significance—and it also indicates the historical moment of Jesus' betrayal by Judas (v. 42)—the historical significance. Of the two, the first is by far the more important meaning for Mark and for the earliest tradition. The Marcan articulation of the second Passion prediction by Jesus, "The Son of Man is being handed over into the power of men" (Mk 9:31), is, in the view of many scholars, the most ancient Palestinian theologoumenon indicating God's initiative in the death of Jesus.[22]

And he was saying, "Abba! (dear Father), all things are possible for you. Take this cup away from me; yet, not what I desire, but what you. ... " To his reporting in indirect discourse Mark now adds for emphasis his version of Jesus' address to God. The Aramaic-speaking Christian community had lovingly preserved the very word *(ipsissima vox Jesu)* that was characteristic of Jesus' intercourse with God, and the later Hellenistic Christian churches had introduced their Greek version of the dominical prayer by means of this bilingual formulation which Mark here uses. In his letters Paul had followed the same procedure (Gal 4:6; Rom 8:15). This precious double expression of "Father" tells us two things. First, it reveals the conviction of the earliest Church regarding Jesus' awareness of the unique character of his own relationship with God. Joachim Jeremias has claimed that here, if anywhere, we have an historical reminiscence of how Jesus, during his earthly life, addressed his Father.[23] It would appear that this form of address was, in Jesus' day, employed in Aramaic-speaking families towards the father of the house. It was thus a family word, equivalent to "papa" or "daddy," and hence was generally considered too familiar for use in prayer to God. Thus, that Jesus should invoke God by a term that no Jew would dare employ (so at least he was reported as doing in the earliest tradition) provides evidence of his own self-understanding. The historical Jesus knew that God was his Father in a profoundly special way. Second, the maintenance even by Greek-speaking Christians of the Aramaic term in the community recital of the *Pater noster* suggests an explanation for the extraordinary care and reverence displayed toward the Lord's Prayer in the early Church into the patristic age.[24] Only after the catechumen had been baptized and had received the Eucharist were the words of this prayer confided to him. It will be recalled that, in

fact, the New Testament has preserved two different formulations of the dominical prayer (Mt 6:8–13; Lk 11:2–4), both seemingly of liturgical provenance. These divergent forms of the
prayer Jesus taught his disciples show how the early Christians
understood the significance of Jesus' gift. It was not a question
of a set formula from which tradition might not deviate. Rather
what was seen as of paramount importance was Jesus' loving do-
nation of his own filial attitudes toward his Father to those who,
after his resurrection, were endowed with the gift of Christian
faith through the Holy Spirit.[25] This privilege of being permitted to identify themselves with the only Son of God in praying
to his Father was the divinely chosen means of growing into full
awareness of their election as adoptive sons and daughters of
God. This uniquely Christian understanding of the function of
prayer in the life of each believer, it would appear, is part of
Mark's pedagogical purpose here. That purpose provides, at any
rate, a plausible explanation for his portrayal of Jesus as adopting the bilingual formula which can only have come into usage
in Hellenistic Christian circles.

   "All things are possible for you." Mark now makes an explicit
cross-reference to the remark of Jesus at 10:27, to which he alluded in his indirect reporting of Jesus' prayer in the verse preceding. On that earlier occasion he had replied to the disciples'
puzzled query, "Who then can be saved?" by asserting his conviction, "With men it is impossible, not with God. All things are
possible for God!" Mark's repeated insistence upon Jesus' attitude as he begins his prayer is significant for the lesson he wishes to impart to his Christian reader. For, to anticipate
somewhat, the evangelist wishes to convince the community for
which he writes that, since God's will for them (and this appears
to involve suffering) is indeed immutable, the Christian under
the impact of constant, fervent prayer can be brought to accept
the divine designs for himself. Such acceptance indeed, as will
become evident in the sequel, is not merely passive or stoical,
but open-hearted, even joy-filled. With the help of his two written sources Mark has constructed his account of Jesus' struggle
so as to pick out three moments. At this initial stage of Jesus'

prayer he is pictured as regarding escape from *his hour* as a real possibility, and moreover, if he is seen to be ready to submit to God's decree as regards his own suffering and death, he is described as quite clearly desiring to avoid it.

Actually in Mark the demand is put bluntly: "Take this cup away from me; yet, not what I desire, but what you. . . . " We shall see later that both Matthew and Luke, each in his own way, soften the seeming sharpness of the Marcan plea. *This cup* is a symbolic expression. What does it stand for, and how does it differ from *his hour?* While many commentators have sought to discern the significance of *this cup* by examining the symbolic usage in the Old Testament, it would seem to be more appropriate methodologically to seek its meaning for Mark in the context of this scene and, further, within the Marcan Gospel. There are in fact two earlier narratives in which the cup is given a symbolic function by Mark. The first is the episode where James and John ask for positions of eminence in Jesus' "glory" (Mk 10:35–45). In reply Jesus tells them, "You do not understand what you ask. Can you drink the cup I shall drink, or be baptized with the baptism I shall undergo?" (v. 38). The obvious allusions to the two chief Christian sacraments, the Eucharist and baptism, through which the saving effects of Jesus' Passion and death are communicated, make it abundantly clear that cup and baptism are symbols of that redemptive death. Moreover, the saying of Jesus with which the incident comes to its climax leaves the matter beyond all doubt. "For indeed the Son of Man has come to serve, not to be served, and to give his life as ransom for the rest of men" (Mk 10:45). What Jesus here promises to the two favorite disciples is the privilege and grace of sharing in the fruits of his life of total service, culminating in his death. In my opinion the view that Jesus here prophesies a martyr's death for these two (as some commentators claim) is dubious. Behind this symbolism of the cup, it may well be, as Father Schnackenburg has pointed out,[26] that Mark intends to suggest the ominous sense of the metaphor as found in the writings of Israel's prophets. There it frequently stands for God's wrathful judgment. If Professor Schnackenburg is right, then Mark means to tell his community that Jesus implied here his acceptance of the dark side of *the cup* and was willing to take on himself the awful consequences of the divine judgment upon sinful humanity.

The second occurrence in Mark of the cup as symbol is found in this evangelist's version of the words of eucharistic institution in his narrative of the Last Supper. "And taking a cup, giving thanks he gave it to them, and they all drank from it. And he said to them, 'This is my blood of the testament to be poured out on behalf of the rest of men'" (Mk 14:23–24). The cup and its contents symbolize Jesus' saving blood, the instrument by which the new covenant was to be struck through his death and resurrection. The sacrificial nature of Jesus' redemptive death stands unequivocally revealed by this symbolic usage. This offering to God of his own life-blood by Jesus as an efficacious sign of a totally new relationship with God on the part of redeemed humanity was accomplished on Calvary by his running the supreme risk of seeming dereliction by God. Mark asserts this by having Jesus utter the terrible words of the psalm, "My God, my God, why have you abandoned me?" (Mk 15:34).

In the light of these two passages, which throw light on the meaning of the cup as symbol for Mark, we are confronted with a problem. If, as has been seen, *this cup* stands symbolically for Jesus' saving death, and even if we accept the dark side of its symbolism, how can the evangelist depict Jesus in Gethsemane as asking his Father to *"take this cup away from me?"* To discover a satisfactory answer to this question, I venture to suggest, we must recall the prophecy by Jesus which Mark has used to frame his entire narrative of Gethsemane. The evangelist introduced the scene with a double prediction by Jesus: his own sufferings and death would in fact cause his faithful disciples to lose their faith in him, and in addition the Passion would cause the break-up of this little band of followers. Their loyalty and fellowship were the only tangible results of his entire public ministry, and now his death for them would destroy even this last fragment of his mission. Accordingly, what Jesus shrinks from, in the view of Mark, at this supreme moment of his life, is the Father's decree that he acquiesce in the complete failure of his public ministry, indeed his whole earthly mission. As Jesus begins his prayer in this narrative, while standing ready to accept God's will for himself, he is portrayed as recoiling from the terrible reality that his very sufferings and death for mankind entailed the dissolution of the little community of believers that alone had remained loyal to him.

And he returns to discover them asleep. At this point we must pause to remove two commonly accepted views of Jesus' attitude toward this traumatic situation. In the first place, it is to be observed that the evangelist nowhere gives the slightest hint that Jesus' revulsion from the ordeal that lies ahead of him is brought about by his foreknowledge of the awful physical torments he is destined to suffer. While in the triple prediction of his Passion in this Gospel (Mk 8:31; 9:31; 10:33–34) there are allusions (and in increasing detail) to the outrages and bodily pain he is to endure, the Gethsemane narrative makes no allusion to such sufferings. The poignancy of Jesus' wish to be relieved of *this cup* then has nothing to do with physical pain. Secondly, the fairly widespread misapprehension that Jesus, at three points in his prayerful struggle, returns to his beloved companions to seek solace or consolation from them has no basis in the Marcan text or in those of the other evangelists. What then is the reason, in Mark's eyes, for this triple return by Jesus to his disciples? It will be remembered that Mark had introduced at the beginning of his account of the scene a text of Zechariah through which Jesus is characterized as the stricken shepherd afflicted by God's design: "I will strike the shepherd and the sheep will be scattered" (v. 27b). Mark here presents Jesus as the Good Shepherd, who confronted with the divine threat of the destruction of his flock returns repeatedly to look after it, to see if they are still together and safe. The familiar Johannine characterization of Jesus as the Good Shepherd (Jn 10:11–16) is not missing from Mark. When Jesus sees the great crowd of five thousand who come to him in an out-of-the-way place, "he was moved to compassion for them because they were like sheep deprived of a shepherd" (Mk 6:34). In Gethsemane then, despite his own traumatic confrontation with the utter destruction of his life's work, our evangelist depicts Jesus as the loving shepherd filled with pity and concern for his own.

The sleep of the disciples during Jesus' trial in the garden has long caused difficulties for the commentators.[27] Is this detail historical? If so, how could the episode be attested and inserted into the evangelical tradition in the absence of any eyewitnesses? This may seem a trivial problem, capable of some fairly easy solution. For instance, the disciples may have dozed off and on, being dimly aware of the tragic situation. Jesus' struggle may well have occurred earlier than the night before his death, as Jn 12:27 would appear to suggest. The wording of his prayer by the evangelists may have been deduced from the disciples' experience of Jesus' long-established custom through his ministry, and articulated with the help of the Psalter. On the other hand, it might be argued that the evangelists would scarcely have had the audacity to present in such a bad light the specially chosen disciples of Jesus, who in the earliest Church appear to have held positions of paramount importance, if their failure to support Jesus in his hour of need—even out of human weakness—were not an historical fact. Such an apologetic argument might indeed carry weight so far as Matthew and Luke are concerned, the two evangelists who consistently defend or excuse the Twelve throughout their Gospels. In the case of Mark however, who insists constantly upon the disciples' lack of understanding, this kind of reasoning may well be regarded as special pleading. Thus whether the disciples actually fell asleep or not remains (in my opinion) an insoluble question. Moreover, whether fact or not, it seems that their sleeping is alluded to for its symbolic value in our Gospels. And the question arises as to the meaning of this symbolism. In the context of the Marcan Gospel a clue appears to be provided by the closing verses of the eschatological discourse (Mk 13:33–37), which this evangelist placed immediately before his Passion narrative, as we remarked earlier in this chapter. If this conjecture is correct, then (whether it is historical or not) the sleep of the disciples is a symbol in Mark's mind of their incomprehension, even at this late date, of the real character of Jesus' vocation as God's Suffering Servant.

"Simon, are you asleep? Did you not have the strength to watch one (brief) *hour?"* Mark has Jesus address this rebuke to Peter alone. As will be presently seen, Matthew interprets it in quite a

different light by making the verb plural. That Jesus here addresses this disciple as Simon need not be taken as a stinging reminder that he is no longer "Rock," as the new name imposed on him by Jesus implies. The use of the name is plausibly an historical reminiscence retained in the tradition, especially in view of Lk 22:31, where at the Last Supper Jesus calls Peter Simon when predicting Peter's future function as the special sustainer of the faith of the Eleven. What is significant here is Mark's allusion to Jesus' incipient awareness that in fact Peter does not yet have *the strength* to stay awake (that is, to guard the eschatological expectancy) even for a very short period of time. The term *hour* here has no symbolic value, but simply signifies a brief period of time.

"Watch, all of you, and pray that you may not encounter the testing." This injunction is given, presumably, only to the three favored disciples. To his earlier command to watch, which they have failed to obey, Jesus now adds a new precept: they must persevere in prayer. As the reader will shortly discover, these disciples are no more capable of praying than of staying awake. Yet Jesus is compelled to urge them to do what they are really incapable of accomplishing (such appears to be Mark's insight) for two reasons. First, when before beginning his public ministry Jesus was "tested by Satan" in the desert (Mk 1:12), he was alone and so had only himself to take care of. In Gethsemane these disciples are with him, and so constitute an added responsibility. If then they are to succeed in avoiding the eschatological testing in which Jesus is already involved, they must take up the weapons of watchfulness and prayer. In the second place, Mark is concerned to have his reader appreciate the fact that Jesus' experience of his disciples' failure to follow out his instructions will prove a turning point in his initial attitude toward *this cup* which the Father wills him to drink.

Our evangelist here implies that Jesus' Passion was for him an experience of that eschatological *testing*, the definitive struggle against the powers of evil in which he will ultimately be victorious. As James M. Robinson has well pointed out,[28] Jesus' battle with Satan for Mark was conducted along various vectors. He challenges Satan's hold upon mankind not only through his exorcisms, but also his miracles of healing, his controversies with adversaries, and his continual rebuking of the timidity, incomprehension, and brashness of his own followers. In his Passion Jesus encounters the definitive testing by the powers of evil as "the stronger" (Mk 1:7), who "binds the strong," and so "loots his house" (Mk 3:27). But his poor disciples are as yet in no position to engage Satan by becoming involved in Jesus' *testing,* for indeed (as the Marcan Jesus will gradually become aware through his prayer) it will only be in virtue of the strength won for them by Jesus' death and resurrection that these future Christians can win through to victory.[29]

In the words *"that you may not encounter the testing"* we have the only allusion by Mark in this narrative to the Lord's Prayer. They recall the petition, "Do not lead us into the testing" (Mt 6:13; Lk 11:4), which in that prayer refers to the eschatological warfare with Satan.

"The spirit indeed is willing, yet the flesh is weak." This remark has the air of an aphorism, yet nothing quite like it is found in either biblical or classical literature. The contrast between flesh (= man) and spirit (God's Spirit = power) is of fairly common occurrence in the Bible. Yet here the evangelist seems to use *spirit* in the sense exhibited in two earlier passages of his Gospel (Mk 2:8; 8:12), where it is used, for the only times in the Synoptics,[30] of the conscious self. In both instances it is a question of Jesus' self-consciousness. The significance of this will appear presently. The phrase "a willing spirit" occurs in the *Miserere:* the psalmist prays, "A willing spirit sustain in me" (Ps 51:12). This "spirit" indeed is God's, as is clear from the preceding verse, "Your holy spirit take not from me" (v. 13). However, the petition in v. 12 speaks of it as a constituent part of the renewed believer, "A steadfast spirit renew within me." It would appear reasonable to assume that Mark employs the term in this latter sense.[31]

An even more difficult problem concerns the application of the maxim here: To whom does Jesus apply it? Obviously it is intended as a warning to the disciples; hence Mark means it to be taken to heart by the suffering community for which he writes. Does the evangelist suggest, in additon, that in this context of Jesus' prayer and struggle it is meant to apply to himself? *Pace* C. E. B. Cranfield,[32] I venture to suggest that the evangelist wishes us to understand that Jesus here speaks out of his own immediate experience as a human being. He is indeed *willing* in that truest part of himself, which Mark designates as his *spirit;* yet he has felt all the weakness of his human nature, the *flesh,* as he struggles to accept his Father's will. And from his own anguished experience he already knows the answer to the question he had put to Peter: the disciples simply do not have the strength to keep hope alive without the divine assistance.

And going off again he began to pray, employing the same words. What is the theme, according to Mark, of this second prayer of Jesus? Usually, *the same words* are understood to refer to the articulated prayer in v. 36, and Jesus is thought to repeat the petition he had already made to be released by the Father from the drinking of *this cup.* While this is, of course, not implausible, I venture to suggest that he now prays to God about the human dilemma, which he has just voiced: *The spirit indeed is willing, yet the flesh is weak.* Jesus has in fact just warned his disciples to *watch* and to *pray that you may not encounter the testing,* because he himself is already caught up in this eschatological combat and has realized his own weakness. As he now prays over this insight gained from his encounter with himself, and as he reflects upon the predicament of his drowsy disciples, unaware of their imminent peril, he comes to see that only by his acceptance of *this cup,* despite its dark side, will his followers ultimately be granted the strength to carry out their mission and to live an authentic Christian existence.

Thus, what I am suggesting is that here, as Mark presents it, we have the turning point in the struggle and prayer of Jesus. He does not repeat his earlier prayer, but now prays for that strength for himself to carry out the Father's design, which only God can give. As will later be seen, the petition Jesus now takes up is akin to that expressed in the Fourth Gospel: "Father, keep me safe throughout this hour!" (Jn 12:27). Moreover, it will also be seen in our discussion of Matthew's presentation of Jesus' second prayer that he has understood Mark to imply a development in Jesus' attitude. For with his characteristic penchant for clarifying what is obscure in Mark, Matthew (the first commentator upon the Marcan text) has created a new formulation which he puts in Jesus' mouth at this point in his narrative (Mt 26:42).

And again he returns to discover them asleep: their eyes seemed to have heavy weights upon them. While Jesus is engaged in prayer a second time, he does not abandon his concern for his beloved disciples, and so he returns as their *shepherd* to see if they are still together, still out of jeopardy. Perhaps, too, he comes back to see if they have taken heed of his twofold injunction to *watch* and to *pray.* In this hope he is to be rudely disillusioned. This repeated lapse of Jesus' followers, despite his grave caution to ward off the *testing,* is the result of Mark's creative use of the two written sources he is employing. By this procedure he is able to underscore the solitariness of Jesus in his plight, and so insinuate that he is God's Suffering Servant, celebrated in the hymns of Second Isaiah (see Is 53:12).

Their eyes seemed to have heavy weights upon them. Here we meet something quite extraordinary in this Gospel: Mark appears to excuse the disciples' failure to comply with Jesus' command to them. As has been observed, it is a predominant feature of Marcan theology to bring out the incomprehension of these close followers of Jesus. Such condoning of their inability to obey the Master, so uncharacteristic of Mark, is a clear sign that we are in the presence of the pre-Marcan traditon. It is of course possible (I think, less probable) to interpret this remark not as an exoneration of the disciples, but as a further indication of their blindness to the revelation of Jesus as a suffering Messiah. Such in fact is the opinion of the distinguished Swedish exegete, Harald Riesenfeld.[33] Luke, however, who like Matthew is one of the earliest commentators on Mark, appears to have understood this remark as an excuse, as may be inferrred from his observation that the disciples had fallen asleep "from grief" (Lk 22:45).

And they did not know what reply to make to him. Two observations are in order here. First, it might conceivably be rendered: "And they did not understand the reply they made to him." However, I accept the judgment of Max Zerwick that "the Greek can not have this meaning."[34] Second, this observation is an echo of that made upon Peter's conduct at Jesus' trans-figuration: "For he did not know what reply to make" (Mk 9:6). Here, as in our text, we have an example of the Marcan theme of the disciples' lack of understanding of Jesus. It will be noted that the evangelist implies that Jesus had wakened them with some remark. Matthew will put the incident in another light (Mt 26:43–44). This Marcan observation indicates that the evangelist has certainly understood the sleep of the disciples as symbolic of their lack of hope and even, perhaps, of faith.

Then he returns a third time. Here we see the creative editori-al hand of Mark at work. He has combined his two written sources (and thus has obtained two intervals in the prayer of Je-sus, punctuated by two returns to his disciples). Now he adds a third moment, but does not venture to say anything here, even by implication, about the character of Jesus' prayer. He is con-tent to show its final results through the subsequent action of Je-sus. Thus Mark appears to stress Jesus' triple return to his friends, while Matthew will display more interest in Jesus' de-parture from his own and his threefold prayer. Mark intends to make his reader aware of Jesus' role as the Good Shepherd who safeguards the flock, for which he is shortly to give his life.

He says to them, "So you are still sleeping and taking your rest?" The absence of any punctuation in the original Greek manu-scripts makes it impossible to be sure whether the remark is in-tended as a question or meant ironically—"So sleep on and take your rest!" However, from the Marcan presentation of Jesus' at-titudes in the entire scene, it would appear improbable that it is to be understood as a stinging rebuke administered with irony. Mark wishes us to realize that, if his disciples' attitude remains consistent with their behavior throughout the story, Jesus' own attitude has now undergone a profound change with respect to his hour.

"Enough of that!" The single Greek word *(apechei)* remains a conundrum. In fact, one may assume that Matthew did not un-derstand its meaning, since he omits it from his own narrative. C. E. B. Cranfield in his commentary gives no less than eight possible meanings.[35] The majority view is content to accept the rendering of the Latin Vulgate *(sufficit)*, and that is the meaning

I have adopted. It probably refers to the drowsiness and sleep of the disciples, although (and this is less likely) it may refer to Jesus' mild criticism of his own.

"The hour has come: see, the Son of Man is being handed over into the power of the pagans." The dramatic announcement of the arrival of *the hour* comes from the tradition, which was known also to the fourth evangelist, who however gives it his own interpretation (Jn 12:23; 17:1). In Mark's view it means that Jesus is about to be arrested (the historical sense); more profoundly, however, it refers to the action of the Father who *hands over* his Son to the forces of evil.

The Son of Man is without any doubt the most controversial expression in the New Testament, and its use in the Gospels is admittedly the greatest piece of unfinished business in modern critical scholarship. The meaning of the phrase itself is quite simple: it is a Semitic way of denoting an individual human being.[36] As it is used in the Book of Daniel, it indicates a symbolic figure which stands for redeemed Israel (see Dan 7:13–18). However, there are several questions about its use by Jesus in our Gospels where he alone is represented as applying it to himself. Did the historical Jesus ever use this expression? Did he use it with reference to himself? A further question which is perhaps easier to answer is: Where did Jesus (assuming he used it) learn the expression? Most likely he took it from the Book of Daniel. That Jesus did make use of the expression during his public ministry is generally admitted by the majority of critics. However, that the historical Jesus ever applied it to himself is very doubtful, the reason being that there are some passages in the Gospels where he clearly distinguishes the Son of Man from himself: "Whoever will be ashamed of me and my words before this adulterous and sinful age, the Son of Man will in his turn be ashamed, when he comes in the glory of his Father with the holy angels" (Mk 8:38; see Mt 19:28; Lk 12:8). Once it is recalled that the Son of Man in Daniel is a symbol for the apocalyptic representation of the future salvation beyond history, it is difficult to imagine the historical Jesus applying the title to himself. He appears rather to have thought of the Son of Man as vindicator of his own preaching and mission in the world, that is, as a symbol for God's vindication of the truth of what he stood for and died for. After the first disciples had realized by the help of the Holy Spirit and his gift of Christian faith that God had indeed vindicated their crucified Master by raising him from death, these earliest Christians became aware that in very truth the risen Jesus was the Son of Man. In the course of further reflection upon Jesus' earthly history, the apostles came to the awareness that already in his earthly ministry Jesus was, although in a hidden, mysterious way, the Son of Man. To express this new-found insight of their belief, they created, upon the basis of sayings uttered about himself by Jesus during his mortal life, new sayings which identified him with the Son of Man. For example, there is the statement, "The Son of Man has not whereon to lay his head" (Mt 8:20). The primitive community also composed sayings in which Jesus predicted his death and resurrection in terms of his role as the Son of Man (Mk 8:31, etc.).[36]

In our present passage we have an instance of this last type of Christian formulation, which is consequently the fruit of the Christological reflection of the very early Church. Awareness of the true nature of this statement enables us to see the theological meaning of the verb *is being handed over*. The theological passive here denotes God as the real initiator of Jesus' Passion and death. The word here rendered as *the pagans*, which only in the Marcan text has the definite article, reads literally "the sinners," a Jewish sobriquet for those who did not possess the divine revelation given to Israel through the Mosaic Law and the sacred prophetic writings. Mark appears to be thinking here specifically of the Romans who executed Jesus. Matthew will speak simply of "sinful men" (Mt 26:45).

"Get up! Let us be on our way. See, he who is handing me over has drawn near!" Mark has composed this statement as the conclusion and climax of the first phase of the Gethsemane episode, in order to link Jesus' struggle and prayer to the second half of his narrative depicting Jesus' arrest by his enemies under the guidance of the traitor Judas. He has however created the verse on

the basis of traditional elements, as the Fourth Gospel indicates by citing the opening words in almost identical fashion, "Get up! Let us be on our way from here" (Jn 14:31b).

The most noteworthy feature of this verse is its delineation of the complete change in Jesus' attitude toward his *hour* from that described by Mark in the initial summary, in indirect discourse, of the tenor of Jesus' prayer with respect to the *hour*. Far from desiring that it *might pass him by* (v. 35b), Jesus now goes forward spontaneously to meet those who seek to arrest him. He moreover insists upon involving his disciples in this tragic outcome of his earthly career. They have not yet deserted him, as they will presently, and so he wishes to keep them with him to protect them as long as he is able. This final gesture of loving solicitude for his tiny band of faithful followers completes Mark's portrayal of Jesus as the Good Shepherd, whose sheep will be scattered according to God's declared will only when he is stricken. It is not accidental that Mark presents Jesus as the first to become aware of Judas' approach and to warn his disciples. Whether the knowledge is attributed to Jesus' divine prescience or simply to his human perceptiveness the evangelist leaves shrouded in obscurity. It is only with a further development of the tradition that Jesus' foreknowledge as the unique Son of God will be insisted upon, Mark is content to imply Jesus' awareness of his divinity by quoting the Aramaic term *Abba* in his address to God and to indicate Jesus' supernatural insight into the meaning of what is now happening to himself through his use of the Son of Man saying created by the faith of the primitive Church.

Mark's Achievement

By way of conclusion we may review the notable accomplishment of Mark from the viewpoint of his structuring, within the compass of his innovative account of the Passion, the narrative of Jesus' struggle and prayer prior to his arrest in Gethsemane. We shall also reflect upon the new as well as the traditional features of his picture of Jesus, Son of God yet fully human, which Mark has succeeded in bringing before his readers in this touching, if terrible scene.

Mark appears to have been the first writer to extend the scope of earlier Passion stories, chiefly by including the account of Jesus' last meal with his own, which reaches its climax in the words and gestures of the eucharistic institution. Mark's quotation strikes us as a terse recital, devoid of detail (hence noticeably un-Marcan in style). Hence it is, in all likelihood borrowed from the liturgy of the Lord's supper celebrated in the community for which our evangelist wrote his Gospel. As a link between the account of the supper and that of Jesus' apprehension by his enemies Mark has inserted the dramatic story of Jesus' struggle and prayer through which he is brought to accept the divine will.

Mark has moreover made use of the device of prophecy—fulfillment in order to unify and coordinate the two chief episodes of his newly minted Gethsemane narrative. With the help of an Old Testament text (Zech 13:7) and a prediction by Jesus preserved in the evangelical tradition, Mark suggests to his reader the principal *leitmotiv* of the Gethsemane cycle. Jesus' sufferings and death will cause the disciples' loss of faith and their dispersal as a community, while Peter will deny him. The accomplishment of the first prediction is noted as the entire scene closes. By inserting the story of Jesus' prayer as a coupling between the eucharistic words and his account of the arrest, Mark has succeeded in showing the dark side of the cup Jesus is to drink.

Within the narrative of Jesus' struggle in prayer with God, the evangelist has creatively employed his two written sources, each containing but one period of prayer, so as to produce three distinct moments in the prolonged dialogue of Jesus with the Father. In the course of his prayer Jesus is seen moving from the plea to have his hour of suffering pass him by and from an attitude of revulsion toward the cup, through the realization of the necessity of his redemptive death to win strength for his disciples in their testing, to a dynamic and voluntary acceptance of God's will as he assumes the initiative in going forward to meet his captors. Thus Mark has managed to impart what in his view is the chief lesson for Christian prayer to be derived from this tragic experience: God's will must indeed be acquiesced in and carried out by the faithful, and it is principally through fervent, prolonged prayer that the believer is brought to accept God's designs for him. Mark shows that he values the dialogue-character of prayer in which the Christian takes up a position as a responsible, mature human being in confrontation with the God to whom he prays.

By his triple structuring of this narrative Mark has also contrived to separate the privileged three, Peter, James and John, from the rest of the disciples, and if our evangelist has forgotten to inform the reader precisely when all are reunited, yet he is able by this division to suggest that the three are chosen by Jesus as recipients of a special revelation of paramount importance: Jesus' role as the Suffering Servant of God.

Mark has judiciously retained the allusion (probably found in the written tradition he uses) Pss 42–43, in order to give a context of confidence in the Father to Jesus' prayer. It will be remembered that this double psalm is categorized as a psalm of confidence, a type of prayer exclusively characteristic of Israel among all her Near Eastern neighbors, whose prayers and psalms we now know from archeological discoveries.

This narrative adds considerably to our appreciation of Marcan Christology. Throughout Mark's account, Jesus is presented as the Shepherd, described by Zechariah, who interrupts his conversation with his Father to return to his little flock that he wishes to protect from the terrible ordeal of the testing he himself is undergoing. Thus Mark insists upon Jesus' loving care by noting expressly his threefold return to his own (Matthew will display more interest in Jesus' triple departure to be with his Father). If Mark does not tell us anything about the third moment in Jesus' prayer, he exhibits its fruit through the complete transformation of Jesus' attitude toward his hour immediately afterward.

More graphically than any other evangelist Mark has underscored the complete humanity of Jesus by his surrealistic description of Jesus' emotional reactions, as also by his profound compassion for his sleeping disciples. Yet Jesus is also depicted as the unique Son of God, whose loving familiarity with his Father is domonstrated by his use of the Aramaic *Abba*. His filial confidence in and obedience to God are also unmistakably brought before the eyes of the reader. The solitariness of Jesus in this scene reminds us of the vicarious nature of his sufferings and death, to which Mark has referred earlier in his Gospel (Mk 10:45; 14:24). Jesus must suffer and die alone, since the Scriptures of Israel had already declared that the Passion was, in the design of God, a "ransom for the many" (Mk 10:45), that is, "for the rest of mankind."

One final question remains to be asked: Does Mark present this agonizing prayer of Jesus as really answered by God? It is possible, I suggest, to give a positive answer to this question. Mark never forgets, in the course of his book, that he is writing for a suffering community menaced by the ominous prospect of persecution, if it is not already enduring such testing. Thus he is, throughout the Passion narrative, desirous that his readers grasp the mysterious paradox of Jesus' sufferings and death. It is by means of this recital of Jesus' struggle through prayer to accept the divine designs for him and for mankind's redemption that Mark dramatically alerts us to the paradox of Jesus' acceptance of the concrete circumstances of his death. So, after his arrest by his captors, the paradox is voiced by Jesus together with his total acceptance of it by the elliptical remark, "Yet, let the Scriptures [which contain the announced will of his Father] be fulfilled!" (v. 49). The divine mystery surrounding Jesus is undoubtedly one of the dominant themes of Mark's little book. Nowhere perhaps in this entire Gospel does the evangelist succeed in expressing the mystery, so poignantly and in such an arresting way, as in his story of Jesus' prayerful struggle in Gethsemane.

NOTES

1. The first example of Redaction criticism, in fact, was a small book by Willi Marxsen, *Der Evangelist Markus: Studien zur Redaktionsgeschichte des Evangeliums* (Göttingen, 1959).

2. M. Kähler, *Der sogenannte historische Jesus und der geschichtliche biblische Christus* (1891), cited by Marxsen, *op. cit.*, p. 17.

3. Especially by his inveterate use of the adverb "immediately," which Mark employs with monotonous repetition. Jesus scarcely concludes one activity when he is off "immediately" to engage in another.

4. R. Bultmann, *Theologie des Neuen Testaments* (Tübingen, 1948), p. 34.

5. W. Wrede, *Das Messiasgeheimnis in den Evangelien* (Göttingen, 1901), an important book that has only recently appeared in English as *The Messianic Secret* (Cambridge/London, 1971).

6. Eduard Schweizer, *The Good News According to Mark* (Richmond, 1970), p. 56.

7. Rudolf Schnackenburg, *The Gospel According to St. Mark I* (New York, 1966), p. 33.

8. *Ibid.*, p. 116.

9. Mark's intention is indicated by his locating of the disciples' question "in the house" and "in private," which thus become symbols that it is the risen Jesus, present to the believing community through the proclaimed word, who continues his teaching.

10. R.Schnackenburg, *The Gospel According to St. Mark II* (New York, 1970), p. 72.

11. *Ibid.*

12. *Ibid.*, p. 154.

13. The introductory phrase, "And while they were eating" (v. 22), an unnecessary repetition of the beginning of v. 18, indicates "a seam" (to use the critics' expression) revealing Mark's editorial interjection of the narrative of eucharistic institution into his own account. These verses (vv. 22–25) with their lapidary formulation, so different from Mark's graphic way of writing, exhibit a liturgical style which is unmistakable.

14. Rudolf Schnackenburg, *The Gospel According to St. Mark*, II, pp. 110f.

15. Thus, for example, J. W. Holleran, *The Synoptic Gethsemane*, p. 49, observes: "And it is easy to miss the significance of Jesus' threefold prayer. Rabbinic literature contains a number of examples of the repetition of prayer, especially under trial. And 2 Cor 12:8 is probably evidence of a tradition of tripling prayer to overcome temptation."

16. August Strobel, "Die Psalmengrundlage der Gethsemane-Parallele Hebr 5:7 ff.," *Zeitschrift für die neutestamentliche Wissenschaft* 45 (1954), 252–266.

17. Literally, "It were necessary" *(dei)*. However in the Greek of the New Testament, the necessity which governs sacred history flows, not from fate (as in classical, pagan Greek), but from the divine will.

18. This suggestion was made by C. H. Turner, "Marcan Usage: Notes, Critical and Exegetical, on the Second Gospel," *Journal of Theological Studies* 26 (1924–25), 231.

19. For a succinct review of the four possible meanings of *heōs thanatou* here, see J. W. Holleran, *The Synoptic Gethsemane*, pp. 14f.; David Daube, "Death as Release in the Bible," *Novum Testamentum* 5 (1962), 94–98.

20. See J. W. Holleran, *The Synoptic Gethsemane*, pp. 17f.

21. This is indicated by his use of the imperfect tense in Greek, which suggests a picture of Jesus in the very act of falling down upon the ground.

22. R. H. Fuller, *The Foundations of New Testament Christology*, p. 151.

23. See the interesting discussion of this point in J. W. Holleran, *The Synoptic Gethsemane*, pp. 22–26.

24. The reader will find very helpful the small monograph, translated by John Reumann, by Joachim Jeremias, *The Lord's Prayer* (Philadelphia, 1964).

25. Jacques Guillet, "Le Christ prie en moi," *Christus* 5 (1958), 150–165.

26. See R. Schnackenburg, *The Gospel According to St. Mark*, II, pp. 54f.

27. R. S. Barbour, "Gethsemane in the Tradition of the Passion," *New Testament Studies* 16 (1969–70), 234–235.

28. James M. Robinson, *The Problem of History in Mark* (London, 1957).

29. For an informative study of the Qumran background of this eschatological testing, see Karl Georg Kuhn, "New Light on Temptation, Sin and Flesh in the New Testament," in *The Scrolls and the New Testament*, ed. Krister Stendahl (New York, 1957), pp. 94–113.

30. A similar usage occurs in the Fourth Gospel (Jn 11:33; 13:21), where also it is a question of Jesus' conscious self.

31. For the opposite view, see J. W. Holleran, *The Synoptic Gethsemane*, pp. 39–45. The view adopted by Eduard Schweizer, *The Good News According to Mark*, pp. 313f., is the one followed here.

32. C. E. B. Cranfield, *The Gospel According to St. Mark* (Cambridge, 1959), p. 434, states, "The suggestion that Jesus is here speaking about himself is unlikely in view of the context (vv. 37, 38a)." On the con-

trary, the context of Jesus' struggle in prayer makes it natural to think of his warning to his disciples as issuing from what he himself has been undergoing.

33. Harald Riesenfeld, *Jésus transfiguré: l'arrière-plan du récit évangélique de la transfiguration de Notre-Seigneur* (Copenhagen, 1947), pp. 281–301. This book is unfortunately unavailable to me; I have taken the reference to it from J. W. Holleran, *op. cit.*, p. 48.

34. Maximilian Zerwick, S.J., *Biblical Greek*, English edition adapted by Joseph Smith, S.J. (Rome, 1963), #348.

35. C. E. B. Cranfield, *The Gospel According to St. Mark*, p. 435, gives in addition to the two senses above: the commercial sense, Judas has received full payment, or the account is paid up, i.e., time has run out; Judas is about to take possession of me; an Aramaic term has been misread for one that means "it is far away," whereas the original Aramaic word meant "it presses" (i.e., the hour); again, if the word "the end" is understood, the sense would be "it is finished"; or (as a question which Jesus immediately answers) "The end is far off?" W. J. Holleran gives two more conjectures (*The Synoptic Gethsemane*, pp. 52–56): "The account is closed" and "That is a hindrance."

36. For a nuanced discussion of this very difficult question the reader is referred to R. H. Fuller, *Foundations of New Testament Christology*, pp. 119–125.

V
MATTHEW'S GETHSEMANE
(Mt 26:36–46)

When one turns to Matthew's Gospel after reading that of Mark, one enters a different world. This evangelist has created as a Prologue to his book five episodes, ostensibly connected with reminiscences of Jesus' birth and early years, to which he has prefixed a genealogy to demonstrate that Jesus is "the Son of David, the Son of Abraham" (Mt 1:1). Upon closer inspection, however, the first four narratives are seen as inspired by four "formula-citations" which are a salient feature of his Gospel—so called because of a stereotyped formula by which they are introduced. They constitute the writer's commentary on a significant situation (they never occur in the mouth of Jesus), and they are notably closer to the Hebrew text than to the Septuagint.[1] This feature, peculiar to Matthew (although employed to some extent in the Fourth Gospel), reflects his special interest in the fulfillment of Old Testament prophecy. The stylized introductory phrase illustrates this writer's (somewhat unimaginative) concern for order and clarity, suggesting a pedagogical and an apologetic preoccupation. A further indication of Matthew's orderly mind is found in the presentation of Jesus' teaching through five lengthy discourses, each terminating with another stereotyped conclusion.[2] In the interstices between these great

155

sermons by Jesus our evangelist has arranged a series of narratives dealing with the public ministry. Their brevity, careful arrangement, and logical sequence (by contrast with the corresponding Marcan stories) exhibit an intention to narrate them chiefly for the religious lesson they contain. For instance, the contrived character of chs. 8 and 9, where a collection of ten miracle stories is inserted almost montonously, leaps to the eye.

While we have accepted as a postulate the priority of Mark's Gospel over that of Matthew, it does not necessarily follow that, in each episode of his account of the public ministry, Matthew has consistently accepted the Marcan version, abbreviating it in line with his own doctrinal concerns. There are stories in Matthew's Gospel which are demonstrably more primitive than the corresponding narrative in Mark. However, what is of principal importance here are the Passion narratives, and specifically the Gethsemane accounts. As has already been observed, the story of Jesus' suffering and death, which comes to its climax with some reference to the resurrection, is universally admitted by scholars to have been the earliest continuous narrative from Jesus' earthly history. This helps to explain (and also to complicate) the interrelationships observable between the four passion narratives. While Matthew and Mark have clearly been guided by one such earlier written document, Luke and John exhibit a closer parentage to a varying tradition, with the result that they frequently agree (even more markedly than in the episodes of the public ministry) against the first two evangelists. Indeed, as will be shortly seen, nowhere possibly in the Passion story is this more striking than in their presentation of Jesus' struggle and prayer toward the close of his life. Accordingly, in this chapter in which a comparison and contrast will be made between Mark and Matthew, we do not wish to give the impression that Matthew has simply operated on the Marcan text, redacting it according to his own image of Jesus and in view of the community for which he writes. In reality, things are more complicated than that; yet in the light of our present knowledge of such interaction it is impossible to account fully for Matthew's editorial methods.[3]

Matthew's Christological and Ecclesiological Interests

Like Mark, our evangelist has been chiefly directed in his redactional activities in revamping the traditions he has received, through Mark as well as from other sources, by his image of Jesus and his concern for a specific early Christian community. Günther Bornkamm has observed: "No other Gospel is so shaped by the thought of the Church as Matthew's."[4] This is perceptible in Matthew's creation of the five great discourses, each of which exhibits some salient feature of the Christian Church, as well as by the great reverence he evinces for the Twelve and the prominence he repeatedly accords to Peter. The thrust of Jesus' instructions, assembled with great care from disparate sayings received in the evangelical traditions, are carefully focused upon two different levels, that of the situation in which Jesus himself operated and that of the very early Church.[5] In Matthew's eyes, then, Jesus' intention of founding the later Christian community (which Mark did not indeed neglect, but did not emphasize) can be readily perceived in Jesus' actions and instructions during his ministry.

Can we discern the particular problems experienced by the church for which Matthew wrote? One may suspect, from Matthew's repeated insistence upon the fulfillment of "the Scriptures" by Jesus, that this community, probably of mixed Jewish and Hellenistic provenance, possibly located somewhere in Palestine, had been deeply troubled by the Jews' refusal to accept the Christian Gospel. It may well be also that some at least within this church have tended to de-emphasize, in their efforts at evangelization and in their exhilaration at their new-found Christian freedom, Jesus' command to "teach them to guard all those things that I have enjoined upon you" (Mt 28:20a). Moreover, for whatever reason, this young church has suffered from a weakening of her faith in the dynamic presence of the exalted Christ to the entire course of history, and even in his special presence within their own community (Mt 18:20), which their own divided state has tended to obfuscate.[6] Another source of their difficulties, occasioned by controversies with the Judaism that still dominated their country, may have arisen from the tension between Jesus' declaration that he "had not come to destroy but to fulfill the Law and the prophets" (Mt 5:17) and his unmitigated denunciation of the religious bankruptcy of the religious establishment (Mt 23), as also of their chauvinistic attitude toward "all the nations" (Mt 28:19a). As Rudolf Schnackenburg has perceptively remarked, "It is only when due account is taken of the two points of view, Jewish-Christian origin and universal outlook, that the themes . . . of the Church in the Gospel according to Matthew can be understood. It is precisely the polemic with unbelieving Judaism with its particularism, its boast of the Torah and its legalist accomplishment, its pride in achievement and striving after merit, which created that consciousness of the Church, which is perceptible in Matthew's Gospel. . . . "[7]

And finally, as so frequently in first-century Christianity, the members of Matthew's community were in confusion about the coming of the kingdom of God. Some were disillusioned with its non-appearance in their day; had Jesus not assured them: "You will not finish the cities of Israel until the Son of Man will come" (Mt 10:23b)? Had he not solemnly declared, "Amen, I tell you: some of those standing here will not taste death until they behold the Son of Man coming in his kingly state" (Mt 16:28)? Had the (Hellenistically articulated) tradition not preserved Jesus' words: "You who have followed me, at the rebirth, when the Son of Man will take his place upon his glorious throne, will also in your turn take your seats upon twelve thrones to judge the twelve tribes of Israel" (Mt 19:28)? We can see two special characteristics of Matthew's redaction of traditional elements which indicate his concern to correct certain serious errors regarding the coming of God's kingdom. In the first place, the evangelist consistently changes the classical expression "the kingdom of God" to "the kingdom of heaven," the exceptions being four (Mt 12:38: 19:24; 21:31; 21:43). While the uniquely Matthean phrase reflects Palestinian idiom—"heaven" being a surrogate in late Judaism for God—the evangelist conceivably uses it also to emphasize the transcendent, eschatological character of the kingdom, announced by Jesus, so that the later historical reality of the Church may not be thought simply convertible with this mysterious, celestial reality. To clarify this distinction between kingdom of God and Church, our evangelist distinguishes the former from "the kingdom of the Son of Man" (Mt 13:41; 16:28) or Jesus' kingdom (20:21), which is the Christian Church (Mt 13:19: 24:14), that awaits the divine judgment at the end of history (Mt 25:34,40). It is not implausible that Matthew was combating some form of primitive Christian millenarianism in his community, or a tendency to think of the Church as composed only of "the elect."

In fact, it is peculiar to this Gospel-writer that he represents the inchoative coming of the "kingdom of heaven" in four stages preliminary to the last judgment: (1) in the mission of the Baptist, who proclaims: "The kingdom of heaven has drawn near" (Mt 3:2) in words identical with the message of Jesus (Mt 4:17); (2) in the teaching, miracles, and especially the person of Jesus during his public ministry; (3) in Jesus' death and resurrection (Mt 26:64 with its interpolation, "*Soon now* you will see . . ."), and (4) in the historical appearance of the Church.

What is the image of Jesus that is distinctively Matthean? In line with our evangelist's concern to show Christianity as the perfect efflorescence of the religion of Israel, Jesus is presented in the first place as the Messiah, "the Anointed" of the Lord, a title more frequently used by Matthew than by any of his fellow-evangelists, except John. For this reason the royal messianic title "Son of David" is given special prominence (Mt 1:1). The point of the angelic annunciation to Joseph revolves about Joseph's transmission of his Davidic lineage to this child, whom he has not begotten in the way his father Jacob "begot" him (Mt 1:16). By naming the child Jesus, Joseph exercises an act of true paternity, thereby also becoming the human intermediary of conferring on Jesus his vocation to "save his people from their sins" (Mt 1:21b). At his messianic entry into Jerusalem the people acclaim Jesus as "the Son of David" (Mt 21:9).

Jesus is also "Son of Abraham" (Mt 1:1). While the evangelist does not frequently refer to Abraham, it is important to observe that in all three instances where he does, it is a question of the fulfillment of the divine promise to Abraham, recorded at

Genesis 17:4: "My covenant with you is this: you are to become the father of a host of nations." Matthew alludes to this in the threatening warning to the Pharisees on the part of the Baptist, "God can raise up children for Abraham from these very stones!" (Mt 3:9). Jesus twice refers to this promise: when he says, "Many will come from east to west and recline with Abraham, Isaac, and Jacob at the banquet in the kingdom of heaven" (Mt 8:11), and in his rebuke to the Sadducees, "You are in error because you do not know the Scriptures nor the power of God" (Mt 22:29), where he cites Exodus 3:6 ("I am the God of Abraham . . .") to recall God's promise of life to the patriarchs, which can only be realized in the general resurrection. As will be shortly seen, Matthew will allude to Abraham in his account of the Gethsemane scene.

The dominant note in Matthew's image of Jesus is, without a doubt, his role as *Christus praesens*, indicated in his name "Emmanuel," which the evangelist explains as "with us is God!" (Mt 1:23b). It is noteworthy that this Gospel, without mentioning the ascension of the Risen One, concludes with his promise, "Remember, I am *with you* always until the consummation of the age" (Mt 28:20b). In the instructions of Jesus to the future Christian community, we have the promise, "Where two or three are gathered together into my name, I am there in their presence" (Mt 18:20). Being with Jesus is to be an important theme of the Matthew Passion, particularly as it there appears in combination with the theme of Jesus' power, a combination perceptible in the evangelist's redaction of the storm on the lake, where "Jesus the Lord of the Church comes to rescue his community when their faith is shaken. This is Matthew's way of saying that as, during his ministry, Jesus was 'God with us,' so too he will be with his Church until the end of the age."[8]

Like Mark, Matthew includes the role of the Deutero-Isaian Suffering Servant in his picture of Jesus. Yet he does so with considerable originality, making it the basis for a theology of the miracles of the public ministry. Where Mark sees in these "acts of power" the initial assault upon the "kingdom" of Satan, for Matthew they fulfill Isaiah's description of the Servant: "He has himself taken on our weaknesses and has shouldered our diseases" (Mt 8:17). One catches an echo of the Servant also in Jesus' reply to the query of the Baptist's disciples (Mt 11:4–5; see Is 35:5–6; 42:18). And at the conclusion of a summary account of Jesus' miracles, Matthew quotes extensively from the first Servant Song (Mt 12:15–21).

It is of course as Teacher that Jesus fulfills his messianic function for our evangelist: "Do not have yourselves called teachers, because your Teacher is uniquely the Messiah!" (Mt 23:10). It is, at first sight, strange then that in this Gospel the disciples (Judas is the one exception) never call Jesus "teacher" or "rabbi," but always "Lord," using the post-resurrection title that indicates his divinity. A clue to this paradox is provided by the final scene in Galilee, where (as already noted) the risen Jesus only speaks (he performs no action) to remind the disciples of his own "injunctions" and to issue new instructions for their mission. If Matthew records the title "Son of God" no more than ten times, he highlights it in three important scenes of this book: after the storm on the lake (Mt 14:33), at Caesarea Philippi (Mt 16:16) and on Calvary (Mt 27:43). For Matthew, Jesus reveals his unique relationship to God nowhere so tellingly as in his teaching of the disciples.

Matthew's Teaching on Prayer

The evangelist devotes more space than Mark to Jesus' teaching on prayer, especially in the Sermon on the Mount, yet surprisingly he does not stress the practice of prayer by Jesus any more than Mark, with one notable exception as will be seen. In fact, Matthew omits the striking Marcan picture (Mk 1:35) of Jesus praying in solitude. He, of course, like Mark (and Luke), mentions the "grace" said by Jesus in the two feeding narratives (Mt 14:19c; 15:36b), and also Jesus' prayer in solitude on the mountain after the first feeding episode (Mt 14:23). On the other hand, Matthew is the only writer to allude to Jesus' prayer over the small children: "Then children were brought to him, in order that he might lay his hands upon them and pray" (Mt 19:13). Our evangelist, in tandem with Mark, articulates Jesus' last cry to God with the help of Ps 22:1; however he cites the Hebrew,

"Eli," not the Aramaic "Eloi," probably to make more plausible the confusion with Elijah.

In total contrast with this poignant cry of dereliction Matthew, as also Luke 10:21, sets down a prayer of Jesus preserved in a sayings-tradition. One unique feature of the prayer is that each evangelist has exactly the same wording (a phenomenon not found in the case either of the dominical prayer or of the words of institution in the Gospels): "I profess my thanks to you, Father, Lord of heaven and earth, for though you have hidden these things from the learned and intelligent, you have revealed them to the simple. Yes, Father, such has been your gracious pleasure!" (Mt 11:25–26). From the beginning of the chapter Matthew has set down a series of reactions: perplexity on the part of the imprisoned Baptist (vv. 2–3), Jesus' praise of John—the only human being Jesus really praises in the Gospels (vv. 7–15), Jesus' condemnation of his contemporaries, who reject him (vv. 16–19), his severe reproaches and threats against the Galilean towns where he has preached (vv. 20–24). More significant, this is one of the rare places in the Synoptic Gospels where Jesus is depicted as divine Wisdom incarnate (v. 19b). This was the *kairos*, the moment of God's choosing, Matthew tells us (v. 25a), in which Jesus offers this public prayer of thanksgiving to God. It is a "confession"—a characteristically biblical form of prayer. Uttered aloud before an audience, it constitutes an invitation to join the one who offers it in praising and thanking God. It is also the result of a theophany, through some oracle (see the *Benedictus*, Lk 1:68–79) or in some threatening situation, as here (see Ps 29, the thunderstorm).

Jesus begins with a solemnly reverent address to God's majesty, and not (as elsewhere in this Gospel) simply with the loving, familiar, "your Father," "our Father," "my Father." Thereby the evangelist presents Jesus as teaching us, creatures as well as adoptive sons, how to approach God as Almighty Creator of all. God's self-revelation given to Jesus to communicate to men is a paradox that at the same time is most consoling and enlightening: consoling because it stems solely from the Father's "good pleasure," enlightening because it turns upside down our human preconceptions about prayer. For in it, Jesus tells us,

God discloses himself to "the simple" (literally, "infants," those unable to speak), while he hides his self-disclosure from the educated and quick-witted. What a reversal of human values! The Matthean Jesus in his own prayer in Gethsemane will present himself before God as one of "the simple."

Matthew indeed has already presented what he has judged to be Jesus' teaching on prayer in the Sermon on the Mount, which defines the "new righteousness" announced by Jesus as being "perfect as your heavenly Father is perfect" (Mt 5:48). It is in fact a striking feature of this discourse, in which reference is made to God constantly, that he is called "my Father," "your Father," "our Father," but very rarely "God." For Matthew Christian prayer is fundamentally an experience of our relationship to God as Father, else it is nothing. This Gospel-writer presents *five lessons* in how to pray through this great discourse.

(1) "Again, when you stand to pray, do not act like the hypocrites: they love to pray standing in synagogue or on street-corners for men to see. Amen, I tell you: they already have their reward" (Mt 6:5). The self-centeredness of such virtuosity is repaid in kind by being turned in upon itself: genuine prayer is an exodus, a going-out of the self, seeking not merit but God as Father. To emphasize his point, Matthew employs the second person singular in the next verse. "Do thou, on the contrary, go to a room by thyself, shut the door, and pray to thy Father, who is there in the secret place; and thy Father who sees in the secret place will repay thee" (v. 6). Real prayer, as its first condition, demands complete absence of any inhibitions, of assuming a mask; it is to stand naked without embarrassment before God, like Adam before his fall. Only when this one-on-one relationship is felt profoundly can one participate in public prayer.

(2) "When you [plural] pray, do not go on babbling like the heathen, who try to win a hearing by sheer force of words. Do not imitate them: your Father knows what your needs are before you ask him!" (vv. 7–8). If prayer is not a public performance, neither is it magic, attempting by rhetoric to bring God to one's own viewpoint, or bringing to his notice a condition of which he is ignorant. The Matthean Jesus in Gethsemane will exemplify all this in his prayer to his Father.

(3) The evangelist now inserts a version of the dominical prayer, as recited at the liturgy of his own community. It is longer than that given at Lk 11:2–4, which omits "Thy will be done" and "Deliver us from the evil one." The Lucan formula is the more primitive according to most scholars, but Matthew's is that which Christians still use. The phenomenon of two variant liturgical formulations in the New Testament indicates that the concern of the earliest Church was not to preserve the exact wording taught to the disciples by Jesus. Rather the Church's esteem of and reverence for this "prayer of the Lord" stemmed from her realization that Jesus' great gift through it was to permit our sharing in his own unique relationship with his Father.[9]

(4) The fourth lesson concerns the necessity of *persevering* in the prayer of petition and its infallibility in being heard. This clearly shows that the historical Jesus placed the highest value precisely upon "asking God" for what one needs. Jesus' teaching according to Matthew contains a demand, and a promise, illustrated by a brief parable. First, the imperative: "Go on asking, and you will receive; keep seeking, and you will find; knock perseveringly, and the door will be opened." Next, the promise: "For the one who goes on seeking receives; the person who keeps seeking finds; to the one who perseveres in knocking the door will be opened" (Mt 7:7–8). What was stated earlier forbidding the suppliant to use "persuasion" or pressure on God (Mt 6:7) was not intended to inhibit perseverance in petitionary prayer, for this "shows whether we really believe. . . . It is not a means of putting pressure on God, but the way of life for the disciple who places himself entirely under God's kingship."[10] Such perseverance will be illustrated by Jesus' attitudes in Gethsemane.

Matthew now adds a readily intelligible example, in which, it is to be observed, the father-child relationship is stressed. "Is there a man among you who will offer his son a stone, when he asks for bread, or a snake, when he asks for fish? If yourselves then, wicked as you are, know how to give your children what is good for them, how much more will your heavenly Father give good things to those who keep asking him?" (vv. 9–11). The homely illustration reveals why Jesus insists that petitionary prayer is always heard. Asking God for our needs is in reality a plea to be accepted as his child, a bid to belong to God's family, and consequently perseverance in petition brings a new and deeper experience of that relationship. The child learns, as well by the wise parent's refusal as by his granting a request, his relationship to mother or father. Jesus' confident promise to us of success reveals his own awareness of his identity as the Son; as such, he ought to know.

(5) Matthew concludes his instructions on prayer at this point in his Gospel with a final *caveat:* "Not everyone who says 'Lord, Lord!' to me will get into the kingdom of heaven; rather, it is the one who keeps doing the will of my heavenly Father" (Mt 7:21). Petitionary prayer, like the earliest credal formula "Jesus is Lord," is to be not a matter of words, but a way of life by which one lovingly accepts *in deeds* God's sovereign rule. St. Ignatius Loyola has remarked: "Love ought to manifest itself in deeds rather than in words" (*Spiritual Exercises,* #230). My relationship to God as his adoptive child, experienced in petitionary prayer (its infallible answer), must also be lived with constancy. That difficult, mysterious lesson will be demonstrated by Jesus throughout the Passion narrative.

Even more than Mark (Mk 11:25), Matthew insists that petitionary prayer can only be efficaciously made in the context of reconciliation (where needed) with one's fellow human beings. In this our evangelist shows how much importance he attaches to such prayer as an experience of, and a living out of, Christian adoptive sonship. Already at the conclusion of his citation of the dominical prayer, Matthew had written, "For if you have forgiven men their transgressions, your heavenly Father will also forgive you; if on the contrary you have not forgiven men, neither will your Father forgive you your transgressions" (Mt 6:14–15). He returns to this important consideration of the necessity of reconciliation in the community discourse. "Again I say to you: if two of you are in agreement [as the result of reconciliation] about any business on earth whatever, it will be done for them by my heavenly Father. For where two or three have been gathered together into my name [through reconciliation], I am there in their presence" (Mt 18:19–20). No matter what mundane business (*pragma*) engages two Christians in partnership, it ought to exhibit true fraternity (hence, presupposing reconciliation where necessary), if the divine assistance of Jesus' Father is to be hoped for. For, as Jesus goes on to explain, this reconciliation is truly a "gathering together into my Name" (as the Son) and entails his intercessory presence in the common petition to the Father.

Like Mark, our evangelist records Jesus' teaching in connection with the cursing of the barren fig tree, in order to draw attention to the absolute necessity of faith for efficacious petition to God. "Amen I tell you: if you have faith and do not yield to doubt, not only can you perform this feat with the fig tree, but even if you say to this mountain, 'Up and into the sea with you!', it will be done. And whatsoever you will ask for in your prayer, as long as you keep on believing, you will receive" (Mt 21:21–22). Wolfgang Trilling comments, "Thus the strange cursing of the tree is taken up and explained in a tolerable way. It becomes a portrayal of the power of faith. Such 'power' comes to each disciple through his prayer, not by reason of his own capacities, but through God's hearing it."[11]

Themes of the Matthew Passion

While it is obvious that in narrating Jesus' Passion Matthew has observed (except for some insertions) the same sequence as found in Mark, it may be helpful to draw attention to the themes that are peculiar to the Matthew Passion in order to appreciate its author's creativeness in presenting the episode in Gethsemane.

By contrast with the Marcan narrative the account by Matthew permits the force of the resurrection to be felt throughout his story, with the result that Jesus is very much more in command of the situation at all times. Attention is directed to the power of Jesus, submerged beneath his humiliation and held in check by the divine will manifested in "the Scriptures." Jesus' "*I can*" is not lost sight of (Mt 26:53, 61; 27:42), since it is "soon now" that, at his exaltation, he will be "seen" (by the eyes of faith) "seated at the right hand of the (divine) Power" (Mt 26:64).

Another Matthean feature is that Jesus speaks continually to his disciples to clarify for them, and through them for the reader, the meaning of his sufferings and death. A characteristic of this Gospel, which is especially significant in the Passion narrative, is the use of the phrase "the disciples" to symbolize the later community of faith.[12] Jesus' freedom is very much to the fore: he offers himself, after a struggle, to his Father with the full liberty of the Son of God. In fact, his endurance of the Passion will create a new freedom after his resurrection (Mt 26:32), when he will be endowed with universal authority (Mt 28:18).

The American scholar, Passionist Father Donald P. Senior, has pointed out several additional traits of the Matthew Passion which we shall simply summarize briefly.[13] He notes that it continues and carries to its climax the on-going debate between the evangelist's Palestinian Christian community and the synagogue concerning the Jewish rejection of the claims that Jesus is Messiah and Son of God. This polemic is visible in two passages peculiar to this Gospel which deal with the blood of Jesus. The first forms the conclusion of the double meeting of the Sanhedrin (Mt 27:3–10). While ostensibly narrating the terrible fate of Judas, it is in reality chiefly concerned with the inestimably precious value of the redeeming blood of Jesus.[14] The second is inserted at the end of the Roman trial (Mt 27:24–25) and contains the terrible imprecation on the part of "all the people" (*ho laos*, viz. Israel), "His blood be upon us and upon our children" (v. 25).

A characteristically Matthean motif, prominent particularly in the Sermon on the Mount, is that of "the new justice" which (as we have noted) is expressed with consummate simplicity (Mt 5:48) in terms of the Christian recognition of the new relationship with God as "our Father." It recurs with special poignancy, as will be observed, in the struggle and prayer of Jesus, in the stress laid on Jesus' awareness of and obedience to "the Scriptures" as the declared will of his Father at his arrest, and as he dies on the cross. Probably also to be mentioned here is our evangelist's dramatic, "apocalyptic" description of the parousia as the immediate sequel to Jesus' death (Mt 27:50–54), and as God's vindication of Jesus' innocence and obedience, whereby he may "reign as Lord of both the dead and the living" (Rom 14:9).

Donald Senior picks out, as the salient feature of Matthew's account, its heightened accent upon the Christological elements. "The repeated emphasis on the name of Jesus ... the enrichment ... by such titles as Christ, Lord, Son of God, the prophetic knowledge of Jesus, his filial obedience, the emphatic testimonials to his innocence ... and the spectacular events that result from his death ... form a consistent pattern that earns ... the label 'christological revelation.' "[15] Finally, there is to be recalled what Senior terms "the subtle insistence on the Old Testament background for the Messiah's history,"[16] which will be seen to be exemplified in the Gethsemane narrative, the immediate context of which we must now advert to.

Gethsemane: Its Context in the Passion Narrative

An attentive reading of our evangelist's lead-up to the scene in Gethsemane in parallel with that of Mark will disclose the striking similarity of the two accounts. Later on, in his Passion narrative, Matthew will insert certain additions, even whole episodes not found in the Marcan Passion. What modifications are introduced by Matthew reveal his special concern to highlight Jesus' mastery of what is happening. Thus, for example, Jesus' foreknowledge of coming events is stressed by having him announce at the start, "You know Passover occurs two days from now, when the Son of Man is to be handed over for crucifixion" (Mt 26:2). In this "handing over" Matthew wishes the reader to discern, beyond any human perfidy and hatred, the hand of the Father. Jesus' prescience of his own destiny is again marked out in the instructions to the disciples for the preparation of the Passover supper, "The teacher says, 'My *kairos* is near' " (Mt 26:18b). It is noted especially by having Jesus disclose to Judas his awareness of treachery, "You have said it" (Mt 26:25).

Especially noteworthy is the Matthean addition to the words of institution over the cup, "This is my blood of the covenant, to be poured out for the rest of men *unto remission of sins*" (Mt 26:28). The redemptive feature of Jesus' mission "to save his

people from their sins" (Mt 1:21) explains this evangelist's continual insertion of the name Jesus in his narrative. In fact, when
describing John's baptismal rite, Matthew deliberately omits the
detail found at Mk 1:4 "for the remission of sins" (see Mt 3:1–4).
Only the blood of *Jesus,* whose theophoric name designates him
as instrument of God's salvation, can remit sins. This preoccupation accounts for the author's additional references to Jesus'
blood, already noted, in his trial narratives.

JESUS IN GETHSEMANE (Mt 26:30–46)

30 And having sung the hymn they went out to the
Mount of Olives. 31 Then Jesus says to them, "All of
you will lose your faith in me this very night, for Scripture has it, 'I will strike the shepherd and the sheep of
the flock will be scattered.'

32 Yet after my resurrection I will go ahead of
you to Galilee." 33 But Peter in reply said to him, "If
they all lose faith in you, I will never lose faith!" 34 Jesus told him, "Amen I tell you: this very night before
the cock crows, you will deny me thrice." 35 Peter says
to him, "Even if it were God's will that I die with you,
never will I deny you!" In similar vein too spoke all the
disciples.

36 Then Jesus comes with them to a farmstead
called Gethsemane, and he says to the disciples, "Sit
down here while I go off over there and pray." 37 And
taking along Peter and the two sons of Zebedee, he began to be sorrowful and distressed. 38 Then he says to
them, "My heart is bursting with sorrow to the point
of death. Stay here and watch with me!"

39 And he went forward a little, and prostrated
himself on his face upon the ground in prayer with
these words, "My Father, if it is possible, may this cup
pass me by; however, not as I desire, but as you do."
40 And he returns to the disciples to discover them
asleep, and he says to Peter, "So you did not, all of you,
have the strength to watch one (short) hour with me?

41 Watch and pray that you do not enter into the testing. The spirit indeed is willing, yet the flesh is weak."
42 Going off again a second time he began to pray in
these words, "My Father, if this cannot pass me by
without my drinking it, may your will be done!"
43 And he returns to discover them asleep again; their
eyes seemed to have weights upon them. 44 And so,
leaving them, once more he went off and began to pray
a third time, employing the same words again.
45 Then he returns to the disciples and says to them,
"So you are still sleeping and taking your rest! Look,
the hour has drawn near when the Son of Man is handed over into the power of sinners. 46 Get up! Let us be
on our way. Look, he has drawn near, the one who is
handing me over."

Before giving a detailed explanation of Matthew's account, it
may not be unhelpful to compare and contrast it with the Marcan version. As already noted, the general similarity of the two
stories is very obvious. André Feuillet[17] notes but two omissions
by Matthew of words found in the Greek text of Mark: the Aramaic word *Abba* (Mk 14:36) and the puzzling *apechei* ("Enough of
that!"—Mk 14:41b). The first variation is however a superficial
one, since Matthew (as is his habit almost always) does not employ Aramaic terms, and for Jesus' address to God he uses the
Greek equivalent, "My Father" (Mt 26:39,42). Since the meaning
of the second word cannot be determined with certainty, Matthew's reason for omitting it cannot be judged; it is possible he
did not know what it meant.

This narrative attests Matthew's *ecclesial* interests. It is
probably for this reason that he has added "of the flock" to the
citation of Zechariah (v. 31), and the same may possibly be said
of the addition "with me," although another reason will be suggested in our commentary. Certainly the modification "the disciples" (vv. 35b, 36, 40, 45), characteristic of the entire Gospel, is
intended to symbolize the Church.

Matthew has subtly altered the text to suggest Jesus' unique relationship to the Father as "the Son of God." If Mark under-scored the solitariness of Jesus (to recall the vicarious nature of his sufferings and death as the Isaian Servant), Matthew con-trives to suggest the view articulated by the Johannine Jesus, "Yet I am not alone, for the Father is with me" (Jn 16:32b). It is for this reason that Matthew puts more emphasis on Jesus' leav-ing the disciples for prayer (vv. 39, 42, 44) to be with his Father, where Mark (14:37, 40, 41) has set in relief Jesus' triple return to the disciples.

The distinctive manner in which Matthew articulates the first and second prayer of Jesus gives the impression that for him the threefold schema, created by Mark, is deliberately played down. Thus the Matthean Jesus reaches perfect confor-mity with the divine will in the *first two* moments of prayer, and so in the third moment he simply rests in that state, beyond which nothing more can be attained. This redactional technique reveals Matthew's sense of the significance of the whole episode. He does not emphasize, as did Mark, the evolution undergone in Jesus' attitude to his "hour"; rather he presents the struggle and prayer as an epitome of all he has previously taught about the Christian character of prayer in his book. The Matthean Geth-semane is a kind of catechesis on the place of prayer in Christian life as lived within the believing community. If in his prayer on the eve of his own death Jesus experiences his unique relation-ship to God as "the Son," the Christian is being schooled by the example of Jesus to experience in his prayer his adoptive son-ship. As with Paul,[18] so with Matthew, the prayer of adoptive filiation is to characterize the prayer-life of the Christian. The importance of the lesson in Matthew's eyes may be gauged by the fact that the Gethsemane scene is the longest in his whole Passion story.

After the introductory verse (identical in Mark 14:26), which serves as the conclusion to the Supper narrative and as the link with Gethsemane, Matthew's distinctiveness at once ap-pears with the use of his favorite introductory "Then" (see vv. 36, 38, 45). The force of the word is difficult to assess; it may be the writer's way of drawing attention to a significant word or action by Jesus, or, not implausibly, Matthew keeps alerting the reader to the pre-Easter, historical ambivalence of what transpired.

Then Jesus says to them, "All of you will lose your faith in me this very night, for Scripture has it, 'I will strike the shepherd and the sheep of the flock will be scattered.'" From the outset this account focuses attention upon Jesus by contrasting him with the disciples, and particularly by making him the subject of every statement (the single exception is found at v. 43b).[19] It is significant that Jesus is represented as the one who acts, the only one who speaks. Matthew specifies the faith lost by the disciples as *in me;* he also specifies the time of this tragic happening as *this very night.* His interest in the community as such, as already noted, is seen in his addition, in the citation, *of the flock.* At several points in his book Matthew has pointed to Jesus as the Shepherd, announced by the messianic prediction of Micah (Mt 2:6): he records the genuine reminiscence of the historical Jesus' attitude to his own people (Mt 9:36), and he uses the symbol (as well as that of king) in his parable of the eschatological judgment, in which the glorified Son of Man is depicted as discriminating between sheep and goats (Mt 25:32). In Gethsemane also, the evangelist observes, Jesus acted as shepherd, assuring the life of the little community he had gathered around himself as long as he could keep them with himself. As in Mark, the Matthean Jesus makes the tragic announcement that his arrest "this very night" and his ensuing Passion, an event that is designed "for the remission of sins" (Mt 26:28) and to "save his people from their sins" (Mt 1:21b), must by God's will cause a loss of faith in himself, indeed, the dispersal of "the flock."

Yet after my resurrection I will go ahead of you into Galilee. As for Mark so for Matthew, it is the Christian knowledge of Jesus' resurrection, announced with his death in the primitive kerygma, which makes the Passion narrative "good news." The fact that the disciples here (as earlier at the triple prediction of his death and resurrection by Jesus) do not react to this statement indicates that it comes from the credal formulae of the young Church, rather than from the historical Jesus' words.

Matthew, despite the great reverence he displays for Peter

through his Gospel, adds, like Mark, the prediction of Peter's denials of his Master, omitting the detail of the double cock-crow, which at Mk 14:30 was probably "a figurative way of emphasizing the triple denial."[20] Peter's fall from fidelity to Jesus is especially tragic in the context of this Gospel, which accords a special pre-eminence to Peter by narrating stories about him found in no other Gospel: his walking on the water, where however he is rebuked as a "man of little faith" (Mt 14:28–32); his confession of faith, which this evangelist has made into a Christian *credo* (Mt 16:16), and which wins Jesus' promise to make him the foundation-rock of the future Church, with powers extending even into the region of the dead (vv. 17–19); Peter's special privilege in having found, miraculously, the amount of the temple levy for Jesus and himself (Mt 17:24–27). Again, in the list of the Twelve Peter not only heads it, as in the parallel lists, but he is expressly called "the first" (Mt 10:2); Peter speaks up for all to ask for an explanation of Jesus' conundrum about the blind leading the blind (Mt 15:15); it is Peter whose question provokes Jesus' promulgation of the Christian law of "retaliation" (Mt 18:21–35); it is Peter's query "What shall we get?" which evokes the great promise by Jesus of the authority of the Twelve in the Christian Church (Mt 19:27–28). It is a curious phenomenon that, after recording Peter's denials, Matthew never again mentions him by name, even in the great post-resurrection scene in Galilee.

Matthew's concluding observation on Peter's brash and egocentric boast provides a clue to his refusal to tone down this sad incident: *In similar vein too spoke all the disciples.* Matthew's phrase *the disciples,* symbol of the Christian community, shows his intention to warn Christians of the perils of a loss of their faith.

Then Jesus comes with them to a farmstead called Gethsemane. The spotlight, in Matthew's redaction, is on Jesus as the shepherd who, as "Emmanuel" (Mt 1:23), is, after the resurrection, to remain always *with them.* Mario Galizzi[21] has pointed out that the Matthean Passion narrative up to Jesus' arrest repeatedly alludes to Jesus' fellowship with the disciples (Mt 26:18, 20, 23, 29, 36, 38, 40, 51). The Greek preposition employed by our evangelist (*meta*) denotes not mere accompaniment (*syn*), but rather indicates the company in which an experience is had, thus explaining the influence one person exerts upon another, which results in the adoption of a corresponding, common attitude.[22] The nuance is an important one for an understanding of Matthew's predilection for the word to suggest Jesus' influence upon the disciples. The evangelist may be subtly hinting at Peter's ignorance of the significance of Jesus' death, when he employs the simple "with" (*syn*, merely accompaniment) for Peter's extravagant, "Even if it were God's will that I die *with* you. . . . " (v. 35a).

And he says to the disciples, "Sit down here while I go off over there and pray." The deliberate insertion of the word *there* into his text suggests that Matthew alludes to the celebrated story of Abraham's sacrifice (Gen 22:1–14), according to the Septuagint version, the Greek vocabulary of which he has incorporated here. This addition by Matthew is apparently meant to recall Abraham's instructions to his two servants, as he and the boy Isaac leave them for the terrible confrontation with God at the sanctuary on the mountain. Paul (Rom 8:32) and John (Jn 3:16) refer to this awful experience when they insist that the divine work of man's redemption has proceeded totally from God's love for sinners. It is useful to recall that in Jewish tradition the episode is known as "the binding of Isaac" (*Aqedath Yizhaq*), an ordeal in which God is represented as initiator both of the *apparently* intended death and of the deliverance of the boy. Matthew introduced his book with a genealogy, not going back, as in Luke, to Adam, but starting from Abraham, to demonstrate that Jesus was "the son of Abraham" (Mt 1:1), in addition to being "the son of David." For our evangelist, as for Paul (Gal 3:16), it is first *in Christ* that the promises made to the patriarch are realized. Thus the typology insinuated here by Matthew is *not* Abraham—Christ (as André Feuillet imagines);[23] rather, it is Isaac—Jesus (hinted at also in Jn 19:17).

Matthew appears to wish his reader to keep in mind the father-son relationship (Jesus to the Father) in order to see in Jesus' filial prayer in Gethsemane an example of the prayer characteristic of the Christian's approach to God. More clearly perhaps than Mark, Matthew depicts Jesus as the loving, obedient Son who accedes to his Father's will because he never loses sight of his Father's love for him. Abraham's love of Isaac was stressed from the beginning of the tragic story in Genesis 22: "Take your son, your only son, Isaac, whom you love" (v. 2). Abraham carries the fire and knife to keep the boy from harm (v. 6), permitting Isaac only to carry the wood on his back (see Jn 19:17). As already noted, Matthew reminds the reader, from the outside of the story of the Passion, that Jesus' "handing over" as Son of Man is the work of God himself (Mt 26:2). The fact that the divine action is deployed in history through men's sinful activity must not be allowed to obscure the vision of faith which alone can intuit the theological and Christological issues.

And taking along Peter and the two sons of Zebedee, he began to be sorrowful and distressed. It is our writer's habitual practice not to identify the disciples by name, with the single exception of Peter. Besides, he shows throughout a singular interest in the Zebedee family (Mt 4:21; 10:2), even the mother (Mt 20:20), whose presence on Calvary he alone records (Mt 27:56). Warren Holleran[24] has made the interesting suggestion that "sons of Zebedee" is used as a reference back to the saying about "the cup" (Mt 20:22). In his description of Jesus' reactions at this point in his story, Matthew pictures Jesus as overcome with a sorrow causing great distress, where Mark depicts Jesus in the grip of stronger emotions ("filled with surprise and terror, and distressed from shock"). Mario Galizzi has remarked, not implausibly, that by using *to be sorrowful* in combination with *be distressed*, Matthew has probably weakened the force of the second verb.[25] Jesus is intended to be seen as the Father's Son who fully accepts, though with sorrow, his Father's will. Earlier in Matthew, it was the disciples who were "filled with (great) sorrow" (Mt 17:23; 26:22); now it is Jesus' turn. What, for this writer, is the cause of such profound grief? Not the prospect of his physical sufferings, which are never mentioned in the scene, but rather the disciples' loss of faith in him and their imminent flight at his arrest.

Then he says to them, "My heart is bursting with sorrow to the point of death. Stay here and watch with me!" The two modifications in the verse are due to Matthean interests. *Then*, that is, in the midst of his sorrow, Jesus is ever mindful of the disciples, and he describes his reaction in biblical terms, expressive of the real meaning of his grief. Matthew is sensitive to the ambiguities of any historical situation, particularly those relating to Jesus' Passion. In his rendition of the first of the triple predictions of it, he observed, "From then on Jesus began *to point out* (*deiknuein*) to his disciples that it was God's will (*dei*). . . ." (Mt 16:21). Here he recalls that Jesus is the Suffering Servant of God, "a man of sorrows and acquainted with infirmity" (Is 53:3). The real action in the Passion, the divine activity, is not readily perceptible; hence in the sequel, at his arrest, Matthew has Jesus enunciate the principles necessary for a Christian comprehension of this suffering and death and for its application to Christian living (Mt 26:53–55).

The second typical change is the command to *watch with me.* Matthew clarifies Jesus' injunction, which is not simply a matter of remaining awake, nor of watching for enemies, but of sharing Jesus' experience. It is highly dubious that Matthew means the reader to think here of "Jesus' humanity and his anguish."[26] The necessity is not on Jesus' side, but that of the disciples. Christian prayer, to be efficacious, must always be "with me." It is instructive that Jesus nowhere urges his disciples to *pray* with me; that would be a human impossibility. "Watching," a symbol of hope in the parousia (Mt 25:1–13), remains ever an ingredient of prayer. Here the evangelist is preoccupied with assisting the believer to enter into the mystery of Jesus' prayer by observing his filial attitudes toward his Father. Insofar as that is possible, it will be accomplished by obedience to the command to *watch with me.* Martin Dibelius has astutely observed that the order, *watch*, is not so much eschatological here as Christological.[27]

And he went forward a little, and prostrated himself upon his face in prayer with these words, "My Father, if it is possible, may this cup pass me by; however, not as I desire, but as you do." To appreciate the thrust of Matthew's presentation of Jesus' prayer, it is crucial to observe its distinctiveness from that of Mark. Jesus' emotional reactions do not cause him to "collapse upon the ground," nor does he ever ask "that, if it were possible, his hour might pass him by" (Mk 14:35). The Matthean Jesus, with great dignity and reverence, adopts the Jewish posture of prostration upon his face in God's presence. Moreover, it is *not* possible, in the context of the Matthean Passion, to present Jesus as asking that "his hour might pass him by," since he announced from the first (Mt 26:2) that God had inaugurated his "handing over," which for Matthew (as for Mark) is symbolized by "his hour." Hence the sole object of Jesus' prayer is *this cup*, which our evangelist distinguishes carefully from what is already effectively willed by God, viz. Jesus' hour already upon him.

He went forward a little. It is instructive to note the progressive separation of himself by Jesus insinuated by Matthew, who underscores, each time more evidently, these departures: "Going off again a second time" (v. 42); "And so, leaving them, once more he went off" (v. 44). In Mk 14, Jesus' third departure, between vv. 40–41, is passed over in silence, for Mark appears more interested in Jesus' triple *return*. Matthew on the other hand seems to evoke the sense of an ever deepening communion with his Father by Jesus. And it is quite out of place to speak of "the loneliness of his hour"[28] in the case of the Matthean Jesus, who goes to be with his Father.

The address *My Father*, a suitable equivalent of *Abba*, is an expression typical of Jesus in this Gospel, where it occurs some seventeen times (never in Mark, only four times in Luke). It suggests Jesus' intimate familiarity with God, and has been used by Matthew's Jesus to declare God's will, which he claims to know (Mt 6:31; 16:17; 18:14; 20:23). To his petition Jesus prefixes *if it is possible*, thus underscoring his obedient submission to God. That a real possibility of escape remains open to Jesus during the Passion, however, can be gauged by his claim at the moment of his arrest: "Or do you think I cannot ask my Father, and he will provide me at once with more than twelve legions of angels?" (Mt 26:53). Yet, as the verse immediately following indicates, God's will, already manifest in "the Scriptures," has decreed otherwise. "How then are the Scriptures to be fulfilled (announcing) that it is God's will (*dei*) that so it be" (v. 54). *May this cup pass me by!* Matthew habitually uses the verb *pass by* in a derived sense, meaning to pass out of existence, become invalid, or (here) not to affect someone. While Mk 14:35 used "pass him by" of "the hour" of Jesus, which as we have seen is impossible for our writer, Matthew uses it for Jesus' prayer which is concerned only with "this cup." What is the thrust of this symbol for Matthew? He has simply clarified the meaning which we have seen Mark attach to it. First, in his version of the logion to the sons of Zebedee Matthew has Jesus mention only the cup (not "baptism") to denote his "service" in giving up his life as a ransom for mankind (Mt 20:22–23). Second, as noted earlier, the Matthean words over the cup speak of "my blood of the testament, that will be shed for the sake of the rest of men, *unto the remission of sins*" (Mt 26:28). Finally, Matthew has highlighted the scandalous side of Jesus' redemptive sufferings by his emphasis on the break-up of the little community by adding *of the flock* to the citation from Zechariah, and has linked the loss of his disciples' faith more specifically with Jesus. It is *faith in me* and the loss occurs *this very night* (v. 31). Thus it is clear that, while Jesus has accepted *what* the Father wills for himself, as declared in "the Scriptures," he is seen by Matthew as hesitating about the sad effects (apostasy and desertion) it is to hold for his disciples. Still, this desire of Jesus, already qualified by the *if it is possible*, is abandoned by his *not as I desire, but as you do*. This may echo the Matthean version of the dominical prayer, "*as* in heaven so also upon earth" (Mt 6:10).

And he returns to the disciples to discover them asleep, and he says to Peter, "So you did not, all of you, have the strength to watch one (short) hour with me?" Three modifications by our evangelist here are noteworthy. First, he has inserted *the disciples* (they represent the Church), and this procedure seems to suggest that for Matthew the previous separation into two groups is insignificant, or only momentary. Second, Matthew has Jesus speak to Peter, but the address is not second person singular, but in the plural. Why? For one thing, ever since ch. 16:17–19 Peter is in charge of the community of disciples. But more plausibly, Matthew hints that Peter was the only one Jesus found awake. At any rate, Peter represents the group.[29] Third, Matthew repeats his Christological interpretation of the watching, *watch with me*. He does not permit the reader to forget that the whole scene contains a profound lesson in prayer for the later Church.

"*Watch and pray that you do not enter into the testing. The spirit indeed is willing, yet the flesh is weak.*" The meaning of *watch* is clarified by what has befallen the disciples: it demands unwavering obedience to Jesus, vigilance over the heart, if the "dispersal of the person" is to be avoided, disponibility toward the divine will, *and* (note the present imperative) perseverance. Thus by the additional imperative, *pray*, these values are made explicit. There is but a single difference in the wording of this verse from the version found in Mark. Instead of "encounter" (*elthete*), we have *enter into* (*eiselthēte*). As Warren Holleran points out,[30] Matthew has employed this word consistently as a technical term for "entering the kingdom of heaven" (Mt 5:20; 7:21; 18:3; 19:23–24; 22:12; 23:13; 25:10, 21, 23). Thus for our evangelist to *enter into the testing* represents the antithesis of eschatological salvation, and consequently he makes it clear that *the testing* is a real threat in the future for the disciples. This may imply that, in Matthew's view, *the testing* does not truly involve Jesus. This impression is heightened when it is recalled that the phrase is an allusion to the second last petition in the dominical prayer (Mt 6:13a), the precious heritage of the believing community. This allusion also alerts the reader to discern the significance of the change in Jesus' second prayer.

Going off again a second time he began to pray in these words, "My Father, if this cannot pass me by without my drinking it, may your will be done!" Matthew carefully enumerates this *second* departure for prayer, thus more clearly emphasizing Jesus' communion with God. The articulation of this prayer is the evangelist's creation. Its antithetic parallelism with the first prayer underlines the fact that Jesus has now reached total acceptance of the Father's design, even in its concrete, tragic effects on his disciples.

Is it possible to perceive from the narrative how our evangelist envisages this great change in Jesus' attitude? Jesus' initial command, *Watch with me* (v. 38b), has not been obeyed. His more express demand, *Watch and pray*, he recognizes to be beyond the strength of the disciples, for *The spirit indeed is willing, yet the flesh is weak.* Indeed, instead of "entering into the kingdom of heaven" they are in grave danger of "entering into the testing" to their ultimate peril. So Jesus' words have made it clear to Matthew that he realizes it is crucial that he "drink this cup." As is his custom, Matthew throws into clearer relief the experience undergone by Jesus. The Marcan Jesus, as we suggested earlier, appears to have felt the weakness of human nature in himself, and so makes that the theme of his second prayer. We have seen that Matthew's Jesus is, throughout this Passion narrative, imbued with power (see v. 53). *May your will be done* is an explicit quotation of the dominical prayer at Mt 6:10b. It is of paramount importance that Jesus resolve his struggle by manifesting the attitude he had taught his followers to adopt. Thus here the words can only mean, "May you carry out your will for the realization of your sovereign rule in history through all the concrete circumstances of my death." For Jesus is represented here as realizing the impossibility of his hypothetical request in the first prayer. Thus, for Matthew, Jesus' prayer now reaches perfection, and consequently the third prayer need not be articulated, since it is simply a repetition and deepening (v. 44) of his attitude displayed here.

And he returns to discover them asleep again. Matthew's redactional genius is disclosed by his shifting the single word *again* (at Mk 14:40 it appears as the modifier of "returning") to emphasize the relapse of the disciples. Like Mark, however, Matthew implies that the disciples were powerless to prevent sleep. It will be noted that *their eyes seemed to have weights upon them* is the single statement in Matthew's narrative where Jesus is not the subject. His purpose is to focus attention totally upon Jesus and particularly on his prayer to the Father, in contrast with the sleeping disciples.

And so, leaving them, once more he went off and began to pray a third time, employing the same words again. Matthew is more concerned with Jesus' withdrawal for prayer than (as is Mark) with his returning to the disciples. Matthew also makes it clear that the third period of prayer was dominated by Jesus' perfect surrender to the Father's will which he had already expressed. It is crucial for an understanding of Matthew's sense of the scene to perceive that Jesus does not (as Mk 14:40c implied) waken the disciples at his second visit to them, but simply returns to renewed converse with God. For, as he did in his account of the transfiguration (Mt 17:4–5), Matthew deliberately omits the Marcan gloss ("And they did not know what reply to make to him": Mk 14:40c).

Then he returns to the disciples and says to them, "So you are still sleeping and taking your rest!" As already stated, *the disciples* symbolize the Christian community for our evangelist; consequently, these words of the now risen Lord are a summons to fidelity to prayer, through which the watchfulness of Christian hope is expressed. It will be recalled that in the Matthew Passion Jesus speaks to *the disciples* (and so to the Church) to throw light on what transpires: they must keep awake and contemplate the deep communion of Jesus with the Father. Moreover, they must understand the force of Jesus' next announcement.

"Look, the hour has drawn near when the Son of Man is handed over into the power of sinners." The Matthean Jesus announced in the beginning of this Passion account that, in two days' time, with Passover, "the Son of Man is being handed over for crucifixion" (Mt 26:2). He now points out the nearness of that hour; even more important, it is not simply a question of chronological imminence (as at Mk 14:41). Rather, Jesus is represented as using the same verb *and* in the perfect tense, as when proclaiming his inaugural message, "Repent, for the kingdom of heaven has drawn near!" (Mt 4:17). Consequently, the evangelist wishes his reader to realize that it is through God's design and activity that the significant "handing over" is to occur. Moreover, it is *into the power of sinners,* and not simply "into the power of the pagans" (as Mk 14:41c appears to mean). Finally, Matthew has introduced this statement by the term *Look* (one of his favorite words) as a caution to the reader to appreciate the force of the announcement. Jesus' handing over is significant not for the historical fact that he is given (ultimately) into the power of the Romans. Matthew reminds us that the meaning of Jesus' death is "unto the remission of sins" (Mt 26:28). He will repeat *Look* in the following verse to underline the parallelism between what transpires in history and the divine initiative in Jesus' death.

"Get up! Let us be on our way. Look, he has drawn near, the one who is handing me over!" Jesus' response to his "hour" was preserved probably also in the other traditional, primitive Passion narrative employed by the fourth evangelist, who reports the first words of Jesus here, although in a different context, in almost identical terms, "Get up! Let us be on our way from here" (Jn 14:31b). They are impressive in the mouth of the Johannine Jesus, presented repeatedly as "knowing that the Father has handed everything over into his power and that he has come forth from God and is returning home to God" (Jn 13:3), and as "knowing everything that is to come upon him" (Jn 18:4). Matthew's Jesus also evinces such prescience (Mt 26:2, 18, 21, 25, 31, 34, 64).

"Look, he has drawn near, the one who is handing me over!" Matthew has set this remark in close parallelism with the similar statement in the preceding verse to indicate that even through the treachery and betrayal of Judas God carries through his saving design for the world. Once again it is through the words of Jesus that the theological dimension of this evil act is manifested. A further indication that the evangelist brackets these two final verses of the scene is that he introduces them by his characteristic *Then*: *Then he returns to the disciples and says to them.* Mario Galizzi[31] has pointed out several other incidents in this Gospel in which a *Then* is the Matthean signature of closure (Mt 4:11; 16:12, 20; 13:43; 17:13). It may be regarded as a kind of indicator that the words of Jesus comment on the incident, underscoring what has characterized the disciples, who sleep, and Jesus' unflagging efforts to rouse them to face his *hour*, to keep them together by taking them with him, and revealing the identity of his betrayer. Implicit too in Matthew's redacted version of Jesus' words is a twofold lesson for the Church: to see the hand of God in what befalls Jesus and to appreciate the efficacy of prayer in confronting with equanimity and courage the dangers besetting the community, death-dealing hatred from without and apostasy from within.

However, to fail to advert to the important redaction by our evangelist in his account of Jesus' ensuing arrest would be to give an inadequate account of his understanding of the Gethsemane incident. Indeed he implies as much by the characteristic gloss he appends to it: "*All this* happened in order that the Scriptures of the prophets might be fulfilled" (Mt 26:56a). Once before Matthew used this same turn of phrase to make his reader catch the significance of his narrative of the annunciation to Joseph (Mt 1:18–25), "*All this* happened in order that the oracle from the lord through the words of the prophet might be fulfilled" (v. 22). In the Marcan account of Jesus' capture by his enemies, Jesus is represented as speaking but once, to utter a logion, found in all four Gospels (Mk 14:48–49), as a protest against the indignity of treating, like a "bandit," one who had taught openly many times in the temple area.

Matthew by contrast has reconstructed the scene with great originality by using the logion cited by Mark to comment upon "the hour": "In *that hour* Jesus spoke to the crowds, 'As against a bandit you have sallied forth with swords and clubs to arrest me? Daily I took my seat in the temple precincts to teach, yet you did not lay hands on me!' " (Mt 26:55). The opprobrious term "bandit" recalls Jesus' pronouncement on the occasion of his solemn entry into the holy city and (according to Matthew) into the sacred area around the temple to perform a prophetic, symbolic action. As he drove out those trafficking, he declared, "My house must be called a house of prayer; you however are making it a den of bandits" (Mt 21:13). Thus the irony of Jesus' reproach at his arrest in Gethsemane can scarcely be lost on the community for which Matthew writes his Gospel: they are called by God to constitute "a house of prayer," a lesson the evangelist intends to be taken from the example of Jesus in Gethsemane.

Matthew has moreover amplified his account of what transpired in Gethsemane by *four* additional logia by Jesus which are to be taken as integral to his interpretation of the struggle and prayer of Jesus. First, Jesus' elliptical (and hence obscure) word, in reply to Judas' greeting and act of reverence to the one he alone (of the Twelve) addressed as "Rabbi" (Mt 26:49), appears to be a command rather than a question, "Friend, [do] what you are here to do!" (v. 51).[32] Even if this remark be interpreted as mildly ironical, it indicates Jesus' acceptance of his betrayal by a disciple with an equanimity that is the fruit of his prayer. Second, two sayings by Jesus are represented as addressed to the unidentified "one of those *with* Jesus" (v. 51), whose recourse to his sword produced such ludicrous results. Matthew, possibly out of respect for Peter, does not reveal the disciple's name, as does the author of the Fourth Gospel (Jn 18:10). The first remark is an ominous warning meant for the later community: "All who take a sword will perish by sword!" (v. 52b). The name given to the weapon denotes the short Roman sword, symbolic (Rom 13:4) of the repressive power of the state. Thus it seems probable that the logion is not to be construed as a principle for pacifism. Rather, it is a rebuke aimed at the risk of unleashing determinism by violence, rampant in society.[33] In his "hour" Jesus has no need of such morally questionable aid, as the next saying will disclose. More important, it is a grave caution to the Church against even condoning (much less employing) force in the propagation or defense of the Gospel.

Jesus' second comment on this comic incident reveals at once his consciousness that God alone is the source of his power and of the total freedom of his own choice in accepting "the cup" held out to him by the Father. "Or do you think I cannot ask my Father, and he will provide me at once with more than twelve legions of angels?" (v. 53). The Father's readiness to rescue Jesus is, for Jesus (and the disciples), the divine guarantee of untrammeled freedom of choice in his filial following of the Father's will. Matthew thus hints that this liberty is the outcome of Jesus' prayerful acceptance of the divine decision for himself. At the same time the evangelist reminds the community that God will not, by any miraculous intervention, deliver the Church from facing the harsh realities of life in the world, and he also manages to instill the lesson of hope in God's ever-vigilant providence over her.

The last saying provides the most fundamental clue to the entire experience of Jesus in Gethsemane—his struggle, prayer, and majestic acceptance of his capture by his enemies. "How then are the Scriptures to find fulfillment [announcing] that God's will is that it happen in this way?" (v. 54). The evangelist points to the infallible source of Jesus' composure and sense of security—the prophetic Scriptures of Israel, that have foretold God's designs for himself. It was this insight, Matthew here seems to hint, that was given to Jesus in the course of his prayer to the Father, between the first petition, "if it is possible" to have "this cup" pass by him (v. 39), and his further prayer of perfect communion with the Father, "May your will be done!" (v. 42). All Matthew had said earlier about the infallibility of persevering petitional prayer as a graced experience of the Christian's relation to God as adoptive son or daughter (Mt 7:7–11) is verified and guaranteed by Jesus' own experience in Gethsemane.

NOTES

1. See the discussion of such citations in Joseph A. Fitzmyer, S.J., *Essays on the Semitic Background of the New Testament* (London, 1971), "The Use of Explicit Old Testament Quotations in Qumran Literature and in the New Testament," pp. 3–58; J. J. O'Rourke, "The Fulfillment Texts in Matthew," *Catholic Biblical Quarterly* 24 (1962), 394–403.

2. "Now it happened when Jesus had finished these words. . . ." (Mt 7:28; 11:1; 13:53; 19:1; 26:1). The first four discourses are followed by some reference to a journey, while the sequel to the last speech is the Passion narrative.

3. André Feuillet, *L'Agonie de Gethsémani: enquête exégétique et théologique. . . .* (Paris, 1977), while accepting the two source theory in general, rightly notes that from this it does not follow that in each episode or saying Matthew is necessarily dependent on Mark, but his text may represent a more "primitive" witness to the tradition. A recent study by Donald P. Senior, *The Passion Narrative According to Matthew: A Redactional Study* (Louvain, 1975), will repay close study for those interested in the topic.

4. Günther Bornkamm, G. Barth, H. Held, *Überlieferung und Auslegung im Matthäus-Evangelium* (Neukirchen, 1961), p. 35.

5. For example, the first section of the so-called "missionary discourse" (Mt 10:5–15) regards the catechetical tour in Jesus' day, while the second (vv. 16–25) reflects principally the experiences of Christian preachers in the apostolic age.

6. See the redactional study of the "community discourse" by Wil-

liam G. Thompson, S.J., *Matthew's Advice to a Divided Community*. *Mt.* *17, 22—18, 25* (Rome, 1970).

7. Rudolf Schnackenburg, *The Church in the New Testament*, trans. W. J. O'Gara (New York, 1965), p. 70.

8. John R. Donahue, S.J., "Miracle, Mystery and Parable," *The Way* 18 (1978), 257.

9. See the article (referred to earlier) by Jacques Guillet, "Le Christ prie en moi," *Christus* 5 (1958), 150–165.

10. Wolfgang Trilling, *The Gospel According to St. Matthew, I*, trans. Kevin Smyth (New York, 1969), pp. 130–131.

11. *Ibid., II*, p. 143.

12. Günther Bornkamm, G. Barth, H. Held, *Überlieferung und Auslegung im Matthäus-Evangelium*, p. 37.

13. Donald P. Senior, *The Passion Narrative According to Matthew*, p. 339.

14. Albert Vanhoye, S.J., "Structure et théologie des récits de la Passion dans les évangiles synoptiques," *Nouvelle Revue Théologique* 89 (1967), 144.

15. Donald P. Senior, *The Passion Narrative According to Matthew*, p. 4.

16. *Ibid.*, p. 396, n. 181.

17. André Feuillet, *L'Agonie de Gethsémani*, pp. 124, 126.

18. See *Boasting in the Lord: The Phenomenon of Prayer in Saint Paul* (New York, 1973), pp. 115–130.

19. Mario Galizzi, *Gesù nel Getsemani* (Rome, 1972), pp. 91ff.

20. Rudolf Schnackenburg, *The Gospel According to St. Mark II*, p. 124.

21. Mario Galizzi, *Gesù nel Getsemani*, p. 128.

22. See *sub voce* W. F. Arndt and F. W. Gingrich, *A Greek-English Lexicon of the New Testament and Other Early Christian Literature*, p. 510.

23. André Feuillet, *L'Agonie de Gethsémani*, pp. 126–128.

24. J. Warren Holleran, *The Synoptic Gethsemane*, p. 168.

25. Mario Galizzi, *Gesù nel Getsemani*, p. 95.

26. André Feuillet, *L'Agonie de Gethsémani*, p. 133.

27. Martin Dibelius, "Gethsemane," *The Crozer Quarterly* 12 (1938), 254–265.

28. As does Warren Holleran, *The Synoptic Gethsemane*, p. 212.

29. Mario Galizzi, *Gesù nel Getsemani*, pp. 131f.

30. Warren Holleran, *The Synoptic Gethsemane*, p. 165.

31. Mario Galizzi, *Gesù nel Getsemani*, pp. 101–102.

32. Ibid., p. 131, where the imperative is taken to suggest that Jesus' prayer was one of acceptance of the cup.—It is to be noted that only this Gospel, alone in the New Testament, employs the Greek word for friend (*hetairos*): Mt 11:16; 20:13; 22:12.

33. Pierre Bonnard, *L'Évangile selon saint Matthieu*, 2d ed. (Neuchâtel, 1970), p. 386.

VI

JESUS' PRAYER ON THE MOUNT OF OLIVES (Lk 22:39-46)

As an aid to situating the Lucan interpretation of the Gethsemane-tradition within the context of the Third Gospel, we begin by reviewing briefly the place of privilege accorded by this evangelist to Jesus' practice of prayer during his public ministry. We shall also take note of Jesus' teaching on prayer as Luke presents it, although in contrast with Matthew this evangelist sets a higher priority upon Jesus' own example of prayer than upon his instructions regarding it. Actually this is a specific instance of the particular emphasis Luke places upon "what Jesus did" rather than upon what he "taught" (Acts 1:1). In this respect the Lucan summary of "the word" God "sent to the sons of Israel" (Acts 10:36-43) is typical. For this compendium of "the word occurring throughout Judaea" contains no saying of Jesus, no reference to his preaching. It simply lists as "the word" the significant experiences of Jesus from his baptism through the post-resurrection appearances to his own.

This Lucan characteristic is reflected in his Gospel by his constant concern to set Jesus before his reader as the great model of Christian living. And in fact it is a peculiar trait of the Passion narrative of Luke to engage his reader in the following of Christ by pointing repeatedly to the exemplary features of Jesus' actions and reactions. In the Matthew Passion it is characteristically a saying of Jesus that habitually dispels the ambiguity of the historical situation for the Christian community, symbolized by "the disciples." Luke is preoccupied rather with the values concretely set forth in the conduct of Jesus as the most effective and attractive motives for imitation.

Role of Prayer in Jesus' Public Ministry

Thus it is of set purpose that Luke presents Jesus, at his first appearance in the narrative of his public life immediately after his baptism by John, as engaged in prayer. "It happened that when all the people had been baptized, Jesus also being baptized was *absorbed in prayer*. The sky opened, and the Holy Spirit descended upon him, in outward appearance like a dove. A voice came out of heaven, 'You are my Son, my beloved; in you I take delight' " (Lk 3:21–22). The reader is alerted concerning the significant role prayer is to play in Jesus' mission as Messiah at the very moment when he is anointed with the Spirit and acknowledged as Son by the Father. Luke appears to imply moreover that this theophany happens precisely in answer to that prayer.

This circumstance is undoubtedly the result of Luke's own editorial activity and his wish to draw attention from the beginning to Jesus' prayerfulness and to its efficacy. Consequently, it is surprising that the evangelist *apparently* passes over a reference to it found in his Marcan source. After recounting Jesus' cure of Simon's mother-in-law Mark notes that he passed the night in Simon's house, but well before dawn "he was up, and out, and away to an isolated place, and there he was engaged in prayer" (Mk 1:35). Luke reports Jesus' withdrawal from the disciples simply as a search for solitude. "When day came, going forth from the town, he proceeded to an isolated place" (Lk 4:41).

However, Luke would appear to have waited to exploit this Marcan reference to Jesus' prayer on a single occasion by incorporating it into a summary description of Jesus' earliest efforts at evangelization. This technique has enabled Luke to generalize and so emphasize how essential prayer was in Jesus' mission.

"Now talk about him kept spreading more and more, and great crowds continued to gather, to listen and to be healed of their ailments. As for himself, he kept withdrawing to isolated spots and *was constantly at prayer*" (Lk 5:15–16). Thus a habit of prayer is made an important and constant feature of Jesus' ministry.

Luke's editorial activity appears again in the introduction to Jesus' selection of the Twelve. On the eve of this decision Jesus had recourse to prolonged prayer. It was a time when controversy with "the Pharisees and scribes" (Lk 5:50; 6:2, 7) had become a regular feature of Jesus' career, and with the first hint of some sinister design on the part of Jesus' opponents,[1] Luke pictures him as employing the weapon of prayer (Lk 6:11). "It happened at that period that he went forth to the mountain to pray, and he *passed the entire night in prayer to God.* When day broke, he called his disciples, selecting, twelve of them, whom he also called apostles" (Lk 6:12–13). The event is fraught with special meaning for Luke's theology. These men are "the original eyewitnesses, who also became ministers of the word" (Lk 1:2). Their personal and collective experience of Jesus' career from his baptism to the ascension (Acts 1:21–22) authenticates their designation as "apostles," the principal guardians of the Jesus-tradition and the leaders of the primitive community. Accordingly it is no surprise that Lucan creativity underscores the crucial role played by prayer in this momentous decision of Jesus. From now on in the Third Gospel Jesus will be seen to pray always in the presence of these followers.

"On one occasion, when he had been praying in private, his disciples, as it happened, were with him. So he put a question to them, 'Who do the crowds claim that I am?' " (Lk 9:18). Peter's reply (v. 20), "You are the Anointed of God," constitutes a "water-shed" (Vincent Taylor) in the disciples' experience of Jesus. This confession expresses the extent to which, during Jesus' life on earth, the Twelve with their traditional Jewish faith were able to pierce the mystery surrounding their Master. Until after his resurrection they could only comprehend his mission and his Person as the divine answer to the messianic hopes of Israel. Luke stresses the importance of this episode by framing it in the context of prayer. He does this, it must be observed, by following a tradition reflected only in the Fourth Gospel (Jn 6:66–69), where this recognition of Jesus as Messiah is linked with the feeding of the five thousand (Lk 9:10–17).[2]

In fact, the Lucan description of Jesus' actions in performing this miracle seems to have borrowed a detail which characterizes Jesus' preparation for prayer in John (11:14; 17:1). Luke pictures Jesus as "taking the five loaves and the two fish, and *after looking up to heaven,* he blessed them. . . . " (v. 16). Jesus' recall of God's presence here acquaints the reader with the role that prayer occupies in the performance of a miracle.

If Luke has followed the Johannine tradition, as we have indicated, in linking Peter's confession with the feeding of the crowd, he has also, once again, made creative use of the brief Marcan conclusion to the feeding narrative: Jesus "retreated to the mountain to pray" (Mk 6:46; Mt 14:23). It is this Marcan observation that lies behind Luke's introduction (Lk 9:18) to Peter's confession alluded to above. Such originality in handling his sources is a salient feature of Luke's genius, as is his reverence and faithfulness in preserving them.

"About eight days after this announcement [the first prediction by Jesus of his Passion and resurrection], taking along Peter, and John, and James, he ascended the mountain *in order to pray. As he went on praying,* his whole countenance was transformed in appearance, and his clothing became dazzling white" (Lk 9:28–29). A connection between the prolongation of the prayer and the extraordinary change in Jesus' appearance, beheld by the three disciples, is intended to be inferred by the reader. Luke implies moreover that Jesus had continued to pray far into the night: the disciples are overcome with sleep (v. 32);[3] it is only "the next day" that the group leaves the mountain (v. 37).

In his version of the curing by Jesus of the boy possessed by a demon, linked by the tradition to the transfiguration, Luke once more surprises us by omitting the logion of Jesus, "This kind can be driven out only by prayer" (Mk 9:29). It may well be that Luke has suppressed this saying purposely in order to bring

out the same lesson more effectively by his account of Jesus'
prayer before his capture (Lk 22:40, 46). For as will be seen,
Luke considers "temptation" or "testing" as descriptive of an
experience wholly diabolical in origin.

The great "confession" by Jesus addressed to his Father (see
Mt 11:25–27) is presented by Luke as part of Jesus' reaction to
the triumphant return of the seventy-two disciples (Lk 10:17–
20), joyfully announcing their victories over the demons. Jesus
warns them that they are to "rejoice that your names have been
inscribed in heaven" (v. 20). "At that moment Jesus exulted in
the Holy Spirit and declared, 'I profess my thanks to you, Father, Lord of heaven and earth, for though you have hidden
these things from the learned and intelligent, you have revealed
them to the simple. Yes, Father, such has been your good pleasure!—Everything has been handed over to me by my Father,
for indeed no one knows who the Son is except the Father, or
who the Father is except the Son, and the man to whom the Son
decides to reveal him.' And turning round to his disciples he
said in an aside, 'Happy your eyes that behold the things you
see. For I tell you: many prophets and kings desired to see what
you are seeing, yet did not see, to hear what you are hearing, yet
did not hear' " (Lk 10:21–24). This is one of the very rare occasions in the Third Gospel when the tenor of Jesus' prayer is disclosed. The tradition which modern critics denominate as "Q"
had retained the memory of this public act of thanksgiving by
Jesus. It took the form of a "confession," which in the Old Testament (Ps 28) was the believer's reaction to a theophany. From
the Lucan redaction the theophany is the revelation of God's
power through the exorcisms of the seventy-two disciples, "the
simple," to whom an experience of the divine power had been
accorded. The power over demons that Jesus had communicated
to these disciples has been given to him by his Father as one of
the means of making the kingdom of God an earthly reality.
These miracles in turn lead to a knowledge of the identity of the
Son, as well as of the Father. Jesus pronounces his disciples
"happy," because they have witnessed what so many Old Testament saints longed to see, the downfall of Satan (v. 18). They

have moreover *heard Jesus' prayer* on this joyous occasion—another manifestation of the presence in him of God's reign on earth.

"Now it happened while he was in a certain place *absorbed in prayer,* that when he finished, one of his disciples said to him, 'Lord, teach us to pray, just as John taught his disciples.' Then he said to them, 'Whenever you pray, you must say,

"Father, make your name holy [in us];
Cause your reign to become an [earthly] reality.
Give us day by day our bread for tomorrow;
and forgive us our sins,
for on our part, we forgive anyone indebted to us;
and do not bring us to the test" ' " (Lk 11:1–4).

Luke's version of the dominical prayer lacks two petitions found in Mt 6:9–13. "May your will (*thelēma*) be carried out!": this is possibly a deliberate omission, since the terms *thelein* and *thelēma* are used in the Third Gospel only of human willing. The last Matthean petition, "But deliver us from the evil one," is probably left out by Luke because of the peculiar meaning he gives to Jesus' temptations (*peirasmos*) as of wholly diabolical origin (Lk 4:1–13), which makes this petition unnecessary.[4] Moreover, it is precisely the paramount importance for Christian prayer of the will of God and deliverance from temptation (in the Lucan sense) which Luke will underscore by his narrative of Jesus' prayer on the Mount of Olives.

The most striking feature of Luke's introduction of the "Our Father" into his Gospel, however, is that he places it in the context of Jesus' own prayer. This enables Luke to suggest that the supreme value of this prayer, already given pride of place in his day within the Christian liturgy, lay precisely in Jesus' allowing his disciples to share his personal sentiments and those filial attitudes he himself displayed toward God when at prayer. Luke's remark about John the Baptist indicates a detail nowhere else mentioned.[5] In the Lucan version of the question about fasting we are told that John's disciples had acquired a habit of prayer (Lk 5:33) which ranked them with the Pharisees, whose devotion and piety were two of their hallmarks.

Once again Luke shows his independence of Mark when he related Jesus' meeting with some "tiny children" brought to him simply "that he might touch them" (Lk 18:15–17). He says nothing about Jesus' blessing them (see Mk 10:16). It is curious that he also omits the observation found in Mt 19:13 that "children were brought to him, that he might lay his hands upon them *and pray.*" In the Third Gospel it is only the risen Jesus who blesses persons (Lk 24:50–51).

This review of the role of prayer in Jesus' public ministry has disclosed *five* notable features of the Lucan presentation of it. First, Jesus is depicted as engaged in prayer at six significant moments in his public life: his baptism, the choice of the Twelve, Peter's confession of Jesus as Messiah, the transfiguration, the reunion with the seventy-two disciples, and the teaching concerning prayer given by Jesus to his followers. Second, Luke intends that repeated recourse to prayer should be regarded as a significant element in Jesus' mission. This is clear from the prominence given to prayer in one of the earliest summaries (5:15–16) which punctuate this Gospel. Third, this evangelist repeatedly suggests the protracted nature of Jesus' prayer by expressly drawing attention to the passing of time (Lk 6:12; 9:29–37), or by the use of the present participle (Lk 3:21; 5:16; 9:18; 11:1). Fourth, Luke has managed to multiply the references to Jesus' prayer either by a clever manipulation of the data supplied by the various strands of tradition he employs (as in the summary at Lk 6:12–13, Peter's confession at 9:18–21, and Jesus' prayer of thanksgiving at 10:21–24), or (as in three instances: Lk 3:21–22; 9:28–29; 11:1) by the creative use of his own imagination. Finally, in only two of these references to Jesus' prayer does Luke give any inkling of its specific content. In both cases (Lk 10:21–24; 11:2–4) Luke is indebted to the evangelical tradition. Otherwise Luke is content to leave the prayer of Jesus surrounded in mystery.

Jesus' Prayer in the Passion Narrative

There are four points in his Passion narrative at which Luke has introduced references to the prayer of Jesus. At the conclusion of the Last Supper, Jesus tells Peter, "Simon, Simon, note that Satan has obtained his request to sift all of you like wheat! For my part, *I have pleaded for you*, that your faith may not fail. As for you, once you are finally converted, you must impart strength to your brothers" (Lk 22:31-32). The term "plead" with which Luke here describes Jesus' prayer is remarkable, suggesting as it does both the intensity of the request and the fact that it arises from a felt need. More arresting still, this is the unique instance in all four Gospels where Jesus' prayer is so qualified. Is Luke here echoing the same tradition (found in Heb 5:7) which speaks of Jesus' prayers as "pleadings"? The term plead (*deomai*) is characteristic of Luke (it occurs elsewhere in the Gospels only at Mt 9:38): it is used for the leper's prayer (Lk 5:12) to Jesus as well as for that of the father of the possessed boy (Lk 9:38), and, as will be seen, in two of Jesus' sayings concerning prayer (Lk 10:2; 21:36). The prayer of Jesus, Luke well knows, is infallible; accordingly he does not speak of Peter as denying his faith in his Master. Peter's sin is not to "deny Jesus" but to deny "knowing him" (Lk 22:32; see 22:54–62).

The next occasion is Jesus' prayer on the Mount of Olives (Lk 22:39–46) to which we shall shortly direct our attention. The third instance is found in the scene on Calvary: "Father, forgive them; they do not know what they are doing" (Lk 23:34). There is some doubt about the authenticity of this verse, the most important Greek witnesses being divided. It is not found in P[75], Vaticanus, the Freer codex or Koredethi. Yet it is attested by Sinaiticus, Alexandrinus, Ephrem Rescriptus, and D (corrector). Certain ecclesiastical writers of the second century cite it: Hegesippus, Tatian, Irenaeus, Justin. The directness and simplicity of the request favor its authenticity; it is moreover in character with Luke's presentation of Jesus, who healed the ear of one of his captors (Lk 22:51b). It is uttered at the dramatic moment of Jesus' crucifixion.

The final prayer occurs at the moment of Jesus' death. "And crying out with a strong voice Jesus said, 'Father, into your hands I commend my spirit,' and saying this he expired" (Lk 23:46). The last, mighty cry of Jesus at Mk 15:37 was left as an inarticulate shout of victory, causing the rending of the curtain in the sanctuary and the conversion of a Roman centurion (Mk 15:38–39). Luke verbalizes this cry with the help of Ps 31:5, the same citation he will put in the mouth of the dying Stephen (Acts 7:59). It is the expression of total confidence in the Father, to whom Jesus turns in trust as he completes his "exodus" (Lk 9:31). Here, it is to be observed, Lucan creativity has (contrary to Mk 15:38 and Mt 27:51) placed the tearing of the sanctuary-curtain *before* the death of Jesus. There is perhaps a theological reason behind this retrojection. Not implausibly Luke has adopted the viewpoint seen in Hebrews' reference to this same phenomenon. "Brothers, we possess free ingress into the sanctuary by Jesus' blood, since he has opened up for us a new and living way through the curtain. I mean his flesh" (Heb 10:19–20). Luke in describing here "that *exodus* of his which he was to realize in Jerusalem" (Lk 9:31) represents the exalted Jesus as greeting the Father at his entry into the celestial sanctuary through the curtain that is already rent in two in order to permit his passage. That the Lucan Jesus should turn to the Father in the supreme moment of his life, dying with a prayer on his lips, is only to have been expected.

Having concluded our survey of Luke's references to the importance of prayer in Jesus' earthly life, we wish to point out how consistently this evangelist draws attention to the protracted character of Jesus' prayer through the use of the periphrastic (Lk 5:16; 6:12; 9:18; 11:1), or the present participle (Lk 3:21), or the imperfect (Lk 22:41; 23:34).

Jesus' Teaching Concerning Prayer

While Luke appears to attach more significance to Jesus' example than to his teaching on prayer, he shows his awareness of a number of sayings relevant to it which are preserved in the other Gospels, and in addition he has included other materials which his own investigations have unearthed. We shall first inspect Luke's reworking of the traditional data, noting how creatively he has exploited it; then we shall recall the teaching on prayer which is peculiar to the Third Gospel.

In the Lucan discourse which corresponds to the Matthean Sermon on the Mount, prominence is given to Jesus' command to love one's enemies (Lk 6:27–36). As in Mt 5:44, the first injunction is to pray for them: "Call down God's blessing (*eulogeite*) on those who curse you; pray for those who treat you badly" (Lk 16:28). If Lk 23:34 is genuine (we saw there is a certain probability in its favor), Jesus will exemplify this teaching at his crucifixion.

Luke records a saying of Jesus found in the tradition he shares with Matthew: "The harvest is indeed plentiful, but workers are scarce; therefore beg the Lord of the harvest to send out workers to the harvest" (Lk 10:2). The text is found verbatim at Mt 9:37. Luke however has made it part of the instruction to the seventy-two disciples and given it priority over all the other injunctions laid on them. The first thing Jesus tells these missionaries as he sends them out in pairs is to pray.

Notice has already been taken of the setting in the life of Jesus, in which according to Luke he taught the disciples the dominical prayer. Luke appends to his version of the *Pater noster* an exhortation by Jesus on the necessity of persevering petition, where Mt 6:14–15 had underlined the crucial importance of reconciliation. While Luke has incorporated some sayings found at Mt 7:7–12, he inserts a brief illustration (Lk 11:5–8) found nowhere else. "And he said to them, 'Suppose one of you has a friend. You go to his house in the middle of the night, and say to him "Dear friend, lend me three loaves of bread. A good friend of mine has landed in on me from a journey, and I have nothing for him to eat." But he replies from inside his house, "Don't bother me! My door is already made fast; my children and I have gone to bed, so I can't get up and give you anything."—I tell you: even if he will not get up and give him whatever he needs because he is a good friend, still he will rouse himself and give it to him at least because of his persistence. So I tell you, keep asking, and God will give it to you; go on seeking, and you will find; continue knocking, and the door will be opened to you. Everyone who keeps asking receives, and the man who goes on seeking finds, and the door is opened to him who continues to knock.—Is there a father among you, who when your son asks for fish, would hand him a snake instead of fish, or if he asks for an egg, would hand him a scorpion? So then if you, bad as you are, know enough to give your children what is good, how much more will your Father in heaven give the Holy Spirit to those who keep asking him!' " (Lk 11:5–13).

There is a saying recorded in the Lucan version of Jesus' prediction of the destruction of the temple and city of Jerusalem which has a partial parallel in the Marcan eschatological discourse. Luke has however revamped it as an invitation to continual prayer. Mk 13:33 reads, "See to it you keep on the alert, since you do not know when the *kairos* occurs." Luke has developed the form so as to focus it on prayer: "But keep on the alert by pleading at every opportune moment (*kairos*), that you may have the strength to escape all these things that will certainly happen, and that you may stand in the presence of the Son of Man" (Lk 21:36). It is interesting to observe a similar development in Eph 6:18: "Keep praying in spirit by using every kind of prayer and entreaty at every opportune moment (*kairos*). Be on the alert about it with great constancy and continual entreaty on behalf of all the saints."

We must now recall three Lucan passages illustrating Jesus' teaching about prayer not found in any other New Testament book. The first is the narrative of Jesus' visit with Martha and Mary (Lk 10:38–42) which forms a prelude to the story concerning the Lord's Prayer (Lk 11:1–4). Since Luke has a well-known habit of grouping materials thematically, it is very probable that he has intentionally inserted the story of this visit here which illustrates the need of "listening to the word" of Jesus in prayer (Lk 10:39). The concluding saying by Jesus discloses the point of the narrative: "Martha, Martha! You are anxious and distracted over many things! Yet there is only one thing we need, and Mary has chosen the best 'dish,' which must not be taken away from her" (Lk 10:41–42). The importance attaching to this logion is here indicated by the peculiarly Lucan usage of

the post-resurrection title for Jesus, which introduces the remark: "In reply *the Lord* said to her" (v. 41).

Within the special Lucan material is a pair of parables
which are juxtaposed since they deal in different ways with the
theme of prayer: the unjust judge (18:1–8) and the Pharisee and
the publican (18:9–14). Each is introduced by an editorial remark
underscoring the principal point of the illustration.

"He told them a parable illustrating how essential it is to
persevere at prayer and never give up. 'Once there was a judge
in a city with no fear of God, nor any respect for his fellowman.
Now there was a widow in that city, who kept coming to him
with the plea, "Protect my rights against the man who is suing
me." Yet he went on for a good while refusing to do anything.
Finally however he said to himself, "True, I have no fear of
God, nor any respect for my fellowman. Still, because this widow keeps pestering me, I will protect her rights, or she will
wear me down with her persistent visits!" '—The Lord said,
'Note what this dishonest judge is saying! Will not God, on the
contrary, protect the rights of his chosen people, who keep crying out to him day and night? Will he take his time answering
them? I can assure you, he will protect their rights in a hurry!—
For all that, will the Son of Man, do you think, find this confidence on earth when he comes?' " (Lk 18:1–8).

The final query indicates Luke's sensitivity to the danger
inherent in misconstruing the thrust of the parable, and he underlines the loving trust (*tēn pistin*) in the God who, as "the just
judge of all the earth" (Gen 18:25), is the very antithesis of "this
dishonest judge" in the story. Thus, while he insists upon the
crucial importance of perseverance in petitionary prayer, Luke
wishes to avoid any misconception of prayer as a way of pres-
suring God into granting the request.

The parable immediately following is meant as a negative
lesson in the art of prayer, as may be surmised from its proximity to that of the unjust judge. It is a warning that prayer is not
"talking to oneself," as the detail about the Pharisee, who "kept
saying this prayer to himself," makes evident. Prayer must not
be allowed to degenerate into a process of self-justification.

"He also related the following parable to certain individuals, who had put their confidence in their own uprightness, and looked down on other people as of no account. 'Two men went up to the temple area to pray, one a Pharisee, the other, a tax-collector. The Pharisee took his stand and kept saying this prayer to himself, "My God, I give you thanks that I am not like other men, thieving, dishonest, adulterers—or like this tax-collector. I fast two days of the week; I pay tithes on all I own." By contrast, the tax-collector, standing at a distance, would not even raise his eyes to heaven, but beat his breast. He said, "My God, take pity upon the sinner that I am."—I tell you: it was this latter man who went home having been made upright, not the former. Each person who makes much of himself will be brought down: it is the man who realizes he is nothing who will be exalted' " (Lk 18:9–14). Prayer is indeed "the raising of heart and mind to God," provided it is realized that it is God's graciousness that "raises up," not man's ineffectual efforts.

What has most appealed to Luke in Jesus' teaching about prayer is his insistence upon the necessity of waiting on God with utmost confidence in his fatherly concern for all his children. Thus Mary symbolizes the fundamental attitude of "listening," so lamentably absent from the self-justifying recital of the Pharisee. Humble, persevering petitionary prayer springs from a profound sense of our own sinfulness (as with the publican) and of our utter dependence upon God's providential care (like the widow whose persistence is a token of "confidence"). The habit of almost perpetual prayer (Lk 21:36) is the only effective means of facing whatever the future may bring, as it is also the only authentically Christian form of retaliation (Lk 6:28). Our study of Luke's narrative of Jesus' prayer on the Mount of Olives will reveal the presence of these values in the Master's attitudes.

Luke's Image of Jesus

Three dominant traits stand out in the picture of Jesus which the third evangelist has taken care to present to the Hellenistic reading public of his times: prophet, martyr, Savior. By contrast with Mark and Matthew, Luke deliberately avoids Jesus' role as the Suffering Servant of God who gives his life as "ransom for the rest of men" (Mk 10:45; Mt 20:28). This saying Luke has dropped from the tradition he received.

In the opening scene of the public ministry, Jesus appears, in his rejection at Nazareth, as the prophet repudiated by his own acquaintances, where he utters the saying which appears in all four Gospels, "Amen I tell you: no prophet is acceptable in his home town" (Lk 4:24). In his discourse on this occasion Jesus compares himself with Elijah (vv. 25–26) and Elisha (v. 27). The reaction of the people at Naim to his raising to life the son of a widow (an exclusively Lucan incident) is shown as the crowd exclaims, "A great prophet has been raised up among us" and "God has visited his people" (Lk 7:16). In another narrative peculiar to this Gospel, Jesus' host, a Pharisee, upon seeing the love displayed toward Jesus by a notorious woman, thinks to himself, "If this fellow were a prophet, he would be aware who this woman is and what sort of person is touching him—a sinner!" (Lk 7:39).

From the common tradition Luke incorporates the rumors that in him "Elijah has appeared, while others were saying that one of the prophets of old had come back to life" (Lk 9:8). Luke alone reports a logion that is certainly authentic, "Look, I am exorcising demons and effecting cures today and tomorrow, and the third day I reach my goal. In any event, it is God's will (*dei*) that I go my way today and tomorrow and the next day, because it is impossible that any prophet perish outside Jerusalem.—Jerusalem, Jerusalem! city that murders prophets and stones messengers sent to her!" (Lk 13:32b–34a). Later on, after his crucifixion Jesus is aptly characterized for Luke as "a prophet powerful in word and work in the sight of God and of all the people" (Lk 24:19). A significant facet of this image of Jesus is perceptible in his permanent possession of the Spirit from the outset of his ministry, as the citation from Isaiah indicates (Lk 4:14). Already "filled with the Holy Spirit" during his sojourn in the desert (Lk 4:1), he returns to Galilee "armed with the power of the Spirit" to inaugurate his ministry there (Lk 4:14). Jesus alone has had this gift bestowed upon him throughout his public life; only after his ascension, as he promises the Eleven, "will I send the promise of my Father upon you; so remain here in the city, until you are endowed with power from on high" (Lk 24:49).

As prophet, Jesus is destined also to be a martyr, according to the popular tradition he appears to apply to himself in the saying (Lk 13:33) already quoted. It is in this specific role that Jesus is cast in the Lucan Passion narrative. In late Judaism a theology of martyrdom, exemplified in the story of Susanna and the books of Maccabees, had been constructed.[6] Several salient features of this Jewish theology have been observed by Mario Galizzi in Luke's story of the Passion.[7]

Proper to Luke's account of Jesus' sufferings and death is the announcement at the outset of the return of Satan, who after "having reached the end of all his temptations [of Jesus] took his departure until the *kairos*" (Lk 4:13).[8] As correctly noted by Schuyler Brown,[9] this return of Satan, who "entered into Judas Iscariot" (Lk 22:3), is not to tempt Jesus once more, but to destroy him. The Lucan Jesus reminds the reader that this "hour" which belongs to his enemies is that of "the power of darkness" (Lk 22:53b). Part of the picture of Jesus as martyr (the Greek term means "witness") is reflected in Luke's peculiar account of Jesus' arraignment by the Sanhedrin; he depicts this hearing as the solemn deposition of testimony by Jesus, omitting any charge of blasphemy or official condemnation, thereby presenting Jesus as the sole, innocent witness (Lk 22:66–71).

In fact, this evangelist has with great originality stressed Jesus' innocence as part of his role as the martyr par excellence. The theme, of course, was not ignored by Mark or Matthew, especially in the Roman trial. In the Lucan discourse after the Last Supper, a composition of this author, a citation from the fourth Servant Song is placed on Jesus' lips, "And he was counted among the outlaws" (Is 53:12). Luke's intention is *not* to recall the vicarious nature of Jesus' death, but to pick out his innocence by contrast (Lk 22:37). Three separate times Pilate attests the innocence of Jesus (as Lk 23:22 expressly notes), and even Herod Antipas is cited by the governor as unable to discover any substance in the charges preferred against Jesus (Lk 23:15).

Compassion is another trait of Jesus the martyr who

throughout this Gospel has manifested compassion for sinners, the afflicted, and the oppressed. Now despite his own sufferings he heals the wounded slave in the hour of his arrest in the garden (Lk 22:51b), expresses pity for the future calamities to come upon the women and children of Jerusalem (Lk 23:28–31), prays for his executioners (v. 34), and promises "paradise" to the well-disposed malefactor crucified with him (v. 43). Thus at Jesus' death the centurion attests, "Beyond any doubt this man was innocent!" (v. 47).

Luke uses the word "spectacle" (v. 47), a term drawn from the literature of martyrdom to describe the scene of the crucifixion. In the celebrated drama of the martyr's death undergone by seven Jewish brothers with their heroic mother under Antiochus Epiphanes (2 Macc 7:1–42), the theme of the glorious resurrection is prominent as the inspiration for the unprecedented courage displayed by these Jewish martyrs. This may in part explain Luke's astonishing departure from the traditional explanation of Jesus' saving death, in shifting the source of man's salvation to his resurrection, as we shall presently observe.

The third notable characteristic of the Lucan Jesus is his role as "Savior," a title not given to our Lord by either of the other Synoptics. Jesus is so designated in the angelic announcement to the shepherds of his birth (Lk 2:11) which is echoed by Simeon (Lk 2:30). Luke is the only evangelist to extend the Deutero-Isaian citation (Is 40:3–5) that forms part of the Baptist's proclamation to include the verse, "And all flesh will see the salvation by our God" (Lk 3:4–6). The canticle of Zachary predicts Jesus' mission as "a horn of salvation for us" (see Lk 1:69, 71, 77). At his visit to Zacchaeus, Jesus announces, "Today has salvation come to this house" (Lk 19:9). The verb "to save" appears more frequently in the Third Gospel than in any other. It is noteworthy that while this evangelist omitted the saying about the Son of Man who lays down his life as "ransom" (Mk 10:45; Mt 20:28), he substitutes a redacted version of it in terms of salvation. "The Son of Man has come to seek and to save what has been lost" (Lk 19:10).

This Lucan preference for the vocabulary of salvation in place of the traditional symbols of expiation or sacrifice can be plausibly explained in terms of acculturation. The Hellenistic world would be repelled by such religious terminology as was then current in Judaism. On the other hand, the term "salvation" (which originally means "health" in Greek) was judged more congenial and fitting by Luke to present Jesus to men of Greek culture as the God-given answer to the highest aspirations of that Hellenism Luke had himself imbibed and of which he was so self-consciously proud.

Reticence Regarding the Salutary Death of Jesus

In the earliest Christian tradition Jesus' death was announced as "good news" because it was "for our sins" (1 Cor 15:3), "for us" (1 Thes 5:10). Jewish sacrificial terminology provided symbols illustrating its saving character (1 Cor 5:7b; Rom 3:25; 8:3), while the Deutero-Isaian Servant by his vicarious, expiatory death as "ransom for the many" (Is 53:12) became the classical type of Jesus (Mk 10:45; 14:24; Heb 9:28).

The great originality of Luke's underscoring of Jesus' resurrection as the source of salvation was pointed out by Augustin George some years ago.[10] As is made clear by the Lucan version of the paschal message to the women at the empty tomb, the mystery of Jesus' death can be grasped only in the light of his resurrection. "Recall what he told you while still in Galilee, 'It is God's will (*dei*) that the Son of Man be handed over into the power of sinful men and be crucified, and rise on the third day' " (Lk 24:6–7). Indeed, it is the chief function of the risen Jesus in this Gospel to interpret the sense of "the Scriptures" regarding the tragedy of his earthly history to the disciples. "Surely it was God's will (*dei*) that the Anointed suffer death and enter upon his glory?" (Lk 24:26). At his first appearance to the Eleven the glorified Lord repeats this good news, later to be enshrined in the apostolic kerygma, that is so often summarized in Luke's second volume (Acts 2:23–24, 33–36; 3:13–15; 4:10–12; 10:40–43; 17:3). At this momentous encounter the Lucan Jesus says to his own, "This is what I meant by saying, while I was still with you, that it was God's will that everything written about me in the Law of Moses, in the prophets and psalms should be fulfilled." And Luke adds: "Then he opened their minds to comprehend the Scriptures, and he told them, 'Thus Scripture has it that the Anointed would suffer death and rise from the dead on the third day' " (Lk 24:44–45). Luke's repeated insistence upon the indissoluble unity of Jesus' experience of death and resurrection, reminding us of Paul, is not to be missed. This twofold event has made Jesus "Savior" and demonstrated that "salvation resides in no other, nor indeed is there any other name under heaven graciously revealed to mankind by which God wills (*dei*) us to be saved" (Acts 4:12).

This Lucan sensitivity for his Hellenistic reading public and its humanistic sensibilities, which (as already noted) led to the abandonment of the traditional imagery for a more personal way of presenting the meaning of Jesus' death, is evinced by our evangelist's redaction of the words of eucharistic institution: "This is my body that will be given over on your behalf. . . . This cup is the new covenant in my blood that will be poured out on your behalf" (Lk 22:19–20). The personal turn of expression is remarkable: Jesus declares that he offers his life for his disciples, inaugurating thereby the new covenant, mediated by himself between God and the new people of God.

One unique characteristic of Luke's account of Jesus' public ministry, marking it out from all other Gospels, is his frequent use of the post-resurrection title, "the Lord" (some fifteen or sixteen times) to designate the earthly Jesus. One reason for this novel usage, it may be suggested here, may be found in his insight that the Risen One is the source of man's salvation.

A Textual Problem (Lk 22:43–44)

Before we examine the Lucan narrative of Jesus' struggle and prayer before his arrest, we must discuss the serious difficulties concerning two verses in the passage. There are strong reasons for considering them an intrusion into the original account, as it came from the hand of our evangelist, by some later (inspired) editor. The questionable verses are these: "There appeared to him an angel from heaven giving him strength. And engaging in the struggle he prayed the more earnestly; and his sweat became like clots of blood, falling to the ground" (Lk 22:43–44).

First, the verses are simply omitted from the text of the best modern critical edition of the Greek New Testament, edited under the direction of Kurt Aland with the collaboration of a group of international textual critics.[11] A strong indication that the verses are an interpolation into the Lucan story is their absence from most of the ancient manuscripts: the Bodmer papyrus, P[75], from the end of the second or beginning of the third century, Codex Alexandrinus and other important witnesses to the Alexandrian recension.[12] From the viewpoint of the science of textual criticism the passage is almost certainly inauthentic.

Second, an inspection of the careful structure of the Lucan pericope (Lk 22:39–46) confirms this suspicion that the verses are a gloss, disturbing the otherwise balanced narrative. This may be readily seen from our presentation of the account.

Third, the description of Jesus' reactions stands in contradiction to Luke's characteristic image of Jesus, never portrayed in this Gospel as exhibiting any violent emotions. The Lucan Jesus thus appears markedly different from the Jesus of Mark, with his show of anger, impatience, and, in Gethsemane, almost irrational fear. Once only does Luke depict Jesus as weeping over Jerusalem (Lk 19:41), and this in a most restrained way.

Fourth, in the Third Gospel angels appear only in the Infancy narratives or in the post-resurrection stories (contrast Lk 4:13 with Mt 4:11). In the garden-scene of Luke, the dilatory advent of an angel "to give him strength" seems ill-timed, as Jesus has already voiced his acceptance of the Father's will in the verse immediately preceding (v. 42). The physical repercussions upon Jesus ("sweat like drops of blood") at this point in the story remain without adequate explanation. Such a belated appendage to an account is typical of Mark (Mk 1:16; 5:43), but is uncharacteristic of a literary stylist like Luke.

Fifth, a number of words occur in these verses which are found nowhere else in the Third Gospel or Acts; indeed, some are *hapax legomena* in the entire New Testament. This phenomenon, of course, does not prove that Luke might not have used them for an exceptional description such as here, but their presence rules out any argument for Lucan authenticity from vocabulary.

Sixth, the omission (if such it be) of the verses in certain manuscripts was once explained as an effect of the Arian controversy: these heretics employed the text to support their unorthodox Christology. With the discovery of the Bodmer papyrus, where the verses do not appear, a document dating about a century before Arius (+336 A.D.), such an argument appears to be fallacious.

In the light of all this, the opinion favoring nonauthenticity of the verses is more than probable.[13] One final observation: granted that Luke did not author this interpolation (any more than Mark wrote the so-called Longer Ending: Mk 16:9ff.), yet its inspired character seems assured, so far as Catholics are concerned, by the authoritative declaration of the Council of Trent, which accepted the entire Lucan Gospel "with all its parts" into the canon of sacred books.[14] For at the time of the Reformation the Lucan authorship of these verses was, like that of the Longer Ending of Mark and the story of the adulteress (Jn 7:53—8:11), the subject of debate. While not presuming to settle the authorship issue, the Council did solemnly declare the passage an integral part of our Christian inspired literature.

It may not be irrelevant to cite here a passage from the Constitution on Divine Revelation (*Dei Verbum*) of Vatican II which defines the authority of the Church in making such a pronouncement. "The office of interpreting with authority the word of God, whether written or handed down in tradition, has been entrusted uniquely to the living teaching office of the Church. . . . This teaching office does not stand over the word of God, but serves it . . . guarding it with all reverence and expounding it faithfully; and all this it draws from this one deposit of faith, which it proposes for belief as having been revealed by God" (*Dei Verbum*, #10).

This may be restated by saying that, in Catholic belief, it is the divinely bestowed responsibility (and, hence, the inalienable prerogative) of the Church through her teaching ministry to preserve in its integrity that living and authentic image of Christ, to which each Christian is by God's design and grace to be assimilated in his living out of the Gospel. In consequence, our exposition of the meaning of Jesus' prayer as presented by Luke will take cognizance of the modalities imprinted on that image by the two verses (43–44).

Luke's Introduction to the Prayer of Jesus

The context of the passage in this Gospel which is of direct concern is the first part of the Lucan Passion narrative. Here, as elsewhere in his book, our evangelist displays familiarity with and reverence for the Jesus-tradition he has received from Mark and other sources, while at the same time employing creative originality in his editorial handling of them, both by what he omits and by the additions made.

Luke notes at the start of his account of the Passion the approach of Passover and the machinations of the high priests and scribes who are conspiring to do away with Jesus. He refers to the festival, however, as "the feast of unleavened bread" (Lk 22:1), not implausibly in view of his quite distinctive account of the eucharistic institution he will soon provide. Immediately he introduces the presence of Satan into his story, depicting Judas' treacherous designs as the result of his possession by the devil (v. 2). Because of this Luke will later speak of the Passion as the "hour" of "the power of the darkness" (v. 57).

The evangelist opens his account of the last meal of Jesus with his disciples by noting that it occurred on "the day of unleavened bread, when the paschal lamb had to be sacrificed" (v. 7). The meal itself began "when the hour came" (v. 14), not implausibly a reminder that it is also Satan's hour. The eucharistic narrative itself is obviously stylized and artfully arranged as a diptych, for the evident purpose of setting out the parallel contrast between the ancient Passover meal of Israel and the paschal eucharistic celebration of the Christian Church.[15] Luke knows an authentic saying of the historical Jesus which expresses his confidence that, through death, he will by God's power share in the future realization of his kingdom. Our evangelist knew it in its Marcan form, "Amen I tell you: I shall never again drink the fruit of the vine, until that day when I drink it new in the kingdom of God" (Mk 14:25). The Lucan redaction has produced, however, two notable modifications. First, he introduces his version before the eucharistic words, thus orientating the meaning to those future repasts of the risen Lord with his disciples during his appearances to them—a feature only found in Lucan accounts of these meetings (Lk 24:30, 43; Acts 1:4). Second, Luke creates two forms of this single saying, one referring to the paschal lamb, the other to the ritual wine of the supper. "With a consuming desire have I longed to eat this paschal lamb with you before I suffer death. Amen I tell you: never again shall I eat it, until it be fulfilled in the kingdom of God" (vv. 15–16). The evangelist then completes his impressionistic presentation of the Passover celebration by remarking, "Then taking a cup, after giving thanks, he said, 'Take this and share it among yourselves. For I tell you: I shall not drink of the fruit of the vine from this moment until the kingdom of God will come'" (vv. 17–18). It appears most probable that Luke wishes the reader to think of those joyous repasts of reunion described by Peter in his sermon at Caesarea, "We ate and drank with him after his rising from the dead" (Acts 10:41b).

Only at this point is the reader given the Lucan version of Jesus' gestures and words, vis-à-vis the future sacrament of "the Lord's supper," which exhibits the influence both of 1 Cor 11:23–25 and Mk 14:22–23. After a long drawn-out debate about the reading of the Lucan text in question, one has the impression that nowadays its authenticity as given here is more and more accepted.[16]

"And taking bread, after giving thanks, he broke it, and gave it to them with the words, 'This is my body that will be given [over to death] on your behalf. Do this as a memorial of me.' And the cup likewise, after supper, with the words, 'This cup is the new covenant in my blood that will be poured out on your behalf'" (vv. 19–20).

The Lucan formula "on your behalf" is more closely related in meaning to the interpretation of Jesus' death in the Fourth Gospel where he is said to "lay down his life for his friends" (Jn

15:13) as a proof of "greater love." They are in contrast with the Marcan words over the cup with their clear reference to the vicarious death of the Suffering Servant, "poured out for the rest of men" (Mk 14:24), or Matthew's "for the remission of sins" (Mt 26:28).

Luke continues his account with a discourse by Jesus composed of elements found in earlier traditions (Lk 1:1–4). Jesus announces his betrayal (vv. 21–23), and then, since "a jealous dispute broke out concerning who among them should rank highest" (v. 24), Jesus teaches his total reversal of worldly standards of precedence, pointing to his own example at this meal, where he has himself waited on the disciples (vv. 25–27). He then promises to make a new covenant with them, as the technical term "to make a will, conclude an agreement" (*diatithēmi*) indicates (v. 29), and he makes a veiled allusion to the functions of these disciples in the future Church, their presiding at the Eucharist and over the local communities (v. 30).

Jesus now issues a warning to "Simon" which involves the entire group, who will be "sifted like wheat" by Satan, during the traumatic events of his own Passion. Yet Jesus declares that he has prayed for Peter personally "that your faith may not fail, and once you have made an about-face, you must lend strength to your brothers" (vv. 31–32). Because this prayer is undoubtedly efficacious, Peter will not "deny" Jesus, as Mark and Matthew put it, but will only "deny knowing me" (v. 34; see vv. 54b–62).[17] The discourse is brought to a conclusion with Jesus' solemn admonition alerting the disciples to readiness for the future eschatological warfare, a consequence of his own execution "with the outlaws"—an explicit reference to his role as the Suffering Servant (Is 53:12). The subtleties of the symbolic language Jesus here employs are lost upon the uncomprehending disciples who remark brightly, "Lord, look! two swords here!" (v. 38a), and Jesus patiently rejoins, "Enough of that!" (v. 38b). This final indication of the lack of understanding of the situation by his followers serves to introduce the Lucan account of what now happens on the Mount of Olives to Jesus, thus giving a clue to the conduct there of the disciples.

LUKE'S ACCOUNT OF JESUS' PRAYER
(Lk 22:39–46)

39 And going out he proceeded, as was his custom, to the Mount of Olives. But the disciples also followed him. 40 Now when he reached the place, he told them, "Pray continually that you may not be exposed to temptation." 41 And he was torn away from them, about a stone's throw, and kneeling down he kept praying, 42 "Father, if you decide to take this cup away from me. . . . Nevertheless, not my desire, but may yours continue to be done!" [43 There appeared to him an angel from heaven, giving him strength. 44 And in anguish of spirit he kept praying the more earnestly. And his sweat became like clots of blood, falling to the earth.]

45 And rising from prayer, upon returning to the disciples, he found them dead asleep from grief. 46 And he told them, "Why are you sleeping? Rise and pray continually that you may not be exposed to temptation!"

Several distinctive features of this narrative will at once strike the reader: its tightly organized unity, the effect of careful structuring, its comparative brevity giving the impression of a terse, laconic story, its relative detachment, both from the account of the supper and of Jesus' arrest, its sharp focus—even more than in Matthew's Gethsemane—upon the person of Jesus, and finally its emphasis, by repetition, on the lesson to be grasped by the believer.

Accordingly, it may be useful to recall the details found in the earlier Gospel accounts that are omitted by Luke, as well as additions he has made. There has been a lively debate among the critics as to whether our evangelist redacted the Marcan account to bring it in line with his Christology, or whether he made use of a different source discovered in the course of his own investigations, or whether—as frequently in the Third Gospel—he is influenced by the Johannine tradition out of which John's Gospel was eventually constructed.[18] The inconclusive results of this on-going discussion do not permit our drawing any conclusions helpful for the understanding of the Lucan scene. Hence, in speaking of "omissions" or "additions," we wish simply to draw attention to significant differences between this presentation and those of Mark and Matthew, without prejudice to the issue of sources.

The detail which signifies the conclusion of the Passover supper in Mark and Matthew, the singing of the Hallel, does not appear in Luke. This strengthens the impression that our evangelist intended to give a highly stylized, not a realistic account of that final meal shared by Jesus with his disciples. Luke's chief purpose was to suggest that the ancient rite of Israel had been fulfilled by Jesus' words and actions in the Christian Eucharist. On the other hand, Luke composed a discourse after the supper which is not found in any Gospel-account except that of John. He was thus able to incorporate in it Jesus' prediction of the "sifting" by Satan of the disciples and Peter's triple denial. Nothing was said however in this context about a loss of faith or an abandonment of Jesus by his own. In point of fact, in this Gospel they will "all" appear with the women on Calvary (Lk 23:49). Such divergence from the viewpoint of his predecessors is probably to be explained by Luke's theology of the apostolic office in the later Church: "the apostles" play a crucial role as "witnesses" in constructing and promoting the apostolic Church (Acts 1:21–22); thus it is imperative that they can from personal experience attest to the various events of Jesus' Passion.

Luke alludes vaguely to "the place," without naming Gethsemane, as earlier he omitted Caesarea Philippi (Lk 9:18–20). The entire group of disciples remains together throughout Jesus' prayer (all must witness what happens), and Jesus' extreme emotional reactions at the start (Mk 14:33–35) are passed over in silence. This is consistent, as was observed earlier, with the Lucan presentation of Jesus. No injunction to "watch" is given: Luke's attitude toward the delay in the second coming of the glorified Christ probably explains his reticence throughout his book in the use of "watch" (Lk 12:37), or "stay awake" (Lk 21:36). No mention is made of the proverb, "The spirit is willing, yet the flesh is weak" (Mk 14:38b). The Lucan Jesus does not interrupt his prayer; it is unnecessary that he return to look after his disciples, who here surround him, nor is he characterized as the Shepherd.

Of the details peculiar to this narrative, probably the most significant is the perfectly balanced format which the whole account exhibits. After an introduction (v. 39), the theme of the necessity of perseverance in prayer, as the means to avert succumbing to "temptation," is set at the head of the episode, to be repeated at its conclusion (v. 46). Jesus then makes his preparations for prayer (v. 41), expressed breathlessly (by means of an anacoluthon) in direct discourse (v. 42). Bypassing for the moment the intrusion (vv. 43–44), Jesus returns to the disciples upon finishing his prayer (v. 45) to repeat the thematic injunction (v. 46). The skillfully tailored schema may be expressed thus: A (v. 40), B (v. 41), C (v. 42), B' (v. 45), A' (v. 46), as suggested by Mario Galizzi.[19] Accordingly, the articulated prayer is carefully set at the very heart of the exposition, its positioning a symbolic pointer to the source, for the community of faith, of its strength and assured success in future struggles against loss of faith in Jesus.

Other small but significant details indicate our evangelist's theological reflection on the incident, as will be noted in the commentary: Jesus goes to pray "as was his custom" (v. 39); he is "torn away" as he withdraws within seeing and hearing distance of the disciples, and he kneels with reverence and self-command (v. 41). All this reminds the reader of the supreme importance and solemnity of this final prayer of Jesus.

And going out he proceeded, as was his custom, to the Mount of Olives. Luke had earlier alluded to Jesus' practice during these final nights of his earthly life (Lk 21:37) of leaving the city. There is no suggestion that it was his purpose to seek safety from his enemies; rather, it was in line with his customary habit, emphasized particularly by Luke throughout this Gospel, of devoting the night to prayer. The word *custom* in both Lucan books has the sense of a religious practice (Lk 1:9; 2:42; Acts 6:14; 15:1). For

Luke Jesus' personal religion centers in his prayer to his Father. *But the disciples also followed him.* The weak adversative (*But*) may well imply that Jesus usually went off alone for prayer; on this night, however, his intimate friends acted as true disciples and *followed him.* In his final discourse to them, Jesus characterized the disciples by saying, "You are the men who have remained with me in my trials" (Lk 22:28). For our author the word "trials" (*peirasmoi*) signifies "*human* snares, or persecutions."[20] By contrast, the singular is used in a distinctive way by Luke, "in a purely pejorative sense."[21] It is rendered "temptation" (vv. 40, 46).

Now when he reached the place. Luke intimates that *the place* is a definite locale. It is, of course, the scene of Jesus' arrest. However, it is probably used to identify *the place* where Jesus was wont to pray during the last nights of his life, and so may be an intentional recall of the evangelist's observation earlier when he recorded Jesus' teaching of the Lord's Prayer: "Now it happened that, while he was *in a certain place* at prayer. . . . (Lk 11:1).

He told them, "*Pray continually that you may not be exposed to temptation.*" This saying from the common tradition was reported by Mark and Matthew to imply that Jesus had himself become engaged in the eschatological *testing* but desired the disciples by recourse to prayer to escape this terrible ordeal. Luke has sensed a different modality of meaning in it. He does not regard the Passion as a test or trial for Jesus engineered by Satan. The source of evil had "exhausted every kind of temptation," so far as Jesus personally was concerned prior to the beginning of the public ministry (Lk 4:13). Conzelmann's contention that Satan's reappearance at the opening of Luke's Passion account was to tempt Jesus has, in my judgment, been successfully refuted by Schuyler Brown, who has shown that Satan's intent was to destroy Jesus through Judas.[22] Luke moreover does not view the Passion as a testing or *temptation* for the disciples who remain with Jesus through his death on Calvary.[23]

In fact, it appears that by *temptation* Luke understands the prelude to apostasy in the case of those whose faith is not deeply rooted and supported by prayer. This is seen from the Lucan redaction of the explanation of the sower. In the Marcan version, the seed scattered among rocks symbolized "those who have no root and last but a short time, so when tribulation or persecution on account of the word occurs, they immediately lose their faith" (Mk 4:17). Luke has reworked the saying to read: "They have no root, these temporary believers, and in time of temptation they apostatize" (Lk 8:13). In his view, *temptation* cannot be the experience of a real Christian who is commanded to avoid such a danger to faith through constant prayer.

By repeating Jesus' exhortation at the end of his narrative Luke shows that he considers it the dominant motif in the whole story; hence it must be viewed as influencing the interpretation of Jesus' prayer which has been put at the center of the account. The Lucan Jesus teaches the disciples how to pray by praying himself (Lk 11:1ff.) in their hearing. Accordingly, to avoid the superficial judgment of Luke's intention that Jesus merely "sets an example" for his followers, that intention must be seen as presenting the prayer of Jesus as *the source* of his disciples' capacity for prayer. Luke's Jesus had effectively prayed for Peter that his faith might stand firm (Lk 22:32); here his solemn prayer to God is not only a paradigm, but the effective mediation of Jesus for his disciples' deliverance from exposing themselves to *temptation*. We may well expect that "this cup" in Jesus' prayer has been given a different symbolic value by Luke than that presented by Mark or Matthew.

And he was torn away from them, about a stone's throw, and kneeling down, he kept praying. Jesus here comports himself as completely self-possessed and in command of the situation (unlike Mk 14:35a). Matthew had imagined Jesus as adopting the reverential Jewish attitude of prostration upon his face. Luke has Jesus adopt the Christian position of genuflection (see Acts 7:60; 9:40; 20:36; 21:5). He hints delicately at the profound emotion Jesus felt at taking leave of the disciples: *he was torn away from them*, like Paul later saying good-bye to the Ephesian Christians, whom he never expects to see again (Acts 21:1). Here Jesus retires a short distance, from where he can be seen and heard by the little group he has left: *about a stone's throw*. Luke's apostles are to be "witnesses." While Jesus' prayer is depicted as brief in its articulation, yet the evangelist's use of the imperfect—*he kept praying*—suggests that the period of prayer was a prolonged one. As remarked, the Lucan Jesus not only provides an example of how to *pray continually;* he must strive to win for his disciples the power to do so in turn.

"*Father, if you decide to take this cup away from me. . . . However, not my desire, but may yours continue to be done!*" Luke's rendering into Greek of Jesus' familiar address to God (*Abba*: Mk 14:36) was already exhibited in the formulation of the dominical prayer (Lk 11:2). Indeed, the Lucan redaction of Jesus' prayer on this occasion in the garden suggests both Jesus' intimacy with God and his awareness of his unique relationship to his Father. Thus "*if you decide*" is more personal than Mark's stilted beginning, "All things are possible for you" (Mk 14:36a), or even Matthew's "If it is possible" (Mt 36:39b). Luke makes the prayer equally conditional on God's will, but he expresses this in terms of the divine decision for Jesus.

In the second place, it should be noted that, in his reformulation of the conditional clause, Luke employs the Greek verb "to will, to decide" (*boulomai*) rather than "to desire" (*ethelein*), as did both Mark and Matthew. While it seems that the distinction in meaning between those two verbs in classical Greek was no longer felt in the popular language employed in the New Testament,[24] it is a Lucan peculiarity to use the second of the pair *only for human preference,* which may partly explain his omission of "Thy will be done" from his version of the Lord's Prayer.

In the third place, by his use of the conditional in Jesus' prayer, Luke seems to suggest that Jesus is still seeking to know for certain whether his drinking *this cup* is truly the Father's will for him. If that should turn out to be the case, then his own *desire* will yield to that of God.

In the fourth place, it will have been noted that our translation presents the first part of the prayer as breaking off unfinished (aposiopesis is the grammatical term for this). Actually the manuscript tradition attests three readings of this sentence. That supported by the majority of the better witnesses coincides with the Marcan form, "If you wish, take this cup away,"[25] but is, for that very reason, suspect as a correction for the sake of homogeneity. A weightier reason for rejecting it, however, is the implausibility of Luke's attributing the imperative "Take this cup away" to Jesus, in view of his earlier emphasis upon Jesus' resoluteness in facing his own death. "He set his face to journey up to Jerusalem" (Lk 9:51). Indeed, Luke alone presents Jesus as impatient to have his ordeal over with as quickly as possible. "I have a baptism to undergo, and what constraint am I under, until the ordeal is over!" (Lk 12:50). And the opening words of the Lucan Jesus at the Last Supper show no change in this attitude. "With a consuming desire have I longed to eat this paschal lamb with you before I suffer death" (Lk 22:15). Thus to have Jesus suddenly exclaim "Take this cup away!" is too abrupt for a stylist like our evangelist.

A second reading, attested only by Byzantine manuscripts and so dubious on that count, uses the present infinitive, "If you wish to take this cup away." At any rate, it is close to the sense of the third reading which—with some hesitation—is adopted here.[26]

The incompleteness in the expression of Jesus' intent, to which attention was already drawn, has the advantage of alluding, more subtly than did Mark, to Jesus' struggle in accepting the will of God. "If you decide to take away this cup ... [I should prefer that!]"[27] Some support for our choice may be gathered from the observation that this is not the first instance in Luke of aposiopesis. "If only you also recognized the things that make for your peace ... [I should be happy]" (Lk 19:42). The Lucan form of this saying manifests the great compassion typical of the Jesus of the Third Gospel. In the prayer under discussion, Luke's hint (through aposiopesis) of the intense quality of Jesus' experience makes plausible our earlier suggestion that in his prayer Jesus is represented as praying also for the gift of endurance and persevering prayer for the disciples.

We have now to inquire into the symbolic significance attached by Luke to *this cup*. The sayings in Mark and Matthew from which we discerned its meaning in the context of their Gospels (Mk 10:38, 45; Mt 20:23, 28), their formulation of the words over the eucharistic cup (Mk 14:24; Mt 26:28), and Jesus' prophecy that his death will cause a loss of faith and the dispersal of the disciples (Mk 14:27; Mt 26:31) are either changed in Luke or omitted altogether, in accordance with his avoidance of interpreting Jesus' death as vicarious or sacrifical. Instead, as has been seen, Luke stresses the new covenant inaugurated by Jesus' death, which he explicitly states to be the symbolism in the eucharistic cup. It was shown earlier that for Luke it is Jesus' resurrection which is the saving event, with which Jesus' death is inextricably linked. Thus it is only in the light of the resurrection that the mystery of Jesus' death can be comprehended. It is to be noted that in his version of Jesus' second prediction of his death (in which the resurrection is not mentioned), the evangelist explains the disciples' lack of understanding of what Jesus announced: "It had been hidden from them, so that they should not grasp its meaning" (Lk 9:44f.). Luke alone refers to Jesus' death and resurrection by two expressions of his own which indicate their inseparability. Jesus at his transfiguration speaks with Moses and Elijah "about his *exodus*" (Lk 9:31), which shortly thereafter is called "his assumption" (Lk 9:51).

Consequently, in the context of the Third Gospel, *this cup* in the prayer of Jesus derives its symbolism from the eucharistic cup, symbolizing in its turn Jesus' death as seen in the light of his saving resurrection. Before this last event, however, this meaning is hidden in God's plan from the disciples, and even for Jesus himself, as Luke seems to hint, this ultimately joyous sense is only shown to him as the fruit of his own prayer on the Mount of Olives. For our evangelist depicts Jesus as seeking to know for certain that his death is an integral part of his "entering into his glory" (Lk 24:26).

"Nevertheless, not my desire, but may yours continue to be done!" Luke is far too respectful of the evangelical tradition to ignore completely the memory of Jesus' struggle to accept the Father's will; consequently it is alluded to delicately in these words. It is important to recall that in this Gospel, where "Thy will be done!" was omitted from the Lord's Prayer, Jesus' acceptance of the divine will is not to be understood as an allusion (as in Mark and Matthew) to that phrase. Rather, *May yours continue to be done* looks forward to those declarations by the risen Christ that

his suffering death in his Passion is to be seen as God's will (Lk 24:26–27, 44, 46).

[*There appeared to him an angel from heaven, giving him strength. And in anguish of spirit he kept praying the more earnestly. And his sweat became like clots of blood, falling to the earth.*]

This pair of verses written by another hand than Luke's are, as has been stated, inspired; they should in consequence be taken into account, *not* to interpret Luke's insight into this moving experience of Jesus, but as an additional interpretation by some anonymous, inspired Christian writer. As such they are indeed worthy of our consideration. What new significance has this unknown commentator seen in Jesus' experience? He lays heavy stress on Jesus' anguished struggle, so dramatically portrayed by Mark; he emphasizes Jesus' perseverance under duress. I am convinced, *pace* Feuillet,[28] that *his sweat became like clots of blood* is intended as a graphic image rather than a realistic description. This writer lays heavy stress upon the humanness of Jesus. It may also be his intention to link the Passion with Jesus' temptations in the desert by inserting the appearance of the angel, since Luke himself had omitted (Lk 4:13) the detail about the ministry of angels in his narrative (see Mk 1:13; Mt 4:11). It is in this sense that Schuyler Brown observes, "Jesus was more in need of heavenly support before the resumption of Satan's offensive than after Satan's first attack had been successfully repulsed."[29] The glossator's observation that Jesus *kept praying the more earnestly* was probably inserted to encourage the Christian reader in his continual combat[30] against apostasy. Finally, this inspired author's explicit affirmation that Jesus' prayer was indeed answered by God indicates that he was in touch with a very early interpretation of the incident, noticed by Hebrews 5:7c as well as by John 12:28b.

And rising from prayer, upon returning to the disciples, he found them dead asleep from grief. The opening phrase, peculiar to Luke, is natural enough, since Jesus had been described as kneeling down to begin his prayer. There may, however, be a symbolic meaning hidden in the expression, since we find an expression used for sleep, employed nowhere else in the Gethsemane narratives, which consistently, in New Testament usage, designates death (Mt 27:52; Jn 11:11; Acts 7:60; 13:36). In Paul's letters it has only this sense. We have suggested this nuance by our rendering *dead asleep.* An intended contrast between Jesus and the disciples will be recalled in the Lucan account of the risen Jesus' meeting with the Eleven, who will be described as "doubting for joy" (Lk 24:41).

And he said to them, "Why are you sleeping?" Only in Luke does Jesus ask the reason for their sleep, an invitation by the evangelist to his reader to seek a deeper meaning in this sleep, rather than a reproach by Jesus to his disciples, who have never been told to remain awake here, as they were in the accounts by Mark and Matthew.[31] Jesus' first injunction following the question is *Rise!* Only by the power of the risen Jesus will his followers be able to throw off their lethargy and despondency in the trials they will have to face and so obtain strength to *pray continually* to avoid the *temptation* that would lead inevitably to apostasy. Warren Holleran's comment is worth citing here: "Now he has risen, and they are to rise with him to face in the constant spirit of his prayer all that lies before them."[32]

NOTES

1. Luke qualifies the attitude of Jesus' opponents as "folly" *(anoia)*, a rare term found otherwise only at 2 Tim 3:9. The evangelist's insertion of the inauguration of the conspiracy against Jesus, if less abruptly introduced than in Mk 3:6, is no less ominous: "They initiated conversations about what they could do to Jesus."

2. Luke displays throughout his book a considerable number of resonances with the Fourth Gospel, particularly in his Passion narrative.

3. Luke here uses a term found at Mt 26:43 in describing the sleep of the disciples in Gethsemane; in his own presentation of that episode he will employ a word that usually means "to be dead" (Lk 22:45).

4. Where in Mt 4:1 it is said that "Jesus was led into the desert by the Spirit to be tempted by the devil," Luke avoids attributing the temptations to the Spirit. He notes simply that Jesus' experience coincided with the period when "he was being led about in the desert by the Spirit" (Lk 4:1–2). See Schuyler Brown, S.J., *Apostasy and Persever-*

ance in the Theology of Luke (Rome, 1969), p. 18: "The temptation does not have the Spirit as its cause or occasion, but is undertaken by the devil on his own initiative and without divine authorization."

5. Despite the fact that John is the only human being unequivocally praised by Jesus, the latter is not influenced by the Baptist in his public ministry. Instead of retiring to the desert, Jesus works in town and villages; he does not take over the apocalyptic style of John's menacing proclamation of the coming divine judgment, and his sociability stands in marked contrast with John's asceticism.

6. R. A. F. MacKenzie, S.J., "The Meaning of the Susanna Story," *Canadian Journal of Theology* 3 (1957), 211–218.

7. Mario Galizzi, *Gesù nel Getsemani* (Rome, 1972), pp. 185–189.

8. In his *Apostasy and Perseverance* already cited, Schuyler Brown criticizes the view expressed by Conzelmann in his *Theology of St. Luke* (New York, 1961); see Brown, pp. 16f.

9. *Ibid.,* p. 7.

10. Augustin George, S.M., "Le sens de la mort de Jésus pour Luc," *Revue Biblique* 80 (1973), 186–217.

11. *The Greek New Testament,* edited by Kurt Aland, Matthew Black, Bruce M. Metzger, Allen Wikgren (Württemberg, 1966).

12. Alexandria, a center of learning from pre-Christian times, was celebrated for textual criticism of classical texts. Many important witnesses to the New Testament are connected with Alexandria, codices Sinaiticus, Vaticanus among them together with papyri.—The Freer codex, now in Washington, D.C., represents by contrast the Caesarean recension.

13. Joseph A. Fitzmyer, S.J., "Papyrus Bodmer: Some Features of Our Oldest Text of Luke," *Catholic Biblical Quarterly* 24 (1962), 170–179.

14. See Denzinger-Bannwart, *Enchiridion Symbolorum,* 28th edition (Freiburg/Barcelona, 1952), #784.

15. Pierre Benoit, O.P., "Le récit de la Cène dans Lc. XII, 15–20," *Revue Biblique* 48 (1939), 357–393.

16. Kurt Aland, *The Greek New Testament,* encloses the disputed verses in his Greek text within doubled square brackets to indicate "passages which are regarded as later additions to the text, but which are of evident antiquity and importance": p. xli.

17. Schuyler Brown, *Apostasy and Perseverance,* p. 70.

18. *Ibid.,* p. 66, n. 266; J. Warren Holleran, *The Synoptic Gethsemane,* pp. 170–198.

19. Mario Galizzi, *Gesù nel Getsemani,* pp. 137f.

20. Schuyler Brown, *Apostasy and Perseverance,* p. 9. See Acts 20:19,

where Paul speaks of the "trials that happened to me from the cabals of the Jews."

21. *Ibid.*, p. 15, n. 46.

22. *Ibid.*, pp. 9ff.

23. *Ibid.*, p. 10.

24. In the classical language *boulomai* denoted the reflective act of will, while *ethelein* stood for the will of spontaneity, that is, "decide, decree" as against "desire."

25. This reading is adopted by Kurt Aland, *The Greek New Testament*, as well as by Holleran, Galizzi, and Feuillet, as it is attested by P[75], Vaticanus, D and many others.

26. The reading of Alexandrinus, Freer codex, etc.

27. This reading has strong witnesses for it, including Sinaiticus. On aposiopesis, see Robert W. Funk, *A Greek Grammar of the New Testament* (Chicago, 1961), #482.

28. André Feuillet, *L'Agonie de Gethsémani*, pp. 146–149.

29. Schuyler Brown, *Apostasy and Perseverance*, p. 8.

30. The Lucan *agōnia* means a desperate struggle and should seemingly not be taken to mean Jesus' death-agony; see Victor C. Pfitzner, *Paul and the Agōn Motif: Traditional Athletic Imagery in the Pauline Literature* (Leiden, 1967).

31. Schuyler Brown, *Apostasy and Perseverance*, p. 67.

32. J. Warren Holleran, *The Synoptic Gethsemane*, p. 217.

VII
INNOVATIVE REDACTION BY THE FOURTH EVANGELIST
(Jn 12:20–32; 17:1–26)

To open the Fourth Gospel, after reading any of the other three, is to enter a world at once strange and familiar. One is conscious of reading the same genre of literature, a book in which Jesus is the central figure, involved in the same activities of gathering disciples about him, teaching and healing, and engaging in controversy with adversaries, both in Galilee and in Jerusalem. The story of his public career is here crowned with a Passion narrative, closer actually to those of the Synoptics in many respects than the singular account of his prophetic ministry. Yet the reader cannot fail to be struck by the divergence from the traditional reporting of Jesus' "words and works" which is the hallmark of this Gospel. The narrative sections in the first twelve chapters contain, in common with the Synoptics, some notice about the ministry of John the Baptist (Jn 1:19–35; 3:23–30). In addition there are further brief references to John (Jn 4:1; 5:33, 36; 10:40–41). John reports also Jesus' symbolic and prophetic action in cleansing the temple-area (Jn 2:13–22) and his miraculous feeding of the great crowd in an isolated locale, followed by his walk upon the lake (Jn 6:1–21). Moreover, there are three miracle-stories which may well be taken over by this evangelist from the tradition behind the Synoptics: the cure of the Jewish official's son at Cana (Jn 4:43–54; see Lk 7:1–10), the restoration of the cripple by the pool of Bethesda (Jn 5:1–9; see Mk 2:1–12), and the giving of sight to a man born blind (Jn 9:1–12), all of which may have been created out of similar episodes in the earlier Gospels.

It is, however, in the great Johannine discourses delivered by Jesus that the most striking contrast with the Synoptic Gospels is evident. Mark has indeed given three impressive instructions by Jesus (the so-called parable sermon: Mk 4:1–34; the exposition of Jesus' ethical teaching: Mk 7:1–23; and the eschatological discourse: Mk 13). Matthew's presentation of the public ministry is articulated by means of five great discourses concerning the various stages in the realization in history of "the kingdom of heaven." Yet in these speeches the Galilean agrarian background and historical circumstances of Jesus' human experiences and his culture are exhibited in a most plausible manner, even while his unprecedented pedagogical skill and commitment to his message and mission from God make him pre-eminent among his own contemporaries. The Johannine Jesus is depicted as a learned, erudite rabbi, skilled in the dialectic of the schools, who through the use of symbols and abstruse concepts ("the truth," "the light," "the darkness") propounds an esoteric, highly mysterious set of doctrines.

The Innovative Redactional Activity of John

What has been said about the dissimilarities between the Fourth Gospel and the three which preceded it, particularly from the viewpoint of content, would appear to indicate that its author had access to another apostolic source than that behind the Synoptic Gospels. This writer, to whom the name John was attributed in the second century of the Christian era, is unknown. His Gospel, at least in the form in which the Church received it, was produced about the middle of the last decade of the first century. His interest in Jesus' ministry in Jerusalem is a feature marking off his book from those of his predecessors.

However, the two features of this evangelist's insight into the meaning of Jesus' earthly history, which have presided over his redaction of the apostolic traditions he received, are, first, his interpretation of Jesus' mission in terms of *revelation*,[1] and, second, his profound conviction of the *transcendence* of Jesus as the divine Son and the *universality* of his message and its appeal.[2]

The first of these conceptions represents a departure from the traditional view of Jesus' work as "redemption" in the Pauline letters (1 Cor 1:30; Rom 3:24; Col 1:14). The Gospels of Mark and Matthew present the same early Christian interpretation with their emphasis upon Jesus' role as the Suffering Servant of God, who "gives his life as ransom for the rest of men" (Mk 10:45; Mt 20:28). Luke may be said to stand midway between this presentation and that of John. As has been seen in the last chapter, that evangelist highlights the saving character of Jesus' resurrection, to which his death is joined in an inseparable unity.

From the end of the Prologue, the fourth evangelist presents the mission of Jesus, the Word of God become man, as "our interpreter of the God no man has ever seen" (Jn 1:18). The Son of God, by living a human life in the world below, has revealed his Father by what he does as well as by what he says. Yet it will only be upon Calvary, as he dies, that Jesus will be manifested as the bearer of the Spirit and by this self-revelation finally succeed in what he had been sent to accomplish.

In our earlier presentation of the Johannine conception of faith we had occasion to discuss some features of the originality of the Fourth Gospel, and we beg the reader's indulgence if we repeat some of its features again briefly. John has placed the spotlight squarely upon Jesus by giving to the received traditions a consistently Christological slant. The Jesus of the Synoptics has been seen to proclaim the imminent coming of the kingdom of God, saying little or nothing about himself. The Johannine Jesus, who only mentions "the kingdom of God" on a single occasion (Jn 3:3, 5), speaks constantly of himself through symbolic utterances and profound discourses. He descends into this world "from above" (Jn 3:13, 21), not to establish God's kingdom here below, but rather, by his return home to the Father, to lead men into that "mansion" of the Father, which remains in heaven (Jn 14:2). During his brief stay in this world,

Jesus, by what he does and what he says, attempts to make his invisible Father desirable, credible, and lovable.

One senses the shift in the notion of God's kingdom by the terms used in the Fourth Gospel to designate Jesus' miracles. Mark had explained these "acts of (divine) power" as Jesus' initial attack on Satan's domination of humanity through disease, deformity, disability, and death—part of his mission in establishing the kingdom of God on earth (Mk 3:27). John calls the miracles of Jesus "signs" (Jn 2:11) pointing to the mystery of his person. For his part, Jesus prefers to speak of them as "works." The reason for this twofold designation, as I have elsewhere pointed out,[3] lies with John's concern about revelation. In their historical facticity, Jesus' miracles are symbols or "signs" of an invisible reality; as "works" they belong to the same category as the ancient, saving acts of the God of Israel, imperiously demanding faith (Jn 10:38; 14:11).

We also alluded earlier to John's insistence on Jesus' failure in his public ministry to disclose his identity to "the world"— the *leitmotiv* of the centerpiece of The Book of Signs (Jn 7:1— 10:39)[4] We also mentioned the theme of "the poverty of the Son"[5] in which all Jesus does, says and *is* comes to him as gift from the Father. In consequence, to see Jesus with faith as "the Son" (Jn 6:40) means to see the Father (Jn 14:9). Why does our evangelist accentuate these two aspects of Jesus and his ministry?

George MacRae explains Jesus' failure: "In view of the movement of the Gospel itself, from the apparent failure of the public ministry of sign and symbolic discourse to the revelation of love in word and actions in 'The Book of Glory,' we must conclude that the Evangelist is actually asserting the transcendence of Jesus over any of the human symbols themselves."[6] It is also evident that the truth that it is God himself who speaks and acts in Jesus explains why he cannot adequately be categorized in any human statement or symbol. This concern to underscore the transcendence of Jesus comes to its fullest expression in The Book of Glory, where the revelation brought by Jesus is depicted as a revelation of divine love.

The Passion: Revelation of God's Love

"The most striking differentiation of the two 'books' [The Book of Signs and The Book of Glory] is that the language of sign and symbol so familiar in the first is virtually abandoned in the second.... What takes the place of the 'figures' is the extraordinary emphasis on love...."[7] This observation by George MacRae indicates that for John the chief hermeneutical principle in his interpretation of Jesus' Passion is love. The author of the first Johannine epistle had already made that clear. "Dearly beloved, we must love one another, since love has its source in God; hence the person who experiences love has been born from God and knows God, while the one who does not experience love does not know God. Now God is love. In this God's love for us has been revealed, that God has sent his only Son into the world, in order that we might have life through him. Such love consists, not in our having loved God, but in his having loved us himself and having sent his Son as an atoning sacrifice for our sins" (1 Jn 4:7–10). The appositeness of this insight into the meaning of the Passion is even clearer if one accepts the view that this epistle was written to defend the orthodoxy of the Fourth Gospel. "Of itself the Fourth Gospel needs to be counterbalanced in the life of Christianity by the rest of the New Testament. So, it seems, thought the member of the Johannine school who wrote the First Epistle of John; for this work—if indeed we are correct in dating it after the Gospel—is best understood as a defense of the Johannine Gospel in the light of a more broadly acceptable early Christian theology. It may be called an attempt to rescue John from the hands of the heretics for the Church at large."[8]

We pointed out earlier in speaking of Johannine faith how for this writer genuine Christian faith must be founded firmly upon the *word of Jesus,* and how in The Book of Glory this word appears as "the new commandment": "You must love one another by virtue of the fact I have loved you" (Jn 13:34; 15:12, 17). We also took cognizance of the innovative character of John's treatment of the theme: its stress on the giving and receiving of love within the Church, and its apparent silence concerning love for God, for Jesus, for enemies. Such reticence is also observable in the late notice, in this Gospel, given regarding Jesus' love for his disciples (Jn 13:1b).[9] Moreover, it is only in this final portion of his Gospel that the evangelist introduces the mysterious figure, "the disciple whom Jesus loved" (Jn 13:23; 19:26; 20:2; 21:7, 20). Finally, only here do we read about the disciples' love for Jesus (Jn 14:15, 21, 23, 28).

Most remarkable by far is John's reticence in speaking, or having Jesus speak, of his love for the Father (Jn 14:31). Jesus' love for his Father is here shown to consist more in deeds than in words (Jn 10:17), as was the Father's love for Jesus as the Son (Jn 3:35; 5:20). This paradigm of a true "community of love" is what is to motivate the believer's obedience to "the new commandment," which in turn is the necessary prelude to the Christian experience of the *mutual abiding* in Jesus and in the Father. "The person who loves me will be loved by my Father, and I in my turn will love him and I will manifest myself to him" (Jn 14:21b). "If a person loves me, he will keep my word, and my Father will love him; and we will come to him, and we will make our abiding with him" (v. 23).

It is in the discourse after the Last Supper that "abiding" expresses increasingly the reality of interiority. Earlier it exhibited a spatial sense: the abiding of the first disciples with Jesus (Jn 1:39–40) and of Jesus with the Samaritans (Jn 4:40), but only rarely *communion* (Jn 8:3; 12:46). In The Book of Glory it denotes the dynamic relationship of Jesus to the Father: "It is the Father abiding in me who is performing his works. Believe me: I am in the Father and the Father is in me" (Jn 10:10c–11a).

It is with the first reference to "the Paraclete" that this "abiding" becomes more personal and interior for the believer. "And I will ask the Father and he will give you another Paraclete to be with you forever, the Spirit of truth. . . . You know him, because he abides among you and is in you" (Jn 14:16–17). In the sequel the parable or symbol of the vine is employed to illustrate the dynamic and vital quality of the personal communion of the risen Jesus and his disciples (Jn 15:1–8), the result of

Jesus' love for them and a created counterpart of Jesus' abiding with the Father.

This rich and highly original development on God's love and that of Jesus is intended as the evangelist's commentary on the Passion narrative which follows. It is also of paramount importance for a proper estimate of John's insight into Christian prayer as communion with Jesus and the Father.

Prayer "In My Name"

Strictly speaking, until he reaches the narrative of the Last Supper, John rarely represents Jesus as praying: there is a brief prayer of thanksgiving before Lazarus' tomb (Jn 11:41–42) and another short petition in the final episode of Jesus' public ministry (Jn 12:27ff.). That prayer, together with "the great prayer" of Jesus (Jn 17:1–26), we shall presently analyze. What is quite extraordinary, given the traditions enshrined in the Synoptic Gospels, is that nowhere in the Johannine Passion narrative, from Jesus' arrest in the garden up to and inclusive of his death, is he ever described as uttering any prayer to God. One has the distinct impression that for our evangelist genuine prayer is a reality too deep for words. As for the mystery of Jesus' own communion with the Father, John dares not intrude upon that sacred domain. He designates it with a word that may suggest the ineffable familiarity of Jesus' relationship to the Father, "ask" (*erotan*), while employing another term, "request, beseech" (*aitein*, once *aiteisthai*), for the prayer of the disciples. Nor is the expression "prayer in my name" altogether original with John. Paul prays for his Thessalonians that "the name of our Lord Jesus may be glorified in you, and you in him, according to the graciousness of our God and of Lord Jesus Christ" (2 Thes 1:12). He comes closer to Johannine phraseology in two passages concerned with Christian public worship. "May the word of Christ dwell among you in all its riches as you teach and admonish one another by songs, hymns, and spiritual canticles, singing gratefully to God in your hearts. And whatever you do by word or action [in the liturgy], [do it] all in the name of the Lord Jesus, giving thanks to God the Father through him" (Col 3:16–18). A parallel in Ephesians runs in a similar vein: "Do not get drunk on wine—that is simply dissoluteness! Rather be filled with the Spirit as you speak to one another by songs, hymns, and spiritual canticles. Sing and make music in your hearts to the Lord, giving thanks always for everything in the name of our Lord Jesus Christ to God, who is also Father" (Eph 5:18–20). An analogous expression is used by Matthew in a reference to the public prayer of the community: "Where two or three are gathered together into my name, I am there in their presence" (Mt 18:20).

The fourth evangelist presents the fundamentally identical saying of Jesus in four passages, with certain variations, the significance of which must be determined by the context into which he has set them.

(1) "And whatever you ask in my name I will do it, in order that the Father may be glorified in the Son; if you ask me anything in my name I will do it" (Jn 14:13–14).[10] The departure of Judas gave the signal for Jesus' announcement of his departure (Jn 13:31). He now explains that he goes to prepare a place for the disciples in the Father's house where "there are many abidings" (vv. 2–3). The resultant fear and grief of the disciples must be controlled by an obedient response to Jesus' call for faith in himself: "You believe in God; believe also in me" (v. 1). Their faith in the God of Israel is henceforth to be specified by their putting the same faith in Jesus (v. 1), and this means concretely a recognition that "I am in the Father and the Father is in me. The words I am uttering to you, I do not utter on my own; it is the Father abiding in me who is doing his works" (v. 10). Hence, to see Jesus himself with real faith is to see his Father (v. 9). For a moment, until Jesus' return to God, the disciples really do not have the full awareness imparted by faith enabling them to see that what Jesus says, does, *is*, is the dynamic presence in him of the Father. When they do attain the perfection of faith, the Father will perform "greater works" in them than those Jesus has done in his earthly life (v. 12). Of these "works," the single example given is the gift of prayer "in my name," a prayer of communion with Jesus and the Father through faith.

(2) John again presents his view of the prayer characteristic of the Christian. This time, it is in the context of the parable-allegory of the vine that illustrates the absolute necessity of the mutual abiding of Jesus and the believer (Jn 15:1–5), since "without me you can do nothing!" Here Jesus remarks, "If you remain in me and my words remain in you, ask whatever you desire, and it will be done for you" (v. 7). The passive indicates God as the agent here. The promise is not qualified in any way, nor is it necessary to add "in my name," since the intimate communion between Jesus and the disciple is presupposed as an essential condition.

(3) The evangelist later represents Jesus as returning to the theme of love to clarify yet once more the meaning of Christian love in which his disciples must continue to abide (Jn 15:9). As with all he does and is, Jesus' love for them springs from the Father's love for himself. To discern whether one's love of Jesus is genuine and not mere sentimentality, the keeping of his commands is imperative (v. 10). This means in effect obedience to the single command of Jesus: love for the community, made possible by his laying down his life for his dearly loved friends (vv. 12–13). This love evinced by Jesus depends upon no quality of lovableness in his disciples; it is totally free because it is creative. Jesus shows his love by communicating to his beloved followers "all I have heard from my Father" (v. 15). Hence it is undeniably clear that their following of Jesus is totally his doing.

"You have not chosen me; it is I myself who have chosen you, and I have determined that you should go and bear a rich harvest, and that your harvest should abide, so that whatever you ask the Father in my name, he will give you" (Jn 15:16). The evangelist now points the direction in which prayer in Jesus' name is intended to develop by his insistence, as has been seen, upon acquiring *the love of friendship* for Jesus. The two previous texts examined could well be interpreted merely in terms of the love of enlightened self-interest. That is to say, the believer may legitimately have recourse in prayer to Jesus with full confidence that he will do "whatever you ask" (Jn 14:13f.). One may turn to God with the same trust "in my name" to obtain whatever is good for oneself (Jn 15:7). This third statement is con-

cerned thus with progress in prayer: through prayer the
believer is led to love Jesus for himself, to enter into a profoundly personal relationship with Jesus, with the result that one no
longer regards him as "useful." Instead the Christian, as he ad-
vances in prayer, turns to God as "the Father" with petitions in
Jesus' name.

The foundation for such filial assurance rests solidly upon
Jesus' untrammeled choice of the believer, a choice inspired
solely by Jesus' love of friendship. It is of paramount importance to interpret the words of Jesus correctly here: "I have determined that you should go and bear a rich harvest." Rudolf
Bultmann, in my view, is correct in noting that the expression
"You go and bear" is a Semitic turn of phrase, equal to "You
bear."[11] Thus in all probability there is no express concern here
for the future apostolic mission of the disciples. Rather, in the
light of the illustration provided by the vine ("I am the vine, you
are the branches; the person abiding in me, even as I abide in
him, bears a rich harvest, because without me you can do nothing"—v. 5), what is meant by our text is the ever deepening relationship of love with Jesus. And one subordinated consequence
of this communion is the infallibility of prayer in Jesus' name.
Because the Christian makes his request to the Father out of his
lived love for Jesus, which involves the love of one's brothers,
the efficaciousness of his prayer is guaranteed by the God who
is, as Paul repeatedly asserts, at once "our Father and the Father
of our Lord Jesus Christ."

(4) The final description by John of Christian prayer, presented as it is, in view of Jesus' final glorification, provides the
most complete characterization of Christian prayer in Jesus'
name. "And on that day, you will no longer ask me any more
questions. Amen, amen I tell you: whatever you will ask the Father in my name, he will give it to you. Up to the present you
have asked nothing in my name; keep asking and you will receive, in order that your joy may find its fulfillment.... On
that day you will ask in my name. And I do not tell you I shall
ask the Father on your behalf; for the Father himself loves you,
because you have loved me and have believed I came forth from
God" (Jn 16:23–27).

The evangelist pictures Jesus as looking forward to "that day" already mentioned (Jn 14:20) as the era of full Christian realization of the truth "that I am in my Father and you are in me, even as I am in you." The source of this newly-awakened Christian consciousness was indicated in that section as "the Paraclete, the Holy Spirit whom the Father will send in my name" (Jn 14:26). Consequently, John appears to remind his reader, by the repetition of "that day," of the role of the Spirit in prayer. The Spirit is designated "another Paraclete" (Jn 14:16), for he is conceived by our evangelist as taking the place of the glorified Jesus on his return to the Father. His role in Christian life has been carefully explained in this sixteenth chapter as initiating the disciples into the meaning of the mysteries of Jesus' earthly history. "When he comes, the Spirit of truth, he will guide you by the full truth. For he will not speak on his own, but will speak of what he hears, and will unveil the future to you. He will glorify me, because he will take what is mine and unveil it to you" (vv. 12–14).

For our evangelist, then, the perfection of Christian prayer is attained through the contemplation of Jesus' earthly history ("what is mine") as "unveiled" by the Spirit, thus providing the fullness of revelation concerning Jesus' words and actions, and, through him, the revelation of God. For the enlightened believer, "on that day" the need for questioning Jesus is past, since, through the Spirit's presence, "an hour is coming when I shall no longer speak to you in riddles, but I shall announce to you in plain words about the Father" (v. 25).

Because they have not received the Spirit as yet, the disciples do not comprehend this prayer in Jesus' name, and so their "joy" has not yet been "fulfilled." The fundamental reason for this is given only in the final verse: they have not realized the deeply affectionate love (*philei*) God as Father entertains for them. Once they arrive at this summit of Christian contemplation, it will be unnecessary for Jesus to "ask the Father" for them. Conscious of their true identity as "sons in the Son," the disciples will be so wholly one with the glorified Jesus that their requests become his. Raymond Brown explains the apparent difficulty with v. 26 "in seeming to exclude intercession on Jesus' part." He states: "Jesus' role in bringing men to the Father and the Father to men (xiv 6–11) will set up so intimate a relationship of love *in and through Jesus* that Jesus cannot be considered as intervening . . . for the Christians' prayer will be Jesus' prayer."[12]

From our consideration of these verses, it has become evident that by asking in Jesus' name the evangelist wishes the reader to understand the *prayer of union*, at once personal and intimate, which springs from genuine faith in Jesus and from the experience of love, given and received, within the believing community. Here, as frequently in the New Testament, the name is synonymous with the person; thus, it is prayer arising from the Christian's communion with the Person of Jesus and, in addition, prayer that proceeds from an intense consciousness of that personal union.

The Closing Scene of Jesus' Ministry (Jn 12:20–36)

Mention was made earlier, in the discussion of John's concept of faith, of the clearly marked division between The Book of Signs and The Book of Glory. I have elsewhere pointed out the significance of the caesura between the two main sections of the Fourth Gospel for the later trinitarian doctrine of the Church.[13] Here it is sufficient for our purpose to remark that it is used to realign certain episodes which belong to the Synoptic Passion narratives, thus placing them in the closing days of Jesus' public ministry, while the Johannine Passion narrative proper begins with the account of Jesus' arrest (Jn 18:1–11). This imaginative use of the Marcan caesura, I suggest, indicates John's acquaintance with at least that other Gospel.[14] The episodes thus retrojected back into The Book of Signs are: the plot of the religious authorities (Jn 11:45–53), and the anointing at Bethany (Jn 12:1–7), which also hints at Judas' dishonesty (vv. 4–6) as the motive for his future treachery. Then follows Jesus' solemn entry into Jerusalem "on the next day" (Jn 12:12–19). The interpretation given to it, as George MacRae has remarked,[15] is "that the crowd acknowledges Jesus as Messiah, 'King of Israel' (see

1:49)." This motif, in fact, of Jesus' kingship is the dominant theme presiding over his account of the Passion.

Raymond Brown has shown that John's presentation of Jesus' entry into the holy city implies the *universalism* of his kingship of Israel.[16] The citation from Zech 9:9 will be found to continue with the promise: "He shall proclaim peace to the nations; his dominion shall be from sea to sea, and from the River to the ends of the earth" (v. 10). The evangelist portrays Jesus' actions as a symbolic prophecy of his future universal kingship. The comment of the Pharisees, ironically, is truer than they realize, "The whole world has run after him!" (Jn 12:19b). We shall presently have occasion to observe how the Johannine redaction of the third prophecy of the Passion by Jesus underscores this universal kingship of the Crucified, "I will draw all people to myself" (Jn 12:32).

20 Now there were some Greeks among those who had come on pilgrimage to worship at the feast. 21 So these men approached Philip (the man from Bethsaida in Galilee), and kept making this request, "Sir, we desire to see Jesus." 22 Philip comes and tells Andrew. Andrew and Philip come and tell Jesus. 23 But Jesus in reply says to them,
    "The hour has come
for the Son of Man to be glorified!
24 Amen, amen I tell you:
unless a grain of wheat dies when it is sown in the earth,
it remains by itself in isolation;
but if it dies,
it produces a rich harvest.
25 The person who loves his life destroys it;
the person who hates his life in this world
will guard it for eternal life.
26 If anyone serves me, he must follow me;
and where I am there also will my servant be:
if anyone serves me, the Father will honor him.
27 Now my heart is deeply troubled,

and [I do not know] what I am to say!
Father, save me through this hour!
Yes, for this reason have I come to this hour.
28 Father, glorify your Name!"
Thereupon a voice came out of the sky,
"I have glorified it, and I will glorify it again."

29 Accordingly, the crowd standing round, on hearing it, kept saying it had thundered; others kept saying, "An angel has spoken to him!" 30 And Jesus said in reply, "Not on my account did the voice occur, but on your account.—

31 Now is the judgment of this world.
Now will the prince of this world be driven out!
32 Yet as for me, when I am lifted up from earth,
I will draw all people to myself!"

33 This he said to indicate what sort of death he was destined to die.

34 So the crowd countered with this answer to him, "We have heard from the Law that the Messiah abides forever; so how can you state that it is God's will that the Son of Man be lifted up? Who is this 'Son of Man'?" 35 And so Jesus said to them,

"Yet but a little while the Light is among you:
walk while you have the Light,
lest the darkness overtake you—
the person walking in the dark
does not know where he is going.
36 While you have the Light,
keep believing in the Light,
in order that you may become sons of light!"

Jesus finished this speech, and he went off and hid himself from them.

While, as Raymond Brown remarks, "there is nothing intrinsically improbable in the basic incident,"[17] yet it seems more plausible to regard the scene as a creation of our evangelist

out of several sayings and events preserved in the Jesus-tradition. Father Brown appears to be of the opinion that the reactions and prayers of Jesus (vv. 27–28) should not be regarded as
"a dismembered form of the Synoptic agony scene. . . . The Johannine picture, where such prayers and sayings are scattered,
may actually be closer to the original situation than the more organized Synoptic scene."[18] One hesitates indeed to differ with
the distinguished American scholar; however, I venture to suggest that, given our evangelist's creativity and his penchant for
reallocating certain narratives (acknowledged elsewhere by Father Brown),[19] it appears more consistent to regard this brief account of Jesus' reaction to his "hour" as a reworking of the
Gethsemane traditions.[20] We shall not comment in detail upon
the entire passage, but mainly on the verses relevant to our
theme (vv. 27–32), contenting ourselves with a more summary
explanation of the opening and closing sections of this powerful
conclusion to the narrative of Jesus' public life.

The passage may be said to consist of an introduction (vv.
20–22) and Jesus' initial discourse in the light of the arrival of his
hour (vv. 23–26). There follows somewhat abruptly a terse narrative of Jesus' struggle, prayer and the divine response (vv. 27–
32). The sequel to this central incident consists of an objection
by the crowd (v. 34) and Jesus' final admonition (vv. 35–36).

The episode is linked with John's account of Jesus' modest
entry into Jerusalem by the despairing remark of the Pharisees,
already cited, "Look! the whole world has run after him" (v.
19b), alerting the reader to the presence of "some Greeks," that
is, pagans well disposed to Judaism, possibly already proselytes,
who have come as pilgrims for Passover. "On the level of the
Gospel—as opposed to that of the history of Jesus—the evangelist is inserting Gentiles, who in his time make up the bulk of
the Christian communities, into the Gospel at the crucial moment when 'the hour has come.'"[21] They present their request
to Philip, who will be told shortly by Jesus, "Philip, the person
who has seen me has seen the Father!" (Jn 14:9). Hence it is not
implausible that the evangelist regards the overture to this disciple on the part of these pagans ("Sir, we desire to see Jesus") as a
longing for Christian faith by the Gentiles. This is the only role

played by these men, who seem to disappear from the scene, as do Philip and Andrew once they have informed Jesus of the petition.

Jesus' articulated reaction is significant for the rest of the episode: "The hour has come for the Son of Man to be glorified!" In the Fourth Gospel "the hour" has a Christological, not merely chronological content, embracing Jesus' Passion and exaltation (in Johannine terminology his "lifting-up"), and also his gift of the Spirit. It is of the utmost importance to note that this announcement, "The hour *has come*," formed the conclusion of the Marcan and Matthean narrative of Jesus' prayer and struggle (Mk 14:41b; Mt 26:45b). By contrast, John has set it at the head of his account of Jesus' experience on this occasion. Henceforth Jesus stands within his hour, from which there can be no question of escape. To be noted also is Jesus' reference to "the Son of Man," a title frequently employed in the Synoptic Gospels, but which has a distinctive meaning for John. Rudolf Schnackenburg is correct in judging that "along with the traditional background of the Son of Man logia in John, there are certain traits which go to make up their special characteristics in John, above all, the dominant thought of the descent and ascent of the Son of Man, and of his exaltation and glorification which are connected with it."[22]

In the light of all this, it is clear that the present moment is the turning point for John in Jesus' entire career, as it is the moment when he begins his return home to God after completing his descent among men in this world. Several times in the Book of Signs the evangelist drew attention to the fact that the hour has not yet arrived (Jn 2:4; 7:6, 8, 30; 8:20). Henceforth the reader will be reminded that Jesus' hour has come (Jn 13:1; 17:1; see 13:31).

The Johannine Jesus through a very brief parable—a parable of *growth*, distinctive of the historical Jesus[23]—describes his saving death as a necessity personal to himself. "Unless a grain of wheat dies when it is sown in the earth, it remains by itself in isolation; but if it dies, it produces a rich harvest" (v. 24). Raymond Brown points out that there is no parable in the Synoptic Gospels that is quite equivalent to this. He does make the interesting observation that a parallel can be found in the Pauline discussion of the future glorious resurrection (1 Cor 15:35ff.), "where Paul speaks of the seed that does not come to life unless it is sown."[24] The Johannine *mashal* aptly illustrates this evangelist's particular view of Jesus' death as the source of life for all who believe (Jn 19:30), inasmuch as it is the source of the Spirit.

While the first fruits of the "rich harvest" springing from Jesus' death are his own glorification that readies his "flesh" to become the transmitter of the "life-giving Spirit" (see Jn 7:39), the thought immediately turns to Jesus' disciples who are to express this dialectic of the paschal mystery in any genuine living of the Gospel. Reminiscent of similar sayings in the Synoptics (Mk 8:35; Mt 10:39; Lk 17:33), the Johannine formulation is distinctive, with its contrast between love and hate, and its use of "guard" for "save." "The person who loves his life destroys it; the person who hates his life in this world will guard it for eternal life" (v. 25). In this Gospel only God and Jesus can "save," an activity beyond mere human nature. Also in this Gospel "life" consistently means "eternal life"; accordingly here the evangelist distinguishes this true "life" from "life in this world."

The following and final saying in the series (v. 26) speaks of "serving" Jesus, a quite unusual way of speaking in the Gospels. At the Last Supper the Lucan Jesus reminds his status-conscious disciples, "I am in your presence as the one who serves" (Lk 22:27b). The Johannine Jesus makes a different point: to serve Jesus means to follow him through a personal experience of the paschal mystery in one's own living and dying. The disciple is to remember however that in this experience he is *with* Jesus and not alone, and being with Jesus ultimately means honor from the Father. "If anyone serves me, he must follow me; and where I am there also will my servant be. If anyone serves me my Father will honor him." In short, the genuinity of Christian existence is to be gauged by the degree to which each believer has submitted, like Jesus himself, to the Father's will for him that he be assimilated to Jesus' earthly history, particularly through death and resurrection. Thus he will ultimately come to share in the "honor" the Father has done Jesus in making his "flesh" the bearer of the Spirit.

Now my heart is deeply troubled, and [I do not know] *what I am to say!* By the word *Now* (which will be repeated twice in this passage [v. 31]), the evangelist reminds the reader of Jesus' statement (v. 23), "The hour has come!" There it was implied that the coming of the Gentiles to seek faith in Jesus heralds the preaching of the Gospel in the apostolic era, but it also presages the tragedy of the rejection of that Gospel by Jesus' own people. The grief over this refusal by Israel to accept Jesus would later be voiced by Paul in a moving passage in his letters (Rom 9:1–5). John employs this *now* meaningfully throughout his Gospel. "But an hour is coming—and it is now—when the true worshipers will worship the Father in Spirit and truth" (Jn 4:23); "Amen, amen I tell you: an hour is coming—and it is now—when the dead will hear the voice of the Son of God. . . . " (Jn 5:25). This *now* echoes through the discourse after the last meal of Jesus with his own: "Now is the Son of Man glorified" (Jn 13:31). Jesus says to Peter, "Where I am going you cannot now follow me, but you will follow afterward" (Jn 13:36). "Now I am going home to the One who sent me. . . . " (Jn 16:5). "Look, now you are speaking with clarity and do not use any riddles. . . . " (Jn 16:29). As in our present passage, the *now* can designate the dark side of Jesus' death: "Accordingly you also have grief now. . . . " (Jn 16:22).

When he was confronted with his enemy death in the presence of the bereaved sisters, Martha and Mary, and their grieving friends, Jesus (the evangelist observed) "shuddered to the depths of his soul and was deeply troubled" (Jn 11:33). For his reserved description now of Jesus' struggle in the face of his hour, John borrows an expression of the psalmist, "My soul is deeply troubled within me" (Ps 41:7 LXX), the source of the Matthean and Marcan phrase "sorrowful unto death." As the crowd at Bethany observed Jesus' distressing reactions and later were privileged to witness his prayer before the tomb (Jn 11:35f., 44f.), so also in this moving episode the crowd, apparently forgotten for the moment, are seemingly witnesses of Jesus' struggle and prayer, like the disciples in the Synoptic Gethsemane.

[I do not know] *what I am to say!* The Johannine Jesus hesi-

tates, as he betakes himself to prayer, about the tenor of his petition to the Father. When he articulates his prayer, however, it is
a *real* prayer, *not* a hypothetical one—as it is made to appear in
modern translations: "Father, save me from this hour?" Some
commentators, in fact, have asserted that this, in John's view, is
not a real prayer at all. The interpretation by the French Jesuit
scholar, Xavier Léon-Dufour, appears to be preferable: what follows this hesitation is a genuine prayer by Jesus, begging the Father with filial confidence to bring him through his hour to
salvation.[25]

Father, save me through this hour! Jesus has already signified
his awareness of the arrival of the hour; thus it is impossible that
he should refuse to accept it, especially as in this Gospel, his Passion and death are his "glory," the divinely appointed means of
revealing his own true identity. That identity is concealed even
from his most intimate friends as late as the Last Supper: Peter
(Jn 13:37), Thomas (Jn 14:5), Philip (Jn 14:8), Jude (Jn 14:22).
Through this hour is literally in the Greek "out of this hour" (*ek tēs
horas tautes*). B. F. Westcott translates, "Bring me safely out of
the conflict," because of a similar expression used by another
writer of the Johannine school.[26] In the Book of Revelation we
read, "Because you have preserved the word of my endurance, I
in turn will preserve you *through the hour (ek tēs horas)* of testing"
Rev 3:10). Moreover, it should be noted that "salvation" for John
has a positive content—it means "eternal life." Nowhere in this
Gospel is there any mention of what mankind is "saved" *from.*
Indeed, in all our Gospels Matthew 1:21 is unique in speaking of
"saving from their sins."

Consequently, it seems more plausible to understand that
Jesus is represented here as petitioning the Father to bring him
to salvation out of his hour, *not* to deliver him from the hour.

Yes, for this reason have I come to this hour. Here again our rendering departs from most other versions: "No, for this purpose I
have come to this hour" (RSV); "No, it was for this that I came
to this hour" (NEB). Edgar Goodspeed renders: "And yet it was
for this very purpose that I have come to this trial," which is
close to the Authorized Version, "but for this cause came I unto
this hour." The presumption in all these translations is that Je-

sus' first prayer is simply hypothetical. In addition, it appears that the casting of this verse as a negative response (to the preceding question), or in the form of an objection, rests upon a misunderstanding of Johannine usage.

For this reason, that is, with full confidence that the Father will keep him safe, Jesus comes to his hour—for the purpose of being glorified. It will be recalled that *revelation* of the unseen God through his disclosure of his own identity is the final aim of the coming of the Word made "flesh" in this Gospel.

Father, glorify your Name! This petition will be expanded at some length in the great prayer of Jesus (Jn 17:1b–5), where the close relationship between these two prayers will become evident. The second moment of Jesus' prayer here appears to be a Johannine variation on the first petition of the dominical prayer "Hallowed be thy name!" when it is recalled that what is asked of God the Father is that he consecrate the believer to his Person. This is further specified by the address "Father." Accordingly, it is a plea to be made holy by God's grace precisely as an adoptive child of God. Once again, this conception is found in the great prayer (Jn 17:11b–12): "Holy Father, protect them with your name, which you have given to me, in order that they may be one, even as we are. When I was with them, I protected them with your name, which you have given to me, and I guarded them and not one of them was lost except the son of perdition." Here the sense of consecration to God as Father is found in combination with the divine protection of the disciples by Jesus during his mortal life. Later in this prayer, Jesus will declare, "I consecrate myself for their sake" (v. 19a).

Thereupon a voice came out of the sky. Like the author of the hymn in Hebrews 5:7, our evangelist expressly states that Jesus' prayer received a response. Moreover, he articulates it. It is noteworthy that this is the first time in the Fourth Gospel that the Father speaks, for John omitted the theophany at Jesus' baptism and nowhere records the tradition, found in all Synoptic Gospels, regarding Jesus' transfiguration. In the Marcan and Lucan Gethsemane, it will be remembered, there were reminiscences of this mysterious episode.[27]

"I have glorified it, and I will glorify it again!" The author of

this Gospel takes the view that, although in an incipient and deeply veiled manner, Jesus had disclosed his true identity through his "signs", which however were "the Father's works" (Jn 10:38). In fact, to his disciples, Jesus reveals that his teaching is also to be included: "The words I am speaking to you I do not utter on my own; the Father abiding in me is doing his works" (Jn 14:10b). The definitive glorification of his name by God will be manifest when he "glorifies" Jesus' humanity by making it, through death, the medium of life by his "handing over the Spirit" (Jn 19:30).

Accordingly, the crowd standing around, on hearing it, kept saying it had thundered; others kept saying, "An angel has spoken to him!" Throughout his public life Jesus had been a source of "division" (Jn 7:43; 9:16; 10:19). While the crowd is depicted as not grasping fully what has happened, yet each group appears to sense the divine presence. Thunder in the Old Testament is a symbol of the voice of God (1 Sam 12:18), and this is dramatically presented by the psalmist who considers the thunderstorm that comes down the coast from Lebanon to the vicinity of the temple to be a theophany for the worshipers in Jerusalem (Ps 29). Likewise, "the angel of the Lord" in the earlier books of the Bible is a surrogate for the self-revealing God of Israel. In the light of these considerations Jesus' next words become less unintelligible.

And Jesus said in reply, "Not on my account did the voice occur, but on your account." At the end of the Prologue, Jesus, "the Word of God," is celebrated as the "interpreter" of the invisible God (Jn 1:18). He has been pointed out, through the allusion to Jacob's ladder, as the bridge between heaven and earth (Jn 1:51). Here Jesus informs the reader that the divine answer to his prayer is intended primarily for those represented as witnessing this experience and prayer of Jesus. In fact, Rudolf Bultmann makes the suggestion that *on your account* is meant to refer to Jesus' prayer, as well as to the heavenly voice.[28] Thus it seems that John here wishes it understood that, as elsewhere in his Gospel, when Jesus prays it is before a group of people who are not only witnesses to his prayer but caught up in it.

"Now is the judgment of this world." One of the characteristics of the Fourth Gospel, surprising in this "spiritual Gospel," as

Clement of Alexandria aptly dubbed it, is its author's predilection for juridical language (testimony, witness, Paraclete, convict, judge, judgment). The term *judgment* is ambivalent: it sometimes signifies "saving judgment" as in Old Testament usage, sometimes "condemnation." "For judgment I have come into this world, that those who do not see may see, and those who see may become blind" (Jn 9:30). "Nor does the Father judge anyone, but he has given all judgment to the Son, in order that all may honor the Son even as they honor the Father" (Jn 5:22). Here *the judgment* is declared by Jesus to be *now*, that is, in his hour, and it is probably intended to display both the positive and negative meanings of judgment, to be distinguished in the two statements which follow immediately.

Now will the prince of this world be driven out. Later Jesus will remark to the disciples, "The prince of this world is coming, yet he has no hold upon me" (Jn 14:30b). While the Lucan Jesus calls the Passion "your hour and that of the power of darkness" (Lk 22:51), in John the hour is that of Jesus' glorification and triumph over evil. Satan, who has taken possession of Judas (Jn 13:2, 27), it is implied in the symbolic scene in the garden, "fell to the ground" with Judas and Jesus' would-be captors (Jn 18:5–6), as Jesus utters the divine name, "I am," thus presaging Satan's overthrow.

"Yet, as for me, when I am lifted up from earth, I will draw all people to myself." This is the final prediction of his death, as the following verse makes clear, *This he said to indicate what sort of death he was destined to die.* John knows the Synoptic tradition of Jesus' triple prediction of his death and resurrection (Mk 8:31; 9:31; 10:33–34) preserved in the kerygmatic formula of the early Church, identifying Jesus as "the Son of Man" who is also the Suffering Servant. Our evangelist however presents the three-fold prophecy in his own inimitable manner. "Yet just as Moses lifted up the serpent in the desert, so must the Son of Man be lifted up, in order that the believer may, in him, possess eternal life" (Jn 3:14–15). "When you have lifted up the Son of Man, then you will know that 'I am'" (Jn 8:28). In this second statement attention is concentrated upon the crucifixion as the means of Jesus' self-disclosure as the One who bears the divine

name "I am" (Ex 3:14). In this third prediction, the evangelist has (for the moment) omitted mention of "the Son of Man" and of the "must" (*dei*) which characterized the Synoptic form of these prophecies, and he invites the reader to contemplate the "drawing power" of the glorified Jesus, enthroned on the cross. Earlier this was described as the exclusive prerogative of the Father: "No one can come to me, unless the Father who sent me draws him" (Jn 6:45b; see v. 65). As the result of his "lifting up" Jesus himself is given this dynamic attractiveness.

To remedy his omission of the title "the Son of Man" and the expression of the will of God as initiating Jesus' death, the evangelist makes the crowd allude to Jesus' statement in a way he did not actually make it—a procedure not untypical of John (see Jn 11:40). *We have heard from the Law the Messiah abides forever; so how can you state that it is God's will (dei) that the Son of Man be lifted up? Who is this 'Son of Man'?"* In this final moment of Jesus' ministry the evangelist points out that the crowd has not changed, has not accepted Jesus, but clings to *the Law.* Jesus has not succeeded, despite his "so many signs" (Jn 12:37) and discussions with the inhabitants of Jerusalem, in disclosing to them his real identity. For that revelation his "lifting up" on the cross remains an absolute necessity. Jesus' last brief discourse picks up his self-characterization as "the Light," and despite its ominous tones it ends on a note of hope. Jesus never gives up, as the great prayer in ch. 17 will make clear, in attempting to win over "the world." John announces the close of the public ministry tersely: Jesus *the Light* has nothing further to communicate to the people at large; henceforth he will devote the last hours of his life to his disciples. *Jesus finished this speech, and he went off and hid himself from them.*

Is it possible to explain our evangelist's retrojection of his account of Jesus' prayer and struggle back into the public ministry? If we can find the answer to that question, we shall have the clue to John's interpretation of this experience of Jesus, which all the earlier evangelists had associated with the time immediately prior to Jesus' arrest. For John, as was noted already, the Passion is the glory of Jesus; consequently he omits anything in his narrative of Jesus' sufferings and death that will distract the reader from that perspective. The scene in the garden (Jn 18:1–11) will become a symbol of Jesus' triumph on the cross. The trial before Pilate, the centerpiece of the entire Passion narrative, is dominated by the theme of Jesus' kingship (Jn 18:28—19:16). In his presentation of what transpired on Calvary, John has carefully excised any of those elements in the earlier tradition that suggest the tragic aspect of Jesus' crucifixion, choosing only to highlight the royalty of Jesus and the universality of his kingship. There is no darkness, no cry of abandonment, no mockery of the crucified, only a passing reference to "two others crucified with him" (Jn 19:18). And Jesus' final statement declares that God himself has finally realized his divine purpose completely: "God has brought it to fulfillment." Thereupon, "bowing his head, he handed over the Spirit" (Jn 19:30).

Given the evangelist's single-hearted purpose, it is clear that he regarded the struggle and prayer undergone by Jesus in Gethsemane as alien to his own presentation of the Passion. Yet because of his profound respect for tradition and because of the values he has discerned in this mysterious experience, John has elected to include it by incorporating it into the first part of his book. The struggle to accept God's will discloses the paradox of the Incarnation, while the Johannine version of Jesus' prayer underscores Jesus' awareness of his unique relationship to God as the Son. Lest the reader miss the significance of that prayer, however, the evangelist has composed a lengthy prayer, which he inserts into the discourse after the Last Supper as its conclusion, and this may be rightly regarded as John's commentary upon that final, meaningful dialogue held by Jesus with God before he suffered.

The Great Prayer of Jesus (Jn 17:1–26)

This longest by far of the prayers attributed to Jesus in the Gospels has been interpreted in various ways which emphasize one or other aspects of this sublime composition by our evangelist. Cyril of Alexandria viewed it as an act of high-priestly intercession, as also did David Chytraeus, a sixteenth-century Lutheran. For Raymond Brown, it is a fitting conclusion to the great farewell discourse to the disciples.[29] Rudolf Bultmann took the rather extraordinary view that it was the evangelist's substitution for the words of eucharistic institution.[30] For Ernst Käsemann, "it is unmistakable that this chapter is a summary of the Johannine discourses, and, in this respect, is a counterpart of the prologue."[31]

In my turn, I wish to suggest that John has created this prayer out of certain elements of the Gethsemane tradition which he judged to be central to its significance, and he has presented these in his characteristically creative way together with certain developments—notably Jesus' prayer for future believers (Jn 17:19–26). One cogent reason for adopting this view is the positioning of this prayer between the Last Supper narrative and the scene in the garden. The Johannine Jesus addresses himself in prayer to the Father at precisely the same point in the Passion story as does the Jesus of the Synoptics.

That our evangelist was familiar with the incident reported in Mark, Matthew, and Luke is acknowledged by all commentators. The evidence for this view is impressive: elements gathered into the Marcan Gethsemane are echoed in various sections of The Book of Glory. We have already seen, from our analysis of the preceding prayer of Jesus, that there is a strong hint of Jesus' struggle to accept the Father's will (Jn 12:27a), and in the scene of Jesus' arrest John asserts the readiness of Jesus to accept his destiny: "The cup which the Father has given me, shall I not drink it?" (Jn 18:11). As in Mark and Matthew, Jesus is presented as prophesying the denials of Peter (Jn 13:38) and the dispersal of the little community of disciples. "Remember, an hour is coming—it has come!—when each of you *will be scattered* [the term found in the Marcan citation of Zech 13:7], each to his own home, and you will leave me alone. Yet I am not alone, because the Father is with me" (Jn 16:32). The last part of the saying was cited as the attitude exhibited by the Matthean Jesus, who is depicted as leaving his disciples to enjoy communion with the Father at prayer. The location of this saying, immediately before the great prayer in John, is also suggestive. Earlier in the Last Supper discourse, at a point which appears to have been its original conclusion, we find a reference to a saying which Mark employs to close the prayer episode (Mk 14:42). The Johannine Jesus says, "However, that the world may know that I love the Father and that I am acting as the Father has enjoined on me, get up! Let us go from here" (Jn 14:31). While the term for "testing" or "temptation" appears nowhere in the Fourth Gospel, Jesus' final saying, immediately before his prayer, conceivably alludes to it in a positive way. "I have told you this in order that in me you may have peace; in the world you will have tribulation, but take heart, I have won the victory over the world!" (Jn 16:33). Further, as we shall have occasion to note in our reflections on the Johannine prayer, several allusions are made to the Lord's prayer, a feature of the Synoptic narratives. Finally, the theme present in the Marcan (and Matthean) Gethsemane, Jesus' concern for his disciples to keep them together as long as possible, receives the fullest development in Jesus' prayer for the disciples present at the Last Supper.

The Johannine prayer revolves about three great themes which in the mind of the evangelist were the principal concerns of Jesus on the eve of his Passion: the fulfillment of his own mission (Jn 17:1–5), the preservation of his disciples as a community of faith and love (vv. 6–19), and the unity of future generations of believers (vv. 20–26). It is remarkable that of the familiar Johannine symbols ("light," "darkness," "peace") only "truth," "joy," and "eternal life" appear, while "love" is brought in only at the very end of the long prayer. Strangest of all, the Holy Spirit is nowhere expressly mentioned.

> 1 Jesus concluded this discourse, and raising his eyes to heaven, said,

> "Father, the hour has come!
> Glorify your Son,
> in order that the Son may glorify you,
> 2 by virtue of the fact
> you have given him power over all flesh,
> that he might give eternal life
> to everything you have given him.

3 This is eternal life,
that they know you, the unique, genuine God,
and him whom you have sent, Jesus Christ.
4 I have glorified you on earth
by bringing to completion
the work you have given me to carry out.
5 So now, glorify me, Father, in your presence,
with that glory I possessed with you,
before the world began to exist.

6 I have manifested your name
to the men you have given me out of the world.
They were yours,
and to me you have given them;
and they have kept your word.
7 Now they know
that everything you have given me is from you,
8 because the utterances you have given me
I have given to them; and they have accepted them,
and they truly know that I have come forth from you,
and they have believed that you have sent me.

9 I am praying about them.
I do not pray about the world,
but about those you have given me,
because they belong to you.
10 Indeed, everything mine is yours,
and yours is mine,
and in them have I been glorified.
11 I am no longer in the world,
yet they are in the world,
while I am coming to you.
Holy Father, keep them with your name that you have
    given me,
in order that they may be one as we are. 12 While I was
    with them,
I kept them with the name you have given me,
and I have guarded them.

Indeed, not one of them has been lost
except him that is doomed to perish,
that the Scripture might be fulfilled.

13 Now however I am coming to you,
so I am saying this in the world,
in order that they may have my joy fulfilled in them.
14 I have given them your word,
yet the world has hated them,
because they are not part of the world,
since I am not part of the world.
15 I am not praying that you take them out of the
    world,
but that you keep them from the evil one.
16 They are not part of the world,
since I am not part of the world.
17 Consecrate them by the truth— -
your word is truth.
18 By virtue of the fact that you have sent me into the
    world,
I in turn have sent them into the world.
19 So for their sake am I consecrating myself,
in order that they, for their part, may be consecrated
    by truth.

20 Not about these men alone am I praying,
but also about those who through their word will be-
    lieve in me:
21 in order that all of them may be one,
inasmuch as you, Father, are in me
and I am in you,
that they in turn may be one in us,
so that the world may believe you have sent me.

22 And I have given to them
the glory you have given me,
that they may be one,
inasmuch as we are one—
23 I in them, and you in me—

in order that they may be perfected in unity,
that the world may come to know you have sent me,
and have loved them inasmuch as you loved me.

24 Father,
with regard to what you have given me
I desire that where I am
there they too may be with me,
that they may behold my glory, which you have given
    me,
because you loved me from before the creation of the
    world.

25 Just Father,
indeed the world has not known you,
but I have known you,
and these men have known you have sent me.
26 So I have made known your name to them
and I shall continue to make it known,
in order that the love with which you have loved me
may exist in them,
and so I may exist in them."

The prayer is introduced by a gesture of Jesus familiar from the evangelical tradition (Mk 6:41; 7:34; see Jn 6:5), symbolizing the entry into God's presence. *Father* is also characteristic of Jesus' address to God in all the Gospels, and our evangelist will repeatedly recall it throughout this prayer (vv. 5, 11, 21, 24, 25). *The hour has come.* Here, as earlier (Jn 12:23), the arrival of *the hour* creates the context for Jesus' prayer. *Glorify your Son.* As throughout the Bible, "the glory of God" symbolizes God's self-revelation in power to his people. God is invoked as the dynamic source of Jesus' glory, the disclosure of his own self-identity begun at Cana (Jn 2:11). For John it is Jesus' laying down his life for his friends (Jn 15:13), the greatest possible demonstration of his love, that brings the definitive disclosure of Jesus' divine Sonship. As already noted, for this Gospel-writer Jesus' dying breath is a symbol of Pentecost, the gift of the life-giving Spirit (Jn 19:30). *In order that the Son may glorify you.* We have observed that it is a salient feature of the Johannine Jesus that everything he says, does, is, as the Son, is part of the Father's "works." This holds good for his mission of revealing the Father: he must receive "glory" from the Father to reveal who he himself actually is, so that he may reveal the God who remains unseen. Throughout his earthly life Jesus has never sought his own glory (Jn 5:41; 8:50), but only the glory of the God who sent him (Jn 7:18). Accordingly in his prayer he asks *to be glorified*, knowing that his glory, like his words, actions and very being, is subordinated to that of the Father.

It is with this "poverty of the Son," as we have called it, that the evangelist connects the Father's gift to him of universal authority or *power over all flesh* (see Jn 3:35; 13:3; esp. 5:19–30). *In order that he might give eternal life to everything that you have given him.* The mission of Jesus is indeed to reveal the unseen Father, yet John understands this "revelation" not as mere theological or abstruse knowledge. Since faith is a deeply personal relationship with God in Jesus, it is a communion with the very life of God that really constitutes this "truth" as *the* Christian mode of existence. Our evangelist occasionally uses the neuter, as here, *everything*, when he intends this to be understood of human persons. This may be the influence of Semitic idiom or simply a Greek means of indicating a quality belonging to a group.[32] John's emphasis upon the gift-character of what God has done in Jesus Christ is not to be missed. In the Fourth Gospel the familiar symbols of light, life, and Truth are so many aspects of the one great grace of "newness" of which the whole New Testament is redolent.

This is eternal life, that they know you, the unique, genuine God, and him whom you have sent, Jesus Christ. In line with his characterization of Jesus' mission as revealer, the evangelist speaks of the new *life* as knowing; however, as will be seen in the concluding verses of the prayer (vv. 25–26), such knowledge must issue in love.

I have glorified you on earth by bringing to completion the work you have given me to carry out. This appears to contradict the rather pessimistic judgment of Jesus' public ministry as failure, which appeared in John's concluding reflections, appended to

The Book of Signs (Jn 12:37–43), where however it was admitted that "many of the leaders believed in him" (v. 42). Actually now the evangelist is thinking of Jesus' successful carrying out of his mission by his gift of the Spirit at his death. In fact, John oscillates between presenting Jesus as already glorified in this prayer (since the hour has come), and viewing him as still upon earth. Jesus' "signs" and his symbolic statements throughout the Gospel are orientated to bringing "the truth" to all who accept him with real faith. The opening movement of Jesus' prayer is, in a sense, for himself; more truly, however, it is to be enabled by the Father's power to reveal God by disclosing his own identity. These verses, with their monotonous repetition, are geared to explaining the very brief prayer of Jesus (at Jn 12:27f.): "Save me through this hour" and "Glorify your name."

So now, glorify me, Father, in your presence, with that glory I possessed with you, before the world began to exist. Jesus is aware that now, in his hour, he stands as the Word become flesh before the Father. The Prologue had spoken of the eternal pre-existence of the Word "in the presence of God" (Jn 1:2) when he was the perfect expression of God before the creation. Now Jesus asks for God's power to reveal God through his human existence, which entails his death—in Johannine terminology, his "glorification." Possibly more clearly than any other New Testament author, this evangelist later emphasizes the truth that Jesus' glorification does not annihilate in him the effects of his Passion: he appears with holes in his hands and the wound in his side even after rising from death (Jn 20:20). As we remarked earlier, another writer of the Johannine school, the seer of Patmos, presents this same truth symbolically, picturing the risen Lord "like a lamb standing with the marks of his slaying still upon him" (Rev 5:6). For these authors, the great good news of the Gospel is that Jesus, at his exaltation in glory, *has chosen to remain human forever.* That is to say, the glorified Jesus *is* and remains the kind of Lord he is by reason of those human experiences he underwent during his life among us. One important consequence of this for Christian prayer is that the contemplation of the mysteries of Jesus' earthly life has now become, by virtue of his resurrection, the privileged means of access to him in glory.

At this point in his intercession, the Johannine Jesus is pictured as praying more specifically for the disciples present at the Last Supper (vv. 6–19).

I have manifested your name to the men you have given me out of the world. They were yours, and to me you have given them, and they have kept your word. While in a sense this is only an extension of Jesus' petition for his own "glorification," still the evangelist wishes to remind his reader that Jesus prayed for the disciples *as a community* of believers. The Synoptic evangelists, as has been seen, implied that Jesus' prayer evinced such an orientation; it is left to the fourth evangelist to state this expressly. Jesus here regards his disciples as a *gift* to himself from his Father. The most striking feature of John's conception of God the Father throughout this book, as was mentioned before, is as a *giving* God. A rereading of the Gospel with attention to the frequency with which the verb "to give" recurs in connection with God will readily reveal this precious characterization.

They were yours. As Jews, Jesus' disciples always possessed the traditional faith of Israel in "the God of the fathers." Jesus had said to them, "You believe in God; believe also in me" (Jn 14:1). The disciples have found faith in Jesus also during his historical existence. Peter declares, "We have known and we have believed that you are the holy One of God!" (Jn 6:69). Their following of Jesus, even during his public ministry, is not to be regarded as the result of merely natural attraction: "No one can come to me, unless the Father who sent me draws him" (Jn 6:44a). Yet their incomprehension of where Jesus is going, as late as the Last Supper, shows how much they have still to be taught regarding him. *And they have kept your word.* They have been faithful to Jesus' word, insofar as they are now able, by loving him (Jn 14:23) and sharing the secrets of his heart as his "beloved" (Jn 15:14–15).

One may ask whether, by *I have manifested your name* to the disciples, the evangelist means, in addition to revealing the person of the Father, a specific name. The divine name "I am" has been pronounced by Jesus as his own in the course of his controversies (Jn 8:24b, 28, 58), and possibly also to the disciples in the Christophany on the Lake of Tiberias (Jn 6:20). Jesus has spok-

en, especially at his last discourse, to the disciples of God as his
Father, assuring them that to know himself is to know the Father (Jn 14:7, 9).

Now they know that everything you have given me is from you.
As the referential term *Now* indicates, the disciples only *know* in
virtue of the hour which is upon Jesus. It is however not yet
completed, and consequently there is a certain ambivalence in
this statement: they actually do not yet know, since they have
not received the Spirit, source of Christian faith and life. Still, it
remains true that they are in a very different frame of mind
from "the Jews" who have earlier demonstrated that they are
closed to any self-revelation by Jesus.

*Because the utterances you have given me I have given to them:
and they have accepted them, and they truly know that I have come
forth from you, and they have believed that you have sent me.* Jesus is
more than the bearer of a message from God, after the manner
of the Old Testament prophets. Jesus' words are the words and
works of the Father; hence to hear Jesus is to hear the Father (Jn
12:50b). This evangelist's criterion of authentic faith is acceptance of Jesus' word, a lesson indicated by the Mother of Jesus,
symbol in this Gospel of a perfect disciple (Jn 2:5), by the Samaritans (Jn 4:42), and by the ruler of Cana (Jn 4:50b). In the
Fourth Gospel the most important "word" of Jesus is "the new
commandment," and it is by the giving and receiving of love in
the community of faith that the disciples will (in virtue of Jesus'
hour) know his origin in God and accept his sending by the Father.

I am praying about them. The reader is reminded of the tenor
of Jesus' prayer; it arises from his concern for their perseverance
in faith and in communion with one another. Jesus' confesses
his responsibility for these followers precisely because they are
those you have given me. Jesus said earlier, "No one can come to
me unless it be given him as gift from the Father" (Jn 6:65). *I do
not pray about the world.* This remark must not be misconstrued
as a refusal by the Johannine Jesus to pray for the world. As v.
20 will indicate, Jesus has by no means given up on the world
and its conversion.

John adds *because they belong to you* to recall once again his theme of the poverty of the Son. Jesus insists in this Gospel that he has nothing of his own.

Indeed, everything mine is yours, and yours is mine; and in them have I been glorified. This verse, with its seeming monotonous repetition, is a kind of summary of what has been said of the disciples in vv. 6–9 and serves as an indicator that Jesus' prayer is shifting to the necessity of his leaving the disciples in the world—a world as hostile to them as it has already shown itself to him.

I am no longer in the world, yet they are in the world, while I am coming to you. Having reached his hour, Jesus can from one point of view, speak of himself as already glorified; he has already begun his departure from this world to the Father. The thought evokes his separation from the disciples, and now in his prayer Jesus looks to their future *in the world,* bereft of his visible, physical presence. A similar dilemma was faced by the apostle Paul in his prayer as he composed his letter to the community of Philippi (Phil 1:20–26).

Holy Father! The epithet *holy* is employed in the Old Testament as proper to God alone. Basically it means "the wholly Other," and it postulates that anyone or anything consecrated to God be withdrawn from profane use. The Code of Holiness (Lev chs. 17—26) in its essentials comes from the ancient past of Israel; its imperatives spring from the notion of God as the Holy One. "Be holy, for I, the Lord your God, am holy!" (Lev 19:2). The Johannine Jesus now prays the Father to keep his disciples together *as a community.* In these verses of the great prayer (vv. 11b–19), our evangelist, who does not cite the dominical prayer, is giving his commentary on its fundamental themes. This is in keeping with the earliest traditions by which Jesus' prayer in Gethsemane was preserved. Jesus himself was acknowledged by Peter in this Gospel as "the Holy One of God" (Jn 6:65). As the "first" Paraclete (Jn 14:16)—a legal expression for a defense-lawyer in Hellenistic law-courts—Jesus has protected the disciples, keeping them together by "manifesting his glory" (Jn 2:11) through the "signs" that awakened their faith in himself. But now he must leave them to return home to God, and so he asks the Father to *keep them with your name that you have given to me.* Is this the ineffable divine Name ("I am") which Jesus bears in this Gospel? Or is it "the King of Israel," a title that designates the unique divine prerogative of the covenanted God which Jesus is given also in this book (Jn 1:50; 12:13)? It is difficult to decide the question; however, it should be recalled that the notion of Jesus' kingship dominates the Roman trial in this Gospel, and the evangelist reinforces this view by his emphasis on the title affixed to the cross (Jn 19:19–22). It is highly significant that the hearing before Pilate comes to a climax with the apostasy from their ancient faith by the high priests when they declare, "We have no king but the emperor!" (Jn 19:15). That God himself was uniquely "King of Israel" had long been a fundamental tenet of Israelite faith; thus the evangelist shows his awareness of the fact that, in their frenzied rejection of Jesus as king, these religious leaders were led to deny their faith in God.

In order that they may be one as we are. The preservation of unity among the disciples of Jesus will be seen as crucial in the third section of this prayer (v. 21) because it is to constitute the challenge to "the world" by which the disciples are to carry on Jesus' own attempts to convert "the world." For Jesus had challenged "the Jews" by his claim to a privileged oneness with God (Jn 10:30). In his earlier prayer (Jn 12:27b) Jesus prays to his Father to keep him safe through his hour; here the evangelist indicates that implicit in that petition was also a plea for the safety of those he was leaving behind to carry on his mission.

While I was with them I kept them with the name you have given me, and I have guarded them. Jesus repeats what he has already said at v. 6: he has revealed God's name to these disciples, *and they have kept your word*, which has *kept them*. Here Jesus adds a further idea: *I have guarded them.* The word *guard* is rare in this Gospel; hence it is a recall of Jesus' instruction to his own about the living out of the paschal mystery—"the person who hates his life in this world will guard it for eternal life" (Jn 12:25). It is reminiscent also of the brief speech with which Jesus closes The Book of Signs: "And if anyone hears my words and does not guard them, I do not judge him—for I did not come to judge the world but that I might save the world" (Jn 12:47). In the narrative of Jesus' arrest, John depicts him guarding his own by demanding of his captors, "If then you are seeking me, let these men go (in safety)" (Jn 18:8), and immediately we are reminded that this was done by Jesus to "fulfill the word he had said, 'Of those you have given me I have not lost a single one of them'" (v. 9). In his prayer Jesus points out expressly the one tragic exception: *Indeed, not one of them has been lost except him that is doomed to perish, that the Scripture might be fulfilled.*

Now however I am coming to you, so I am saying this in the world, in order that they may have my joy fulfilled in them. Twice during his final discourse to the disciples, Jesus spoke of his hope that their joy might find its fulfillment. It is one of the reasons he gives for "keeping my commandments," that is, the "new commandment" of giving and receiving love in the community (Jn 15:10–12); it was also mentioned as motivation for obeying the injunction to "ask in my name" (Jn 16:24). Jesus' concern is that the joy he imparts to them may be fulfilled in their communion with one another, out of which they will be enabled to pray in communion with himself, so that their prayer becomes infallible. It is significant that John makes no reference here to the Holy Spirit, who in Pauline theology is associated with true Christian joy, felt even in the face of persecution (1 Thes 1:6).

I have given them your word, yet the world has hated them, because they are not part of the world, since I am not part of the world. It is still more curious that, in this context of the hostility of the world, John does not mention the Paraclete. Raymond Brown has observed that the first mention of the Paraclete spoke of the world's failure to recognize him (Jn 14:17), while later there is marked hostility between the Paraclete and the world (Jn 16:8–11).[33]

Earlier (v. 6) Jesus has referred to the way he had formed his disciples: *I have manifested your name to them . . . and they have kept your word.* Jesus, the Word, the perfect expression of the Father, formed his followers by revealing the Father to them. Now he mentions another effect of this gift of *your word:* hatred by the world. This is John's way of alluding to the "testing" (*peirasmos*), one of the petitions in the dominical prayer. The hatred already manifested toward Jesus, and shortly to be unleashed in all its fury against himself, will also be directed against his disciples.

I am not praying that you take them out of the world, but that you keep them from the evil one. While the second half of the verse is an obvious reference to the last petition of the *Pater noster,* the first part would appear to be John's attempt to clarify the "Do not lead us into the testing." It is no part of the religion of Jesus to exempt the Church from attacks by the evil power-structures aligned against her in the course of history. He only promised her the final victory over the forces of evil (Mt 16:18c; Jn 16:33). As the Father will keep Jesus safe through his hour (Jn 12:27), so will he ensure the salvation of the disciples. Their destiny is the same as that of their Lord, and for the same reason: *They are not part of the world, since I am not part of the world.*

Consecrate them by the truth—your word is truth. As the Johannine Jesus concludes this part of his prayer for the disciples who are present, he returns to the idea of God expressed in his initial address in this section: *Holy Father.* The correlative of *holy* is the exclusive consecration of the believer to God's service. As he began to pray for his disciples, Jesus asked the Father, as *holy,* to *keep them with your name.* Now he repeats this idea in other words: *consecrate them by the truth.* In the Fourth Gospel *the truth* is the revelation of the unseen God committed to Jesus to disclose to men. This revelation is epitomized in the precious revelation that God is our Father. In his commentary on the passage, Raymond Brown suggests somewhat hesitatingly: "Perhaps 'truth' in xvii 17 is meant to be identified not only with God's word but also with the Paraclete who is the Spirit of Truth."[34] Without denying such a possibility, I should like to suggest that this is John's version of the first petition in the Lord's Prayer, "Hallowed be thy name," as was also implied by the opening invocation, *Holy Father, keep them with your name* (v. 11).

"Hallowed be thy name" is a plea to God to *act* (the passive indicates that God is agent) by consecrating us to his Person, and that is specifically with reference to the name already invoked, "Our Father." The sense of this petition is preserved by *consecrate them by the truth* and by *keep them with your name.*

Your word is truth. God's word is Jesus' word, as Jesus is himself the Word of God incarnate. Faith for John is a deeply personal relationship with the risen Jesus, into which one is "drawn" (Jn 6:44) by the Father, since it "has been given" only by the Father (Jn 6:65). Jesus' word is the unique, radical basis for genuine faith which produced that abiding in Jesus which, in turn, makes possible Christian prayer in Jesus' name.

By virtue of the fact that you have sent me into the world, I in turn have sent them into the world. The communion with Jesus, which John prefers to call "abiding," is one fundamental ingredient in Christian discipleship. There is however a second, equally basic element set forth in this verse: to be a disciple of Jesus is to continue the mission of Jesus to the world. As I attempted to demonstrate in a study of Christian mysticism,[35] this apostolic, centrifugal movement is, for the great theologians of the New Testament, particularly Paul and John, a matter of paramount importance. Attention to this dynamic aspect of Christian mysticism has, I believe, tended to be left in shadow by much of the classical writing on mystical theology.

So for their sake am I consecrating myself, in order that they, for their part, may be consecrated by truth. The evangelist interprets Jesus' progress through his hour as a process of being assimilated to the divine holiness, that is, separation from the profane, becoming totally devoted to the will of the holy God. The Synoptic narratives of Gethsemane indicated this by depicting Jesus' struggle through prayer. John, who, as has been seen (Jn 12:27), has not neglected the struggle aspect, presents Jesus through this lengthy prayer as consecrating himself to the will of the Father for the sake of his disciples, *in order that they, for their part, may be consecrated by truth*. Thereby, this writer indicates his profound insight into the inestimable value of Jesus' gift to Christians in the Lord's Prayer. It is his self-giving to his Father that has imparted its specially privileged effectiveness to this greatest of Christian prayers, as *the* means of acquiring that consecration to God as our Father, in which the essence of Christianity consists. This verse therefore also throws new light upon the meaning of that "prayer in my name" imperatively demanded by the Johannine Jesus.

One may say that this verse also represents Jesus' self-offering to God as a *priestly* oblation: it is through his hour that Jesus, for John, brings his priesthood to its fullest realization. The view echoes that already seen in the ancient hymn cited by the author of Hebrews (Heb 5:7–10), which is probably one of the most ancient Christian interpretations of the Gethsemane-experience. Not implausibly, the Synoptic portrayal of Jesus' acceptance to drink "this cup," a symbol in part related to the Eucharist, implies this priestly character of Jesus' prayer.

With the ensuing verses, a third moment in the great prayer is picked out by this evangelist: Jesus directs his attention and his heart to future generations of believers, including them also in his last petitions to the Father. It will be recalled that it is upon those "who have come to believe without seeing" (Jn 20:29b) that the risen Jesus pronounces, in this Gospel, his final beatitude. We noted how, for Matthew, the characteristic expression "the disciples" symbolizes the later Church. This insight has been taken up and fully orchestrated by John. This is nowhere so strikingly evident as in the ever deepening stress upon *ongoing unity* (no longer a question of keeping together the little band of original disciples) which characterizes the closing lines of Jesus' prayer.

Not about these men alone am I praying, but also about those who through their word will believe in me. In the preceding section Jesus spoke to the Father about his disciples as the men who *have kept your word* (v. 6), and he summarized his own instruction of them by saying, *I have given them your word* (v. 14). Now there is a new development: he speaks of *their word* as the source of faith for future Christians. It is a reference to the apostolic preaching, and also, not improbably, to his own Gospel and those of his fellow-evangelists. This writer in an explicit statement of purpose will end his book by saying, "These things have been written down in order that you may believe that Jesus is the Messiah, the Son of God, and by believing find life in his name" (Jn 20:31).

In order that all of them may be one, inasmuch as you, Father, are in me and I am in you, that they in turn may be one in us. The oneness of Jesus with the Father is, of course, a dominant theme in the Fourth Gospel. And if John carefully reserves any mention of love until the very end of this prayer, he has made it clear that this unity of Jesus with the Father has its source in God's love. "The Father loves the Son and has given everything into his hands" (Jn 3:35); "The Father loves the Son and shows him everything he himself is doing" (Jn 5:20a). Thus by hearing Jesus the disciples have heard the Father (Jn 12:50); because they have seen Jesus they have seen the Father (Jn 12:45; 14:9–10). Indeed, it is this abiding of Jesus in the Father that makes possible their coming to make an " abiding" (*monē*) with the believer, on the condition of his loving Jesus by keeping his word (Jn 14:23).

So that the world may believe you have sent me. Indescribably precious as is this abiding of Jesus and the Father in the believer, it is not, for John, an end in itself; it is orientated to *mission*, as Jesus never gives up hope for *the world*. This unity that is to reign among future disciples is intended by Jesus to have an apostolic orientation. It is, as we have said, to provide the continuing challenge to the world which Jesus himself issued by saying, "The Father and I are one!" (Jn 10:30).

And I have given to them the glory you have given me. This statement may at first seem cryptic. In speaking of the disciples present, Jesus had declared, *I have given them your word* (v. 14). Now he prays for future disciples, that is, in the period after his own glorification (*glory you have given me*). These believers, as yet unborn, will have no personal experience of Jesus and his earthly history, as did the first disciples. They will, on the other hand, live in the era when the Spirit will have been given, who *"will glorify me.* For he will take what is mine, and unveil it for you" (Jn 16:14). Thus it would seem that the evangelist hints at the work of the Paraclete here.

That they may be one, inasmuch as we are one. This unity that is to link all future Christians appears to be something more than a moral unity, since it is caused by, and modeled upon, the communion of Jesus with the Father, which later theology will describe as a metaphysical oneness in the Godhead. John is attempting to express what the Christian community is in its most profound reality. Paul had asserted this by his use of a comparison with the body: "You are Christ's body!" (1 Cor 12:27). John himself had portrayed it, with equal realism, by his figure of the vine (Jn 15:1ff). Raymond Brown has called it "a vital, organic unity."[36] He adds that it is conceived moreover as a *visible* unity. This communion of Christians is to be in fact nothing short of *awareness of their new-found self-identity* in the risen Jesus, as the emphasis here upon *glory* indicates.

I in them, and you in me. Jesus as the incarnate expression of the Father vis-à-vis all believers is always the bridge, or "Jacob's ladder" (Jn 1:51). It is an important theorem of Johannine theology that the Word once become incarnate remains human forever.

In order that they may be perfected in unity. Eschatological salvation, of which the preservation of the original disciples as a vital community of love (a concern of Jesus in Gethsemane as the Shepherd) was a symbol, receives great stress here. Only thus can the divine "abiding" of Jesus with the Father be realized in human terms in the Church.

That the world may come to know you have sent me. This oneness in community, for which the Johannine Jesus prays so fervently in the future of history, has an apostolic orientation to challenge the world *to come to know* Jesus' origin from the Father. This "knowledge" involves moreover an awareness of the Father's love: that *you have loved them inasmuch as you have loved me.* This is the first mention of love in Jesus' great prayer. The Father's love is the originating source of Jesus' mission, which remains always a mission to the world. "God so loved the world as to give [over to death] his only Son" (Jn 3:16). It is God's love of the *incarnate* Son from which the divine love of all mankind springs.

The final lines of the prayer return to expand upon the promise Jesus made in connection with his first announcement that the hour had arrived (Jn 12:23ff.) and that those who "serve" him must "follow" him in the experience of the paschal mystery to come ultimately with him into the Father's presence, where God will "honor" them.

Father, with regard to what you have given me, I desire that where I am there they too may be with me. In the Synoptic accounts of Jesus' Gethsemane prayer, the drama revolved around his *desire* and the will of the Father. In this Gospel, Jesus' struggle was delicately suggested in the scene with the Greeks, while in this prayer Jesus' desire is from the beginning in total conformity with that of his Father. It is to be recalled however that Jesus' initial repugnance to "this cup" (Mark) or, at least, his hesitation in drinking it (Matthew) was presented as arising from the traumatic realization that his sufferings and death would cause a loss of faith in the disciples and the break-up of this little community of faithful friends. In the present verse, the *desire* of the Johannine Jesus also involved his disciples, in the future as well as at present: *that they too may be with me*. The last phrase *with me* is reminiscent of the phrase characteristic of the Matthean Jesus. *That they may behold my glory, which you have given to me, because you loved me from before the creation of the world*. While, as has been noticed, the early Church proclaimed, "We have beheld his glory" (Jn 1:14b), yet here, it appears, the evangelist thinks of the final contemplation in heaven of the *glory* of the exalted Christ. The love of the Father is again commemorated (as in v. 23).

Just Father, indeed the world has not known you, but I have known you, and these men have known you have sent me. It may seem strange that the title *Just Father* has been reserved to the end of this prayer. However, the evangelist's purpose here is to recall the new covenant which (in the Synoptic tradition) Jesus struck with his disciples at the Last Supper through the eucharistic institution.[37] The title also recalls a prominent theme in the Fourth Gospel, the judgment, at once a saving judgment and a judgment of condemnation. The statement *the world has not known you* is a recall of "the sin of the world" which Jesus as "the lamb of God" has come to take away (Jn 1:29). "Not to know God" in the Bible is always sin, indeed the worst of sins. In this Gospel "the Jews," that is, religious leaders of Judaism in Jesus' day, exemplify this "sin of the world" by their obduracy in remaining closed to Jesus and his message. By contrast, as Jesus states early in this prayer, "to know God" is to share in "eternal life" (v. 3) which Jesus possesses in abundance. For those who believe in Jesus, it also means that *these men have known you have sent me*. Such "knowledge," of course, is not "gnostic," but it presupposes a personal relationship with Jesus and an experience of love, given and received, in the Christian community.

So I have made known your name to them, and I shall continue to make it known. Jesus has already stated, with respect to his public ministry, that he has in a real sense succeeded in revealing God to his disciples. However it is only through his hour that he can complete this work of revelation of divine love by laying down his life for his beloved friends (Jn 15:13). The parallel between this final statement by Jesus and the assertion by the heavenly voice, "I have glorified it, and I will glorify it again" (Jn 12:28), in response to Jesus' plea, "Father, glorify your name," is not to be missed. Accordingly, it may be asserted that vv. 25–26 actually contain the divine response to the prayer of Jesus before his Passion, a response that for John assumes the dimensions of a new covenant. And what is the purpose of this covenant? As stated at Jn 13:1–3, the covenant was ratified by Jesus who "having loved his own, who were in the world, loved them to the end—to perfection" and who struck this covenant with full awareness that "the Father has given everything into his hands." The covenant, as John chooses to depict it, was acted out as a kind of prophetic charade by Jesus through the washing of his disciples' feet. This symbolic act was purposely inserted into his narrative of the Last Supper by John, instead of the traditional words and gestures by Jesus in the eucharistic institution. John appears to have intended his readers to understand that this act of loving service symbolized Jesus' death "for his beloved friends" as well as "an example" (Jn 13:15) of "the new commandment" of giving and receiving love in the community of faith. Thus it is a dramatic representation of the "new covenant" of love.

In order that the love with which you have loved me may exist in them, and so I may exist in them. Here is the almost incredible purpose of the new covenant: the abiding of Jesus and of his Father's love in the disciples.

We suggested initially that the great prayer of Jesus stands where it does in this Gospel because our evangelist intended it to be understood as his commentary upon the Gethsemane tradition. If that view be accepted as valid, then this lengthy, somewhat obscure, frequently monotonous and repetitious passage must be regarded as the crown of the entire development, within the New Testament, of so many efforts to grasp the meaning of this mysterious episode in the earthly life of Jesus. With profound insight, John has seen, in Jesus' acceptance of "this cup," the ratification by Jesus of the Eucharist, "the new covenant in my blood, that will be poured out on your behalf" (Lk 22:20). He has chosen to present Jesus' acceptance of his Father's will regarding his own death as the divine answer to his prayer for his "glorification," the successful completion of his mission from God by the disclosure of his own self-identity as the Son, who thereby interprets for us the love of the "God no man has ever seen" (Jn 1:18). By what one can only call a stroke of genius, the fourth evangelist has disengaged the painful struggle experienced by Jesus, which he recorded at 12:27, from his version of the final, great prayer, and thus has been free to exploit to the full the depth of meaning it contained.

NOTES

1. Pierre Benoit, O.P., "Paulinisme et Johannisme," *New Testament Studies* 9 (1962–63), 193–207. An English version appeared in *Cross Currents* 15 (1965), 339–353, entitled "Pauline and Johannine Theologies: A Contrast."

2. George MacRae, S.J., "The Fourth Gospel and *Religionsgeschichte*," *Catholic Biblical Quarterly* 32 (1970), 13–24.

3. "Believe the works," *The Way* 18 (1978), 272–286.

4. The division of the Fourth Gospel into "The Book of Signs" (chs. 1–12) and "The Book of Glory" (chs. 13–21) was originally the work of C. H. Dodd. More recently, it has been used by Raymond E. Brown in his two-volume commentary.

5. "Experience in the Apostolic Church," *The Way* 17 (1977), 202–216.

6. George W. MacRae, *Faith in the Words: The Fourth Gospel* (Chicago, 1973), p. 58.

7. *Ibid.*, p. 52.

8. *Ibid.*, p. 9.

9. An exception to this is the mention of Jesus' love for the family at Bethany, Lazarus, Martha, and Mary (Jn 11:3, 5, 36).

10. I wish to acknowledge my indebtedness here to the doctoral dissertation, as yet unpublished, from the Pontifical Biblical Institute, Rome, by James McPolin, S.J., *The Name of Father and Son in John and I John.*

11. Rudolf Bultmann, *The Gospel of John: A Commentary* (Philadelphia, 1975), trans. G. R. Beasley-Murray, R. W. N. Hoare, J. K. Riches, p. 545, n. 2.

12. Raymond E. Brown, S.S., *The Gospel According to John XIII—XXI* (Garden City, N.Y., 1970), Anchor Bible, p. 735.

13. My reasons for this view are given in "The Purpose of the Fourth Evangelist and the 'Trinification' of the Christian," *Trinification of the World* (Toronto, 1978), pp. 259–278.

14. *Ibid.*, p. 262.

15. George W. MacRae, *Invitation to John* (Garden City, N.Y., 1978), p. 149.

16. Raymond E. Brown, S.S., *The Gospel According to John I—XII* (Garden City, N.Y., 1966), p. 463.

17. *Ibid.*, p. 470.

18. *Ibid.*, p. 471.

19. Raymond E. Brown, S.S., "John and the Synoptic Gospels: A Comparison," *New Testament Essays* (Milwaukee, 1965), pp. 192–213.

20. George W. MacRae, *Invitation to John*, p. 153, observes: "Verse 27 shows us John's reinterpretation of that scene in the garden." See also Rudolf Bultmann, *The Gospel of John: A Commentary*, p. 428, n. 1.

21. George W. MacRae, *Invitation to John*, p. 153.

22. Rudolf Schnackenburg, *The Gospel According to St John*, Volume I (New York, 1968), transl. Kevin Smyth, p. 537.

23. Rudolf Schnackenburg, *Das Evangelium nach Markus*, I. Teil (Düsseldorf, 1966), p. 99.

24. Raymond E. Brown, S.S., *The Gospel According to John I—XII*, p. 472.

25. Xavier Léon-Dufour, "'Père, fais-moi passer sain et sauf à travers cette heure!' (Jn 12, 27)," *Neues Testament und Geschichte: Historisches Geschehen und Deutung im N.T.: O. Cullmann zum 70. Geburtstag*, Eds. Heinrich Baltensweiler, Bo Reicke (Tübingen, 1972), pp. 157–165.

26. Cited by X. Léon-Dufour in the article just listed.

27. Anthony Kenny, "The Transfiguration and the Agony in the Garden," *Catholic Biblical Quarterly* 19 (1957), 444–452.

28. Rudolf Bultmann, *The Gospel of John: A Commentary*, p. 428.

29. Raymond E. Brown, *The Gospel According to John XIII—XXI*, p. 744, cites the parallel with the Book of Deuteronomy, an example of the farewell discourse genre like Jn 13—16, which concludes with two prayers by Moses, viz. Deut 32 and 33.

30. Rudolf Bultmann, *The Gospel of John: A Commentary*, p. 486. Actually our evangelist has substituted the foot-washing for the pericope of eucharistic institution found in the three Synoptics.

31. Ernst Käsemann, *The Testament of Jesus: A Study of the Gospel of John in the Light of Ch. 17* (Philadelphia, 1966), p. 3.

32. Max Zerwick & Mary Grosvenor, *A Grammatical Analysis of the Greek New Testament*, vol. 1 (Rome, 1974). See the comments on Jn 17:2.

33. Raymond E. Brown, *The Gospel According to John XIII—XXI*, p. 711.

34. *Ibid.*, p. 766.

35. "The Elements of Christian Mysticism Exhibited by Certain New Testament Documents," in *Mystique*, a volume of essays on Eastern and Christian mysticism, *Studia Missionalia* 26 (1977), 1–35.

36. Raymond E. Brown, *The Gospel According to John XIII—XXI*, p. 776.

37. The word "covenant" appears in the words of eucharistic institution over the cup (Mk 14:24; Mt 26:28; Lk 22:20). Jesus' eucharistic body and blood constitute the instrument of covenant-making with "the Twelve" (Mk 14:17; Mt 26:20) or "the apostles" (Lk 22:14), representative of the new Israel, the future Church.

AFTERWORD

Our investigation into the texts in the New Testament which deal with the harrowing experience of Jesus toward the end of his life, when he was confronted with the prospect of his own sufferings and death and his agonizing search for the will of God for himself in all this, has disclosed the paramount interest displayed by earliest Christianity in the episode popularly known as "the agony in the garden." While Paul's total silence about this crucial turning-point in Jesus' earthly history has admittedly left us the poorer, still we do possess deeply moving accounts of it by each of the four Gospel-writers which exhibit its many-faceted meanings for faith and prayer. We have moreover been handed the precious insights into this incident by an anonymous Christian poet in the hymnodic scrap preserved by the author of Hebrews. In addition, our appreciation of the dynamic of Christian faith that strives to seek an ever deeper understanding of the mystery that is Jesus, Son of God become fully human, has been sharpened by the contributions of two unknown authors whose brief expositions of the Gethsemane event can, with some degree of probability, be recovered from the Marcan account. And if finally we include a variant interpretation of the experience by the inspired glossator on the Lucan story (Lk 22:43–44), we may enumerate—together with the five Gospel narratives—nine "essays in contemplation" bequeathed to us by the young Church. Thus the evidence that Jesus' struggle and prayer in the closing hours of his life made an undying impression upon the first Christian century is indeed impressive.

The resources provided to us by contemporary scriptural studies, particularly by Form and Redaction criticism, have proven their usefulness for an assessment of the way in which the living evangelical traditions developed through the efforts of the evangelists to serve the interests of the various communities for which the Gethsemane narratives were originally composed. As a consequence, our awareness and appreciation of the values for prayer and for the living of the Gospel, which the inspired writers have intuited in this emotionally charged episode, have been immeasurably enriched.

At the end of our study, however, we cannot avoid taking notice of a problem which has inevitably arisen from the use of these modern tools of New Testament scholarship: the unfortunate shift of attention away from the central figure of our sacred books, the historical person of Jesus of Nazareth. The valid and lasting contributions made by Form criticism, in the first place, cannot be gainsaid. It had alerted us to the remarkable evolution occurring within the Jesus-tradition as it was translated into Greek from the Aramaic language, subjected to selection and adaptation to new needs and a new culture, and reflected on and reformulated, as two or three generations of Christians found nourishment and inspiration for their faith in its living testimony. This achievement of the Form critics meant, of course, that the focus of attention was directed to the character and complex concerns of the earliest communities of believers. In its turn, Redaction criticism has fixed its sights, with happy results for our increased sensitization to the enormous worth of the Gospel narratives for the art of prayer, upon the specific theological viewpoints of each sacred writer, with his individual image of Jesus and his preoccupation with the tensions from within and the threats from without experienced by the particular community for which he wrote his Gospel. Once again, the upshot has been to enhance our respect and admiration for the creative achievements of these authors, the resultant of a profound insight into the mystery of Jesus and a delicate sensitivity for the needs and aspirations of their fellow Christians. At the same time, this newer kind of criticism has, of necessity, diverted its practitioners from the Jesus of history to the distinctive, highly personal spiritualities of each evangelist.

In consequence of all this, a new question has been posed for contemporary New Testament scholarship: What import, if any, has the historical Jesus for Christian living? Can the claim that Jesus remains the principal source for our comprehension of God's mysterious dealings with mankind be substantiated? Is one any longer able to assert with confidence that in the person of Jesus of Nazareth, through his demonstrably authentic words and the series of events we call his earthly history, God did in fact make his definitive offer of salvation to humanity? Or are we now forced to admit that Christianity takes its rise from the post-resurrection beliefs of Jesus' first followers?

As might have been expected, these crucial questions have received divergent answers from the biblical scholars of the twentieth century. In a perceptive article on Christology, Rudolf Schnackenburg has remarked: "Basic for New Testament Christology is the question whether it is solely the product of the Easter faith of Jesus' disciples, or has its roots already in the self-understanding of Jesus."[1] The distinguished German Catholic critic answers this question in the affirmative. At the other end of the spectrum Rudolf Bultmann has declared, with the first sentence of his now celebrated *Theology of the New Testament*, that "Jesus' preaching pertains to the presuppositions of the theology of the New Testament, and is not in itself a part of it."[2] This position Norman Perrin came, in the course of his academic career, to endorse emphatically: "As revealed by redaction criticism the nature of the Gospels and of Gospel material is such that the locus of revelation must be held to be in the present of Christian experience."[3] It is sufficient here to point out how such a view would appear to cut away the historical basis for Christianity, despite Perrin's previous assertion that "there is real continuity between these two things," that is, "the ministry of the historical Jesus" and "the reality of Christian experience."[4]

An interesting phenomenon in modern critical Gospel studies may be mentioned here in passing. While from the outset the Form critics announced that their new-found methodology had made it impossible to write a life of Jesus, and hence the nineteenth century abortive attempts to discover the historical Jesus on the part of liberal Protestantism were hunting a will-o'-the-wisp, a remarkable number of these scholars, led by the originators of Form criticism, Martin Dibelius and Rudolf Bultmann, wrote a book about Jesus by employing the principles of *Formgeschichte*. I call the phenomenon interesting, because it attests the fascination, which the central figure in our Gospels continues to exert even upon those scholars whose research has led them in other directions than that of the historical Jesus. The irresistible appeal of the Jewish peasant-rabbi from Galilee is still felt by the critics, despite their academic scrupulosity in sifting out a bare minimum of Jesus' "authentic" sayings and their acceptance of a pitifully small number of events in his life as historically certain. It has accordingly become more and more apparent that, despite all signs to the contrary, the immediate followers of Jesus and those early Christians who created our inspired literature were not in fact above the Master!

The chief aim of this small book has been to examine those scriptural passages which bear upon Jesus' striving with the help of prayer to accept his own death in all the concrete circumstances willed by God his Father. It was moreover mainly to view the relevant New Testament texts as the fruit of the Christian contemplation of his painful experience in the life of Jesus in order to learn in the school of the evangelists and other inspired writers the art of prayer. An ancillary purpose was to assist the thoughtful Christian to see the inadequacy of any fundamentalist approach to these sacred texts, which, as has been seen, present divergent, even contradictory views of this dramatic occurrence. Did Jesus remain continuously at prayer, perhaps through an extended space of time (Luke), or did he interrupt his dialogue with the Father at intervals, returning to his disciples (Mark and Matthew)? Did the disciples actually fall asleep, and did they flee at the arrest of Jesus? Indeed, is the entire scene simply to be regarded as the imaginative creation of one of these writers or some nameless author of the antecedent tradition? What was, in reality, the attitude of the historical Jesus to his own death, once he realized through the overt hostility of the religious authorities that it was unavoidable?

With regard to this last question, it is well to bear in mind the caution expressed, among others, by Edward Schillebeeckx, O.P., about attempting to invade the privacy of Jesus' unique self-awareness, the sacred domain of One who is at once God and man.[5] It is therefore well to distinguish carefully that self-awareness of Jesus from his self-understanding, which can be reached indirectly by what is implicit in his words and actions. In a recent review of the trends in contemporary Christology, Gerald O'Collins, S.J. states, "A modern consensus is emerging. A good number of sound historical conclusions are available about Jesus' road to death."[6] In the same article the Australian theologian observes: "On the eve of his death, the agony in the garden strikingly exemplified this free obedience toward the Father's will. There are, of course, difficulties in settling the details of the episode. Here, as elsewhere, the Gospels do not provide uniform evidence. Nevertheless, it seems reasonable to accept an historical basis for the story of that agony."[7]

The questions regarding the actual conduct of the disciples on this memorable occasion are, in my opinion, capable of solution. The difficulty raised about their reliability as witnesses to Jesus' reactions and his prayer because of sleep has, I venture to suggest, been blown up out of all proportion. Even if one grants that their falling asleep was written into the record as something more than a symbol of their incomprehension of the ordeal Jesus underwent, it is highly implausible that all would have simultaneously fallen asleep. Moreover, if one regards the Marcan division of the disciples into two groups as a literary device, introduced to illustrate Mark's interpretation of Jesus' prayer, it is very probable that these men were well aware of Jesus' struggle and privy to his prayer, which in Jewish fashion would have been uttered aloud. On the other hand, the flight and dispersal of the little group of Jesus' followers—at least, in the first flush of their surprise and fear at the arrest of Jesus—seems factual enough (Mark and Matthew). The absence of any reference in Luke to such lamentable conduct in those nearest to Jesus, as we observed, is explicable in terms of Lucan theology,

which demanded that "the twelve apostles" be personally involved as "witnesses" in the significant eventualities of Jesus'
public life and death.

The situating of Jesus' prayer within the historical anteced-
ents to his capture by his enemies is, from the evidence, most
plausible, especially in view of the position assigned by the
fourth evangelist to "the great prayer of Jesus" immediately pri-
or to the events "in the garden."

The gravest problem unquestionably is the location of Jesus' terrible struggle to accept God's will, *after* what transpired
at the Last Supper, when Jesus had clearly expressed his firm
confidence that God would vindicate him beyond his death and
give him a place in the eschatological kingdom. As we have seen,
the saying reported in the Synoptic Gospels is acknowledged by
contemporary Gospel critics as historically authentic. "Amen I
tell you: I shall never again drink the fruit of the vine, until that
day when I drink it new in the kingdom of God" (Mk 14:25). In
view of this expression of his trust in God's power and love for
himself, is it plausible that within a few hours Jesus could have
hesitated to accept the divine will for his death? Moreover, this
reported reaction of Jesus in Gethsemane may well appear dis-
cordant with his consistently manifested attitude toward the
will of God through the course of his public ministry, an attitude generally admitted to be characteristic of the historical Jesus. In that event, the implication in the Johannine narrative of
Jesus and the Greeks (Jn 12:22ff.) that this struggle occurred
during the course of the public ministry may be accepted as an
historical reminiscence. For my part, however, I hazard the
opinion that the reported reaction of Jesus on the very edge of
his earthly life, within hours of his arrest, is certainly not implausible. When one recalls the truth, central to the entire
Christian tradition, that the Son of God became completely a
member of the human family in every respect except sin, such a
momentary vacillation, as the full import of his tragic destiny
struck him, is very plausible indeed.

My purpose in raising the issue of the historicity of the
Gethsemane experience of Jesus and his disciples by way of epi-
logue has not been to present a definitive solution to any of

these questions. The aim has been simply to provide the reader with some indications of the unsettled nature of the on-going quest for the historical Jesus and to invite him to further reflection upon the significance of history as the chosen place of operation by the self-revealing God of Israel and Christianity. It is abundantly clear that the earthly history of Jesus of Nazareth, even if it were attainable by more refined techniques than we now possess, would never constitute the adequate basis for our belief, which remains always the work of God in Christ. Nonetheless since believing in Jesus means most basically entering into a personal relationship with him who "died and came to life that he might reign as Lord both of dead and living" (Rom 14:9), and since the maintaining of that personal relationship depends, as the history of Christian spirituality attests, on the contemplation of Jesus' earthly history, it is imperative that we acquire as accurate a picture as we can of the historical Jesus. For it is through the mysteries of that incomparable human life that we come to know in faith the kind of Lord we acknowledge and serve, since as Christians we confess with Paul that "he died on behalf of all mankind in order that the living might no longer live for themselves, but for him who on their behalf died and was raised to life" (2 Cor 5:15).

NOTES

1. Rudolf Schnackenburg, "Jesus Christus: II. Ntl. Christologie," *Lexikon für Theologie und Kirche* Vol. V. (2d ed., 1960), col. 932.

2. Rudolf Bultmann, *Theologie des Neuen Testaments* (Tübingen, 1948), p. 1.

3. Norman Perrin, *What Is Redaction Criticism?* (Philadelphia, 1969), p. 79.

4. *Ibid.*, p. 75.

5. Edward Schillebeeckx, *Jesus: An Experiment in Christology*, trans. Hubert Hoskins (New York, 1979), p. 54.

6. Gerald O'Collins, S.J., "Jesus' Concept of His Own Death," *The Way* 18 (1978), 223.

7. *Ibid.*, 220.

TOPICAL INDEX

INDEX OF AUTHORS

INDEX OF PRINCIPAL SCRIPTURAL TEXTS